Thirteen Roman Defeats

Thirteen Roman Defeats

The Disasters That Made The Legions

Ian Hughes

Pen & Sword
MILITARY

First published in Great Britain in 2023 by
Pen & Sword Military
An imprint of Pen & Sword Books Limited
Yorkshire – Philadelphia

ISBN 978 1 52672 667 4

A CIP catalogue record for this book is
available from the British Library

Typeset by Mac Style
Printed in the UK by CPI Group (UK) Ltd, Croydon, CR0 4YY.

Pen & Sword Books Limited incorporates the imprints of After
the Battle, Atlas, Archaeology, Aviation, Discovery, Family History,
Fiction, History, Maritime, Military, Military Classics, Politics,
Select, Transport, True Crime, Air World, Frontline Publishing, Leo
Cooper, Remember When, Seaforth Publishing, The Praetorian Press,
Wharncliffe Local History, Wharncliffe Transport, Wharncliffe True
Crime and White Owl.

For a complete list of Pen & Sword titles please contact

PEN & SWORD BOOKS LIMITED
47 Church Street, Barnsley, South Yorkshire, S70 2AS, England
E-mail: enquiries@pen-and-sword.co.uk
Website: www.pen-and-sword.co.uk
or
PEN AND SWORD BOOKS
1950 Lawrence Rd, Havertown, PA 19083, USA
E-mail: Uspen-and-sword@casematepublishers.com
Website: www.penandswordbooks.com

Contents

Introduction   vi

Chapter 1   The Gallic Terror: The Battle of the River Allia,
                c.387/6 BCE   1

Chapter 2   The Ferocious Samnites: The Caudine Forks, 321 BCE   21

Chapter 3   Pyrrhic Defeats: Pyrrhus of Epirus
                The Battle of Heraclea, 280 BCE
                The Battle of Asculum, 279 BCE   34

Chapter 4   Hannibal: The Battle of Lake Trasimene, 217 BCE   59

Chapter 5   The Gallic and Germanic Tribes:
                The Battle of Arausio, 6 October 105 BCE   75

Chapter 6   The Persian Menace: The Battle of Carrhae, 53 BCE   94

Chapter 7   The German Wall: The Battle of the Teutoburger
                Wald, 9 CE   111

Chapter 8   The Gothic Threat:
                The Battle of Abritus, 251 CE   128

Chapter 9   The Sasanid Threat:
                The Battle of Edessa, 260 BCE   147

Chapter 10 The Sasanid Threat Continues: The Siege of
                Amida, 359 CE   164

Chapter 11 The Sasanid Threat Yet Again: Julian's Campaign in
                Persia, 363 CE   183

Chapter 12 Civil Wars: The Battle of the (River) Frigidus,
                5–6 September 394   211

Chapter 13 The Vandal Disaster: The Battle of Cape Bon, 468   223

Conclusions   238
Notes   240
Index   249

Introduction

The Roman Empire usually strikes the casual reader as a monolithic structure, its rulers intent upon dominating the majority of Europe in the West and, at times, attempting to recreate the Empire of Alexander the Great in the East. This is a fair assumption, based as it is upon the size, longevity and extensive campaigns undertaken by the rulers of the Roman Empire. This should not blind us to the fact that, over the many centuries during which the Empire existed and in the centuries prior to the creation of the Empire during which Rome was a Republic, Rome underwent many changes: for example, different times and different rulers had different ideas regarding whether or not the Empire should expand. This contradiction in strategy is nowhere more clearly displayed than when comparing the aggressive, expansionist emperor Trajan (r.98–117 CE) and his more defensively-minded successor Hadrian (r.117–138 CE). The former conquered Dacia and annexed the Nabataean Kingdom before launching a major campaign that conquered large areas of the Parthian Empire: the latter retreated from Parthia and firmly established the frontiers by ordering the building of major defensive works such as Hadrian's Wall. In reality, the growth and consolidation of Roman power was far more varied than is sometimes appreciated.

A similar assumption is often made concerning the Roman army, a military force which is perceived as having more in common with modern military practices than with the 'primitive' systems in use by its contemporaries. Again this is a fair supposition until a closer assessment is made: for example, the army's composition and equipment changed over time, and analysis of Rome's later contemporary opponents shows at least some similarities beginning to emerge.

A study of the army may also give the impression of a military juggernaut, obliterating every enemy placed in its way and advancing the borders of the Empire to the furthest extremes possible. Again, this is understandable: the story of the Empire is one of repeated victories and comparatively few defeats. Yet in some ways the defeats almost certainly had a greater effect on the psyche and history of the Empire than the victories.

This book is an attempt to highlight how the many enemies of Rome inflicted at least some of these defeats on the Empire and how these setbacks affected the Romans and influenced both their future actions and those of their enemies. It is not an attempt to give an extensive list of the defeats suffered by Rome, nor is it necessarily aiming to highlight only the greatest, most devastating defeats in terms of casualties. Rather it is an attempt to focus upon examples where the outcome, both in military and, just as importantly, in psychological terms outweighed the story told by the simple loss of men and matériel.

There is one major difficulty in compiling this list of battles. Many readers of a military bent will hope to see both strategic and tactical maps involving the events leading up to the battle and of the battle itself. This is a common feature of modern military assessment, but while in most cases the former remains a distinct possibility, the latter is often impossible, either due to a lack of information in the surviving sources (e.g. the Battle of Edessa, Chapter 9) or because the nature of the battle is such that a standard textbook illustration is impossible (e.g. the disaster of the Teutoburger Wald, Chapter 7).

It is hoped that what is included here will give the reader an insight into why and how the Roman military machine suffered defeat and, just as importantly, what effect the defeat had on the future of the Empire. Whether this aim has been achieved is for the reader to decide.

As a final note, due to the vast numbers of books written about all these battles it would be impossible to include in the bibliography even the smallest number without omitting important texts, so except where quotes are used only primary sources are being included, where possible with links to translations available on the internet to allow readers to access the information for themselves and so give them the ability to assess the information for themselves.

Chapter One

The Gallic Terror: The Battle of the River Allia, c.387/6 BCE

The Sources

There are four main extant sources for the Battle of the Allia. Analyzing these in chronological order can help to explain some of the difficulties when using them.

The earliest is Polybius, a Greek historian who lived in the second century BCE and wrote *Historiai* (*The Histories*), a work covering events from 264 BCE (the start of the First Punic War between Rome and Carthage) to 146 BCE (the date of Carthage's final destruction by Rome). Polybius is acknowledged as being a historian of the highest calibre, one who attempted to report events accurately. Despite the fact that his history covers a later period, he does include a description of the Battle of the River Allia. The main difficulty with his description, as with all of the accounts, is that it was written long after the event and so relies partly upon oral history – which is liable to distortion due to the nature of the audience – but mainly upon accounts written long after the event that are now lost.

The second source is Diodorus Siculus ('of Sicily'), another Greek historian who lived and wrote in the first century BCE. His main work is the *Bibliotheca Historica* (*Library of World History*), on which he worked between 60 and 30 BCE. Like Polybius, he used surviving written accounts that have now been lost. Until recently, modern historians have been critical of Diodorus' work, noting that he simply collated earlier works to produce his own opus without any critical analysis or attempt to improve upon the earlier compositions. More recently it has been accepted that he succeeded in his main aim, which was to 'write an easily accessible world history. The title, *Library of World History*, proves that Diodorus did not pretend to offer more than a collection of summaries. As a historian, he is simply as good as his sources.'[1]

The third source is Livy (Titus Livius), who wrote his major work, *Ab Urbe Condita* (*From the Founding of the City*), starting sometime in the third quarter of the first century BCE. Livy attempted to cover all of Roman history from the earliest times to the modern day. His work is criticized for including much that is both legend and is obviously distorted to fit with Livy's attempt to write a 'moral' history of Rome. It is also noted that he is uncritical of his sources and that he makes errors; for example, sometimes failing to recognize that two sources are giving separate accounts of a single event, thus copying them separately and covering the same event twice at two different dates. However, modern historians are coming to realize that he was a better writer than had been accepted in the past. For example, in places he noted where his sources were poor and so simply recorded them rather than accepting them as true history, and in others he discounts events that are clearly misrepresented.

The final historian is Plutarch, another Greek historian, who lived from the mid-first century to early in the second century CE. His main work is *Parallel Lives*, a series of biographies comparing two ancient personages with each other. His coverage of the Battle of the Allia is included as part of the *Life of Camillus*, the Roman commander renowned for eventually defeating the Gauls and the man usually associated with major military reforms after the defeat and the Sack of Rome. As with all the sources, his work is reliant upon histories written long before his own time but long after the battle itself.

The last two points highlight the major difficulty faced both by the ancient writers and by modern historians: the sources upon which all modern work is based are themselves based upon lost sources, themselves written long after the event and based upon either oral history (which can be distorted to fit the sensibilities of the audience) or upon family history as maintained by the great families of Rome (which can be twisted to fit with the family's political ambitions). The net result is that the history of early Rome is confused and much of the information passed down is either heavily distorted or completely false. Consequently, it should be noted that much of what is written here is liable to reinterpretation in the light of new archaeological and historical discoveries.

Background

The period around the turn of the fifth century BCE was one of turmoil in Italy. In the centre of the peninsula, the small town of Rome was expanding its influence, slowly pushing back the Etruscan Confederation (a group of loosely-allied cities) to the north and the hill tribes to the east. In addition, a group of Gallic tribes had crossed the Alps and established themselves in the Po valley, and one of the tribes – the Senones – had reached as far south-east as the Adriatic and settled in the region of Rimini. Again, the main political power-block that was forced to retreat in face of the Gallic expansion was the Etruscans. After colonizing the region, the Gauls quickly established political contact with the towns

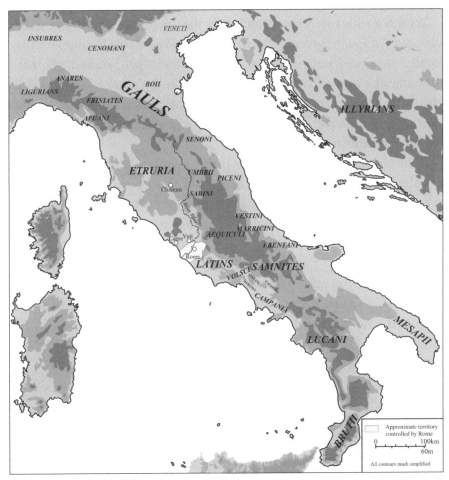

Italy in the fourth century BCE.

in north and central Italy and soon became a major force in northern and central Italian politics. Their martial skills were appreciated, and the Gauls soon gained a reputation as mercenaries.

The events surrounding the outbreak of the Romano-Gallic War are unclear as the sources give different accounts. According to Plutarch, one of the citizens of the town of Clusium, a settlement about 80 miles north of Rome, asked the Gauls to intervene in a dispute in the city.[2] Requesting support from external entities was not unusual: many of the Italian towns were riven by political discord and personal ambition, and external states were seen by some political players as potential allies. The Gauls were simply a new faction to be used for personal gain wherever possible. When the Gauls marched into Clusian territory other citizens of the town asked Rome for support and the countdown to war began.

Yet this is only one account, and sadly the other sources give alternative versions. Although agreeing that the citizens asked Rome for support, Livy implies that the Gauls were expanding on their own, without the need for requests from individuals in Clusium.[3] On the other hand, Diodorus claims that the citizens of Clusium had not requested help from Rome: 'At this very time the Roman people sent ambassadors into Tyrrhenia to spy out the army of the Celts.'[4]

If the circumstances surrounding the first contact between the Romans and the Senones are slightly confused, so are the accounts of the causes of the war. Again, the main accounts give different versions of the outbreak of hostilities, but all accept that three members of the Fabian clan were sent as envoys to the Senones.

Plutarch suggests that the Gauls were laying siege to the city when the Roman envoys arrived and demanded that the Gauls halt the attack. Brennus, the Gallic leader, compared the Gauls to the Romans in that they both wanted the excess lands of their neighbours. Baulked, the envoys entered the city and joined the defence with the Clusians and one of the envoys, Quintus Ambustus Fabius, killed a Senone chieftain.[5]

In his account, Livy gives a slight variation. Rather than defending behind the city walls, he states that after the first meeting there was a set-piece battle and that the three envoys were conspicuous by their valour. However, he too states that it was Quintus Fabius who killed a Senone chieftain.[6]

In some ways Diodorus supports the account of Livy, but he claims that when the ambassadors arrived at Clusium battle had already begun and 'with more valour than wisdom [the ambassadors] joined the men of Clusium against their besiegers, and one of the ambassadors was successful in killing a rather important commander.'[7]

In a slight variation, the fourth source, Diodorus, claims that Quintus Fabius had attacked a Senone foraging expedition and killed their leader rather than having taken part in a set-piece battle.[8]

Whatever the true events, the sources all accept that the envoys joining the Clusians fighting the Senones was against tradition concerning the accepted behaviour of envoys, and unsurprisingly after the 'battle' the Gauls sent ambassadors to Rome demanding reparations and the surrender of the three Fabii. Again the sources give slightly conflicting accounts of ensuing events, but it would appear that the Senate was on the point of acceding to the demands when the Fabii brought the matter before the people and the Senones' terms were rejected.[9] Obviously the clan of the Fabii had a great influence within the city. To add insult to injury, when the angry Senones began to advance towards Rome, the Fabii were elected to command the army as tribunes, alongside Quintus Sulpicius Longus, Quintus Servilius and Servius Cornelius Maluginensis.[10] Enraged, and forsaking all other targets, the Senones announced to all other cities on the journey that 'their destination was Rome'.[11] The war had begun.

The Opposing Forces: Rome

The exact form of the Roman army at this date is unknown. Later writers claim that Servius Tullius (r.578–535 BCE) reformed the army – the Servian Reforms – which divided the population into five classes based upon wealth. In theory, the first class could afford to have body armour, greaves, a shield, a sword and a spear, the second class omitted the body armour and the third class omitted the greaves. These troops served in the phalanx, with the first class in the front ranks, backed by the poorer citizens, as was probably the case in the majority of the Italian city states. Supporting these troops were the fourth and fifth classes, who were the skirmishing arm, equipped with missile weapons such as javelins, spears and slings.

In recent years, historians focusing on the nature of warfare in the Greek and Roman world have disputed with each other concerning how both the 'hoplite' army of the Greek city states, and by inference that of the early Roman Republic, were organized and fought. In the traditional evaluation, the major Greek city states deployed their infantry in a solid 'hoplite block' – the phalanx – and it was assumed that the Romans at this time simply imitated this, following an example set by the Etruscans.

However, although the frescoes of the period show warriors equipped as hoplites and archaeologists have found hoplite panoplies, analysis of the written evidence portrays a different image. Consequently the traditional view has been disputed, with various theories being promoted, ranging from a slightly fragmented hoplite line to a far more uneven deployment based on family, personal loyalties and relationships.

This interpretation has also been questioned, especially as there is a fresco in Poseidonia/Paestum that shows hoplites in close formation. However, a closer inspection suggests that these men were kneeling behind the protection of their shields as skirmishers engaged in front of them with missile weapons. In this context, the kneeling formation and interlocked shields were likely simply a reaction to missile fire rather than preparation for close combat.

Consequently, it is possible to suggest that Rome did indeed adopt Greek equipment, even though Rome may have been a more 'primitive' society based largely upon extended families or 'clans'; however, this may also have been the case in at least some of the Greek city states. The clans were intent upon following family-based feuds and usually more concerned with cattle-raids or revenge attacks upon neighbouring cities or clans – which were also organized upon the same formula – rather than upon inter-city aggression. This clan-based view may be reinforced by the fact that the Roman envoys to the Senones did not represent a wide spectrum of Roman society, but were instead all members of one powerful clan: the Fabii.

As a result of these reinterpretations, rather than being seen as the traditional close-knit phalanx as traditionally assumed to be practised by the larger Greek states, the Roman army is now seen as still in the process of transitioning from 'heroic' warfare based upon individual or clan reputation to the more 'community-based' force as traditionally depicted by later sources.[12] In that case, individual prowess may have played a central role in Roman warfare.

This interpretation is to some degree supported by more recent research aimed at analyzing how ancient sources depict warfare and in interpreting this research with regard to individual behaviours in battle. This suggests that the majority of warriors would be more interested in self-preservation than in killing an enemy. Consequently, the clan-based formation would be composed mainly of men fighting defensively. These in turn would not tend to advance to close quarters unless they believed that the enemy would waver and run as they charged.

In this context, it is up to the clan leaders and any aggressive individuals within the formation to encourage a charge; going out from the 'phalanx' and engaging in hand-to-hand combat. If this was with opposing individuals, a victory would greatly encourage their followers whereas a defeat could easily lead to a loss of confidence. If no single opponents emerged from the enemy formations, this would help their followers to believe that the enemy was unwilling to fight. At this point, a leader entering combat with the enemy formation could lead to a mass charge and an enemy rout.

If this portrayal is in any way accurate, then it is probably unlikely that the army formed up as a single line of hoplites in an extended phalanx: the Roman army was unused to serving together as a large, elite hoplite phalanx, but was more a loose collection of clans whose members tended to remain together in separate close-knit clusters resembling miniature phalanxes rather than acting in unison with other clans as a single cohesive force to defeat the foe, with gaps between covered by the skirmishers.

The same lack of organization is probably true of the skirmishers and the cavalry. When deployed for larger-scale battles rather than the more customary raids, the skirmishers were not trained in close combat, and although the aristocratic cavalry may have had personal training exercises that they performed regularly, they do not appear to have drilled as units. Consequently, they would have been unprepared for the Gallic assault. In addition, the cavalry especially was not a large proportion of the army and were almost certainly outnumbered by their counterparts among the Gauls, so may have had little chance to affect the course of the battle.

In some respects, this new model explains why events at the Battle of the Allia transpired as they did. Rather than being a coherent army committed to serving together to defend the city, the Roman army may have been a more disjointed, family-based force which was not adequately prepared and experienced to face the new threat posed by the Gauls.

In an aside, the model as portrayed above would further explain why the Gauls had enjoyed great success in the north of Italy: their foes, and especially the Etruscans, were largely similar in fighting tradition and technique to Rome and these also struggled to repel the Gallic invaders.

The confusion in the sources can be ascribed to the 'antique' fighting techniques used by the Romans at the Allia not being understood by later Roman writers steeped in the history of the reformed Roman army's major conquests and success. This fact would help to explain their misinterpretation of events. In addition, the authors of these sources were also living in a large city with an ever-expanding population rather than the much smaller town of the fourth century BCE. This would account for the great disparity in the numbers of troops given by the sources when compared to modern assessments based upon the probable size of the city at the earlier date.

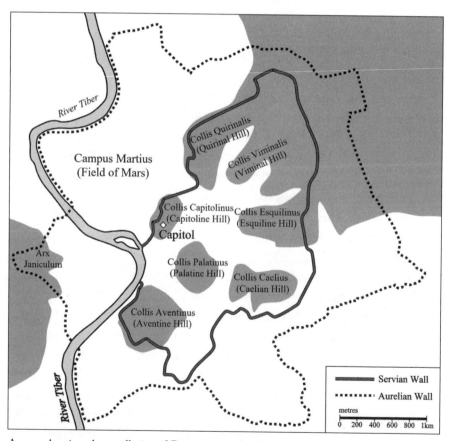

A map showing the small size of Rome in the fourth century BCE: it is unlikely that this small town (c. 2 × 3km) could support the large army portrayed in the sources, even though a proportion of the population would live outside the urban area.

As to the numbers involved in the battle, Livy does not give a figure, but Diodorus claims that the Roman army comprised 24,000 men.[13] Dionysius states that the Roman army consisted of four experienced legions and a larger levy of untrained citizens.[14] Plutarch gives a figure of 40,000 men for the Roman army, but notes that most lacked training, which can be roughly computed to the same number given by Diodorus.[15]

Interestingly, at the time of the Servian Reforms (see above) the army was estimated to have numbered 3,000 infantry and 300 cavalry, a far lower number. Although the city had grown since the sixth century BCE, it is unlikely that it had expanded eight-fold by the early fourth century BCE, so this number appears to be a mistake.

Modern estimates based upon this information vary widely, giving the Romans between c.15,000 and upwards of c.30,000 men. However, close analysis makes it impossible for the information contained in the sources to agree with modern estimates of the size of the city – and hence of the number of troops that could be raised – or of the composition of the army in this archaic period.

For example, a close reading of Diodorus and his four-legion army makes it clear that he is giving information about the army of a later date: at most, the city of the early fourth century could raise two legions per year, not four.[16] Moreover, the assertion by Livy that six tribunes were elected (see above) implies that this was a year in which a phenomenon dated to between 444 and 367 BCE occurred.[17] This was where in one year two military consuls commanded the army as expected, but in alternate years the army was commanded by 'military tribunes with consular power' known as 'consular tribunes'. The year of the battle would appear to be a year of consular tribunes, as a consequence of which the suggestion by Diodorus that Rome had four legions, presumably two each per consul as was the custom later, is obviously in error.[18] Furthermore, the suggestion that the three Fabians were among those in command reinforces the concept that this was a year of the consular tribunes, with the Fabians joined by three other tribunes.

Alongside the misapprehension in the sources that, as later, consuls commanded two legions each, there is also the problem of the number of men in a legion. In later times the legion numbered between 5,000 and 6,000 troops. According to Livy – who interestingly fails to include a number for the Roman army at the Allia – in this earlier period the legions numbered in the region of 4,200–5,000 men, along with 300 cavalry.[19] As a result, if it is accepted that at this time Rome only fielded two legions, the number of experienced men available would probably be at most around the 10,000 mark. In addition, Livy states that the levy 'was not larger than had been usual in ordinary campaigns', meaning that only the normal two legions had been raised.[20]

A final factor reinforcing this analysis is the size of the city itself. Modern estimates vary, but at this early date the population was at most 40,000. As a consequence, the army would likely have numbered at most 10,000, and so the huge numbers given in the sources cannot be supported. Nor can it be assumed that the Roman army was supported by troops from allied cities. The speed of the attack and the ensuing lack of time to prepare precludes there being time for an allied city to both raise an army and march to Rome. The Romans were on their own.

The conclusion must be that the Roman army at the Allia was composed of a maximum of 7,000–8,000 men with military experience, possibly supported by a maximum of c.7,000 other citizens with no experience, but probably fewer as otherwise this would have included the elderly, plus women and children. It was this smaller military force that marched to meet the Gallic advance.

The Opposing Forces: The Senones

When it comes to the Senones, the little information we have from the sources is easy to misinterpret as it is largely a comparison to the Roman forces, which have already been demonstrated as being mistaken. Earlier historians have accepted the figures given almost at face value, and so the image of an entire tribe on the move is sometimes portrayed.

In reality, this is unlikely. The speed at which the Senones moved and their actions during the war imply that they were a smaller group. The events earlier at Clusium reinforce this concept. The Gauls who were 'hired' to intervene in the city were in reality a mercenary group being paid to intrude into what were otherwise internal political events, not a tribe on the move.[21]

A further factor is that, not long after their victory at the Allia and the ensuing Sack of Rome, the same band of Gauls was defeated by the citizen army of the town of Caere, at that time at war with the Greek city of Syracuse in Sicily.[22] It is possible that the Gauls had moved on from Rome to Sicily, as a Gallic mercenary force is attested as being hired by Diodorus of Syracuse a few months after the Sack, possibly the same 'Senones'.[23] If they were indeed a mercenary band, then that explains much: their involvement at Clusium, the speed of the attack on Rome, and their activities between the Sack and their defeat by Caere. It may also place a limit on the size of their army.

Given that the maximum force employed by Rome was c.15,000, it may be that in reality the opposing army was not the overwhelming force portrayed by the sources, as a mercenary band of 20,000 would be extremely large. It is likely that the sources, derived from biased Roman information, have exaggerated the number of Senones in order to give an excuse for the defeat, a factor that may have been common in antiquity. Yet if the concept of this being a mercenary force travelling to the south of Italy looking for work is accepted then a further possibility emerges.

Although usually being seen as a single entity – the tribe of the Senones – it may be that, as noted above, although Brennus was a Senone, the force he commanded was a conglomeration of warriors who had come together with a view to seeking work as mercenaries, first in the south of Italy and then perhaps by travelling further abroad from one of the ports in the south. Consequently, although starting as a large 'army', many of these men would break away from the main force when work was offered. This would help to explain why the Gauls easily defeated the Romans but lost to an army from the city of Caere: it was the extremely large, outward-bound force that defeated Rome, but a smaller army that had lost components to employment elsewhere that was later defeated.

If the Senone army was in the region of 15,000, it would be a very large mercenary force but, being mercenaries, it may have been smaller, with a core of very experienced and battle-hardened men. It is also likely that it was not composed solely of foot troops, but included a large proportion of cavalry and, as it was a Gallic army, perhaps a force of chariots.[24] Although it is possible that Gallic mercenary forces did not include chariots as these may have been seen as too cumbersome for long-distance journeys in search of employment, at this early date at least some of the nobles probably retained them to ensure that their status was recognized. Chariots would also have been useful when travelling for carrying the nobles' equipment and supplies.

The proportion of chariots in a Gallic army is unknown. One of the few numbers given is that by Livy for the Battle of Sentinum (295 BCE):

> Great as the glory of the day on which the battle of Sentinum was fought must appear to any writer who adheres to the truth, it has by some writers been exaggerated beyond all belief. They assert that the enemy's army amounted to 1,000,000 infantry and 46,000 cavalry, together with 1,000 war chariots. That, of course, includes the Umbrians and Tuscans who are represented as taking part in the battle.
>
> *Livy, 10.30.4–5.*

As Livy notes, this battle was fought by Rome against a coalition of Samnites, Etruscans, Umbrians and Gauls. Assuming that Livy's 'some writers' have given each of the four enemies an equal share of the troops, this means that the Gallic army was allegedly composed of c.250,000 infantry and c.12,000 cavalry. On the other hand, the 1,000 chariots would have only been Gauls as the other nationalities no longer used chariots in warfare. Although extremely exaggerated, the proportions given *may* reflect some form of army composition.

Although extremely ambiguous as there is no means of validating the theory, using the numbers given it is possible to estimate the composition of the Gallic forces. If, as postulated above, there were c.250,000 infantry, 12,000 cavalry and 1,000 chariots in the Gallic army at Sentinum, giving a ratio of 250:12:1, then if there were c.15,000 troops in the Gallic army at the Battle of the Allia, proportionally that would equate to c.14,000 infantry, c.750 cavalry and c.100 chariots. Although only an extremely rough estimate, when this is compared to the numbers of the Roman army above it appears to be a sensible number and so a possible description of the battle can emerge.

Location

According to Livy, the two armies met 'where the river Allia, descending from the Crustuminian Mountains in a very deep channel, joins the river Tiber not far below the road.'[25] This is reinforced by Plutarch, who states: '[The Romans] advanced from the city about eleven miles, and encamped along the river Allia, not far from its confluence with the Tiber.'[26]

It is hard to gain a picture of the terrain as the region has changed in the last 2,000 years. It is just as difficult to ascertain the initial deployment of the two armies, in large part due to the lack of any detail in and the conflicting nature of the sources. The main difficulty here is that although the River Allia is described as being in a 'very deep channel', neither the river itself nor its 'deep channel' feature in the accounts of the battle. The question then is whether either the Romans or the Gauls deployed along the Allia and thus the need to cross the river was a major factor in the outcome. A possible answer to this question can be obtained by the sources' description of the battle.

Deployment

There are three 'detailed' accounts of the battle. Diodorus states that the Roman army was drawn up in a long line on the plain, with the raw recruits placed on the right flank on a hill. He goes on to say that the Gauls also formed a long battle line, but with their best troops on the hills facing the Roman levy. Giving slightly more detail, Livy states that the Senones were already at the river, and that the Romans failed to follow their traditional military practices of constructing a camp but immediately formed for battle. As they were outnumbered, they thinned their line in an attempt to avoid having their flanks turned, but in doing so weakened the centre. Diodorus is in agreement that the raw levy was placed on a hill on the right flank. It seems likely that Livy and Diodorus are following the same older source, as neither describes the Senones' deployment, noting simply that Brennus saw the Roman deployment and took measures to counter it. In a very brief description, Plutarch claims that the Roman army camped along the Allia but gives little indication of the deployment.

It would seem clear then that the sources agree that the Romans formed their line of battle in front of the River Allia and rested their left flank upon the River Tiber. They placed the raw troops on a hill to the right and it may be that a portion of the experienced troops were deployed to support the levy. In doing so, the remaining troops were stretched in the centre and the Romans were unable to retain a reserve – if this was part of their tactics at this early date – due to the desire to avoid having their flanks turned. It would appear that the position of the raw troops, on the

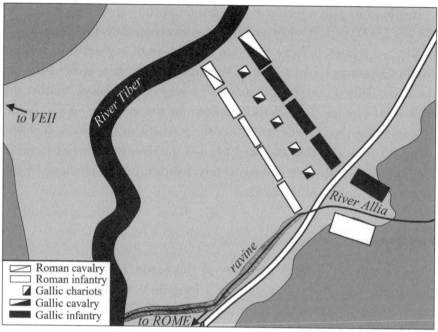

The Battle of the River Allia: deployment.

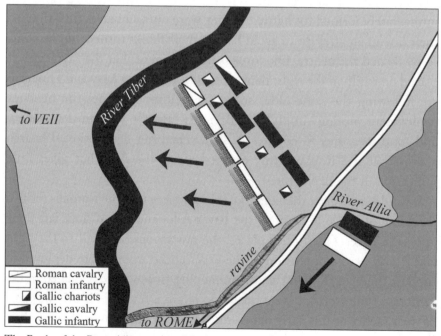

The Battle of the River Allia: course of the battle.

right flank in a large block and possibly behind a thin line of experienced troops, would in some respects determine the course of the battle.

This is due to the fact that, for their part, the Senones appear to have simply lined up against the Romans, probably after the Roman deployment: Brennus, the Senones' commander, is attested as having deployed to counter his perception of the Roman plan. He allegedly believed that the Roman strategy was to hold the main line, but then to use the 'reserve' (the large block of raw 'volunteers') on the Roman right to defeat his left flank and then swing onto the centre and rear of the Senones' main body.[27] He would not have known that the large force on the hill was in fact men with little to no experience of fighting. Thanks to his interpretation, Brennus deployed his strongest troops – i.e. his battle-hardened veterans – to counter the Roman threat. This would mean weakening his right flank and/or centre, but to counter this he may have relied upon his superiority in cavalry, along with the mobility and morale effect of his chariotry, to pin the centre and flank of the Roman army while his left flank defeated the expected Roman assault.

Course of the Battle

Although there are differences between the sources concerning the battle, a reasonable description can be attained. The main cause of confusion is Diodorus, who writes that as the two armies met in battle, the Gauls quickly drove the recruits from the hills. He claims that it was the recruits fleeing in panic and disrupting the Roman centre and left that caused the entire Roman army to rout. At first glance this seems reasonable, but it may actually reflect Roman propaganda: obviously, to Roman minds, the unexpected defeat must have been due to the brittle nature of the raw levies, not the loss of fighting spirit of the main body of troops. Diodorus appears to be following Roman tradition in blaming the levies rather than the main body of fighting troops, but this is not what is depicted in the other sources.

Livy states clearly that the 'reserve' on the hill for a time withstood the attack and that it was the centre and especially the left that routed at the first onset. Plutarch supports Livy, suggesting that Brennus directed the main body of the Senones against the recruits on the hill, but that the raw troops – or more likely a thin line of intermixed raw and experienced troops fighting desperately – conducted a fighting retreat and so many escaped. In Plutarch's account it was again the left that instantly collapsed and was 'driven into the river'.

None of the accounts describes any of the fighting or of the manoeuvres used by the Senones, largely because the sources are intent upon highlighting and excusing the defeat of the Roman army rather than the success of the barbarians. As a consequence, the specific course of the battle as seen by the Gauls remains a matter of debate and it is necessary to resort to conjecture.

As noted earlier, the Roman army, though theoretically based upon the 'hoplite' system, was not fully experienced in the concept of close cooperation, being largely a conglomeration of small clan-based forces normally used for cattle-raiding or for inter-city warfare against states using the same or a similar system. By contrast, the Gauls were an expanding military force using a combination of warriors, cavalry and chariots which in some ways may have been more sophisticated than their 'civilized' counterparts. Consequently, it may have been close cooperation between the different arms that gave the Gauls their stunning victory. However, if the description of antique warfare outlined above is in any way accurate, with few individual soldiers risking their safety by venturing beyond their own lines, then the Senones had one further advantage: the anger of their leaders against the 'treacherous' Romans may have instilled in the troops a similar anger, leading to a far greater proportion being willing to risk danger and charge the Roman lines.

Combining the sources can lead to the following description of the battle. Arriving after the Senones, the Romans immediately deployed in a thin line from near the River Tiber to a hill, with a large 'reserve' of recruits being placed on the latter, possibly protected by the stream of the Allia flowing in front of them before it formed a deep channel, in front of which the remainder of the Romans deployed. In addition, the main body of troops probably formed in groups related to the number of tribunes rather than as a single coherent body.

Observing the enemy's deployment, Brennus placed troops to face the hill and, as this included the need to force a river crossing, this force likely contained his veteran troops. The result was that on the Roman right the recruits – reinforced by a few veterans, along with a height advantage and defending the river line – managed to repulse the first attack by the

Senones. Furthermore, it is possible that, as these troops were a raw levy and so not deployed in the 'dispersed' manner theoretically used by the main body of 'clansmen', they massed as a solid body, fighting to defend each other.

However, on the Roman left things were different. The plain near the river was more suited to cavalry, so the Romans may have deployed their cavalry on the extreme left flank. Both these and the left flank of the infantry would have been faced by the Senones' cavalry and chariots. These troops heavily outnumbered the Roman cavalry, and although the chariot arm was small, this was a force to be reckoned with. Three centuries later Julius Caesar would remark upon the outstanding qualities of the British chariots and it may be here that a clue may be found to the actual nature of the battle:

> In chariot fighting the Britons begin by driving all over the field hurling javelins, and generally the terror inspired by the horses and the noise of the wheels are sufficient to throw their opponents' ranks into disorder. Then, after making their way between the squadrons of their own cavalry, they jump down from the chariot and engage on foot. In the meantime their charioteers retire a short distance from the battle and place the chariots in such a position that their masters, if hard pressed by numbers, have an easy means of retreat to their own lines. Thus they combine the mobility of cavalry with the staying power of infantry; and by daily training and practice they attain such proficiency that even on a steep incline they are able to control the horses at full gallop, and to check and turn them in a moment. They can run along the chariot pole, stand on the yoke, and get back into the chariot as quick as lightning.
>
> *Julius Caesar, Gallic War, 4.33.*

Even the veterans in Caesar's legions invading Britain were unsettled by the British chariots. The Romans of the fourth century BC had no such experience, especially the poorer men serving as skirmishers in front of the main line. Terrified by the large numbers of cavalry and the dashing, noisy chariots, they turned and fled, taking the main body with them. It may also be that they saw the Senone attack upon the hill and assumed that the levy would instantly turn and run. A further possibility is that the three Fabians were terrified of being taken alive, so were among those who first turned and ran, followed by their three *cohorts*.

At this point, it is possible that events may give added support to the theory that the Roman army had deployed largely in front of the River Allia. Livy bemoans the fact that, rather than heading back down the road to Rome, the survivors from the centre and left flank fled towards the Tiber and then on to Veii. Contrary to his hyperbole, it is likely that, having the deep gorge of the Allia to their rear and being compressed in the centre by the Senones' attack, they had no choice but to head for the Tiber where they still had a chance of escape.

As the Roman left and centre fled to the Tiber, the Roman right fought a defensive withdrawal before finally returning to Rome. Rather than pursue the Roman right, who had fought bravely and who appear to have been more willing to turn and defend themselves in the hills, the majority of the Senones' army seems to have spent the last of their energy attempting to kill the Romans floundering in the Tiber. The battle was lost for the Romans. The raw Roman recruits returned to Rome with the report that the main body of the experienced Roman army had been lost.

Aftermath

In reality Roman losses are not attested as being high, largely due to the fact that the majority of the Roman troops fled at the first contact. Losses among the Senones would have been even lower as only the troops on the Roman right flank resisted their attack. However, as the majority of the Roman survivors of the battle were forced to head towards Veii rather than Rome, the city was largely undefended when the Senones finally arrived at the walls. The remaining Romans either retreated to the citadel or fled to nearby cities, especially Caere, which was allied to Rome: this was the destination for the *flamen*, the vestals and their sacred objects. A few elderly senators refused to retreat and were killed in their homes. The result was that the city was captured and sacked, except for the citadel.

What happened next is hidden in myth and legend, but it would seem that the Romans eventually paid 1,000 pounds of gold to make the Senones go away.[28] On the other hand, according to the pro-Roman sources, the Senones were defeated either due to Brennus offending the gods and his army being struck down by illness, or the Romans recalling their general

Camillus to regroup the Roman army and defeat the enemy: the latter has been described by one modern historian as 'incredibly dubious'.[29]

Strabo, writing at the turn of the first millennium, instead states that it was the army of Caere that defeated the Gauls as they headed north from the south, but that this fact was lost as it reflected the glory of Caere rather than that of Rome.[30] It is possible that, rather than attacking Caere as mercenaries for Syracuse, the Senones headed from Rome to Caere to demand that the city surrender the Romans that had fled there. If so, the attack has nowhere been recorded as such and so is discounted here, but must remain a possibility due to the poor nature of the sources.

Effects

Although the battle was not a major military disaster and Rome quickly recovered its lost prestige, the capture and sack of the city of Rome was to leave an indelible mark on the Romans' psyche throughout the rest of the period of the Roman Empire. Afterwards the Romans held 16 June, the *Dies Alliensis*, to be a *dies nefastus*: an unlucky day.[31]

It is probably following the defeat at the Allia that the Roman elite recognized that the methods being used by the army were no match for the Gauls and that major changes were needed: the army was ineffective and needed improving to make it fit for purpose. These reforms are hard to date, and what form they took and how long they took to implement is unknown. They are traditionally associated with the general Camillus, who according to Dionysius was recalled to Rome following the Gallic victory at the Allia after being exiled earlier for embezzlement.[32] It was allegedly he who defeated the Gauls – rather than the Caerans – and who then undertook to reform the army to make it capable of defeating the Gauls and any other opponent in Italy. Although this is doubtful, and it is likely that the reforms were a gradual process taking place over many years, it may be that Camillus did in fact begin the process by implementing their first stage.

The 'loose' clan-based formations used against the Gauls were transformed into a more efficient, well-organized army based upon troops working together and following the commands of an individual general rather than those issuing from many clan leaders. The lack of contemporary information means that certainty is impossible, but it may be that at this point the Romans finally adopted the linear 'hoplite' formation used by the Greeks, although with some local amendments: namely, the implementation of a three-line system, with ample reserves to prevent the instant collapse of the army as had happened at the Allia.

With this new reformed army, over the next two centuries Rome gradually extended its control over Italy, including Cisalpine Gaul (Gaul 'this side of the Alps'), but even these victories could not erase the disgrace of the Gallic defeat, and it was only following Julius Caesar's conquest of Gaul in the first century BCE that the *metus Gallicus* ('Gallic Fear') began to fade. Yet the memory remained: when the Goths sacked Rome in 410 CE the event was compared to that of the Senones more than 800 years previously. The events of the Battle of the Allia and the ensuing Sack of Rome were to remain forever ingrained upon the memory of Rome.

Select Bibliography

Diodorus Siculus, *Library of History*, Book XIV, pp.113-117
http://penelope.uchicago.edu/Thayer/E/Roman/Texts/Diodorus_Siculus/14G*.html
Dionysius: http://penelope.uchicago.edu/Thayer/E/Roman/Texts/Dionysius_of_Halicarnassus/home.html
Livy: http://www.gutenberg.org/files/19725/19725-h/19725-h.htm#e38
Plutarch Camillus: http://penelope.uchicago.edu/Thayer/E/Roman/Texts/Plutarch/Lives/Camillus*.html
Polybius: http://www.gutenberg.org/files/44125/44125-h/44125-h.htm#b1_6

Chapter Two

The Ferocious Samnites:
The Caudine Forks, 321 BCE

The Sources

The main source for the battle is Livy (8.30–37, 8.38–39, 8.40.5 and especially 9.15.7). There are mentions in other sources, most notably in the works of Cicero (*De Officiis* (*On Duties* or *On Obligations*) 3.109, and *De Senectute* (*On Old Age*) 41), but these are merely minor comments that appear to rely on the account given by Livy for their information.

As noted in Chapter 1, the works of Livy have traditionally been regarded as of dubious value – especially when concerning the early years of the Republic – due to obvious inaccuracies and internal contradictions. Yet recently his work has slowly become more accepted as of higher value. Although Livy makes mistakes and assumptions concerning the nature of the early Republic, these are understandable given the nature of the evidence available to him.

One example of this internal contradiction concerns the aftermath of the Battle of the Caudine Forks (which is outlined below). Yet here it is not necessarily Livy himself that is at fault, but more that he was unable to make sense of the sources he was using. This episode highlights the difficulty Livy faced when composing his *History*: for example, the evidence available was either hardly legible, was extremely biased (as it was based on the 'family histories' maintained by important families), or was based on oral history. Obviously the 'histories' of different families highlighted different episodes and aimed to bolster the image of the family's ancestors; oral history contained the 'facts', but interwoven with myth and changes to emphasize the victories and minimize the defeats of the Romans; and even 'official' history was highly doctored in an attempt to make past mistakes palatable to Roman sensibilities. When these differences appeared Livy attempted to make some sense of them, but he was unable to do so at every turn so he simply recorded them for posterity, hence the contradictions.

Consequently, the events as recorded by Livy always have to be assessed carefully and not simply taken at face value. However, where Livy is the only source – as here – his account has to be used, but needs to be checked for plausibility at every available instance.

Background

There were to be three wars between Rome and the Samnites, a group of tribes centred upon the Apennines. The First Samnite War (343–341 BCE)

Roman expansion in Italy during the fourth century.

began when the Samnites attacked the Sidicini. The Sidicini appealed to their allies, the Campanian League – more specifically the city state of Capua – for aid. This was given, but the Samnites defeated the alliance in two battles before advancing and laying siege to Capua itself. The Capuans then sent envoys to Rome, who at this time were allied to the Samnites, asking for support.

The Romans hesitated as they were unwilling to break the treaty with the Samnites, but when the Campanians voluntarily acknowledged Roman suzerainty the Roman hesitation was removed. Rome sent envoys asking the Samnites to desist in their attacks. When the Samnites refused, Rome declared war. It may be in part due to the 'treachery' on the part of the Romans that from this point onwards the Samnites were extremely hostile to Rome.

Rome was victorious in the ensuing war after victories in several engagements, and a peace was agreed in 341 BCE. Yet the war against the Samnites had only been suspended due to growing friction between Rome and her Latin allies. This tension finally broke into the Latin War of 340 to 338 BCE. Ironically, the region that had asked for support against the Samnites and thus caused the break in the Romano-Samnite alliance now joined the Latin League in the war against Rome. Triumphant in the war, Rome took revenge by expanding into the territory of the Sidicini and the Aurunci and began operations to take control of Campania.

Yet Rome had not forgotten that the previous war against the Samnites had been halted due to the unrest of the Latins. In 334 BCE Rome established a colony at Cales. The Samnites were unable to respond as war had begun between them and the Greek colony of Tarentum. To add to the confusion, Tarentum had called in support from Alexander, King of Epirus. This war would only end in 331 BCE.

With the end of the Tarentine War, tensions between Rome and the Samnites took central stage, and in 328 Rome established another colony, this time at Fregellae. When the Samnites complained, the Romans countered with the claim that the Samnites were encouraging the city of Naples to expand into Campania as rivals to Rome, so the establishing of new colonies was simply a counter to this threat. In response, the Samnites sent troops to garrison Naples. As usual with Greek city states, the Neapolitans were politically divided and some of the elite class of the city sent messengers to Rome to ask for help against those internal politicians allied with the Samnites. Accordingly, in 327 BCE a Roman army arrived and evicted the Samnites. The Second Samnite War had begun.

In the first years of the war the Romans were victorious, prompting the Samnites to sue for peace, but the terms demanded by Rome were unacceptable and the war continued. Shortly after the rejection of the Roman terms, the Roman Consuls Titus Veturius Calvinus and Spurius Postumius Albinus joined their legions together at Calatia and, having formulated a plan to defeat the Samnites, began their march into Samnite territory.

The Opposing Forces: Rome

After the defeat by the Gauls at the Battle of the Allia the Roman army underwent major changes. In the sources this reorganization is attributed to the Roman general Camillus and so is known as the Camillan Reforms. However, the scale and drastic nature of the change probably reflects an evolution over a period of time rather than a revolution under one individual as implied by Livy when he states that '*At length* they [the legions] were divided into several centuries' [author's italics].[1] It is clear that over time the Roman army changed from the earlier disparate clans fighting individually into a single 'phalanx' fighting in a line, into a triple line, and eventually into a configuration that was more flexible, based upon *maniples*, small 'companies' of men, fighting in a *quincunx* formation.

It is believed that experience of fighting in the Samnite Wars prompted the change from linear tactics to the new 'manipular' tactics, but whether this was during the First, Second or Third Samnite War is disputed. However, it is likely – given later evidence – that although at this time the Roman army was fighting in three lines, it had not begun using the *quincunx*: for example, there is the implication in Livy that in 340 at the Battle of Veseris the army was still fighting as a hoplite phalanx.[2] If this assumption is correct, the three lines of the Roman army were the *Hastati* ('Spearmen'), the *Principes* ('First') and the *Triarii* ('Third'). It is unclear why the first two lines were so named as it would be expected that the *Principes* would be the front line and not the *Hastati*.

There remains one other problem concerning the Roman army at this early date:[3] Livy records the presence of 'troops' named *Accensi* and *Rorarii*.[4] Debate has raged over whether these troops existed, and if so what their function was in the Roman army. In Livy's description they appear to be '*Triarii* of inferior quality', and this has been accepted by some authorities in the past.[5] However, recently it has been noted that, for example, in Cato's work *Accensi* are the equivalent of 'attendants'.[6] Consequently it would seem that the *Accensi* were 'messengers and orderlies', possibly acting as servants to the hoplites, but in battle acting as light troops.

This concept is reinforced somewhat by the fact that, although Livy uses the word *Leves* for skirmishing infantry, *Rorarii* is sometimes used to represent 'men who opened the battle', i.e. skirmishers.[7] Moreover, the term was still in use in the second century, although by then it was giving way to the term *Velites*.[8] Consequently it is here assumed that the *Accensi* were attendants and that *Rorarii* was the original name for the legion's skirmishing arm.

Concerning armament, it is possible that at this date all three lines of troops still retained the use of the *hasta*, the thrusting spear associated with the earlier 'hoplite phalanx'.[9] However, it is also possible that by this date at least some of the troops used the *pilum*, a 'javelin'/'throwing spear' c.2m/6ft 6in in length, with an iron shank of c.60cm/2ft joined to a wooden shaft of c.1.4m/4ft 6in. The date of the adoption of the *pilum* is unknown. It may have been copied from the Etruscans and so already have been in use, or it may have been copied from the Samnites, so again may have been in use if adopted after the First Samnite War, or it may have been copied later from the Iberians serving Carthage in the First Punic War (264–261 BCE), in which case it would not have been in use in the Second Samnite War.[10] If the *pilum* had been adopted, it may only have been by the first line, the *principes*, which used it as the second line, the *hastati*, named after the *hasta*, retained their name for a long time. Consequently it is here assumed that the *principes* now carried the *pilum*, but that the *hastati* and *triarii* retained the *hasta*. Each legionary also carried a *gladius* (sword) and a *pugio* (dagger) for close-quarter fighting.

Defensively, those who could afford it – usually the veterans of the *triarii* – bought mail shirts, but the vast majority had at most a version of the Italic *pectoral* to cover the chest. The *hoplon/aspis* of the earlier army had now become obsolete, and all of the main body carried the *scutum*, a long semi-cylindrical shield, and most of the troops wore versions of Etrusco-Corinthian and Attic helmets.

The lightly-armed troops were armed with *hastae velitares* ('spears of the velites'). These were c.30in long, including a c.10in iron head. Without protection apart from a helmet and a small shield, these were not separate formations, but were formally attached to *maniples* of *principes*, *hastati* and *triarii*, although in battle they formed a skirmishing screen to combat enemy skirmishers and to attempt to disrupt enemy formations with a hail of javelins.

The Roman cavalry, being composed of the political elite, was defended by mail or bronze body protection, a similar helmet to the infantry and a small round shield. They were armed with a spear suitable for close-quarter fighting but less well-suited to skirmishing with opponents.

There is one further factor to be borne in mind. This is that, contrary to the expectation of later writers including Livy, it would seem that at this early date each consul was in command of only a single legion: this would seemingly only increase to two after the defeat at the Battle of Heraclea (see Chapter 3).[11] Finally, there is no guarantee either that the recently-defeated Latin allies immediately supplied troops to fight alongside the Roman legions: it may have taken time to reorganize the military command to assimilate the Latin allies, given their recent animosity. Consequently, it is probable that the Roman army at the Battle of the Caudine Forks consisted of only around 9,000 infantry and 600 cavalry, and not the huge numbers – for example, 40,000 and 50,000 – given by later writers.[12]

The many complex caveats noted above concerning the numbers, equipment and disposition of the Roman army may result in the exact course of the battle being difficult to assess. However, the character of the two armies and the nature of the terrain mean that to some degree the manner in which the Roman army deployed for set-piece battles may be irrelevant.

The Opposing Forces: Samnium

The Samnite *Meddix* (similar to a Roman consul or *magistratus*) in command at the Caudine Forks was a man named Gaius (sometimes Gavius) Pontius. He was in command of approximately 9,000 infantry and 1,000 cavalry. The Samnite infantry of this period is well attested from the wall paintings found in tombs. The wealthy would wear an

Italic *pectoral* or breastplate, whereas the less well-off would have no body defence, relying for protection on a shield of varying forms, either similar to the Roman *scutum* or a round or flat-topped tapered version of the *scutum*. They also wore variants of the Italic Etrusco-Corinthian and Attic helmets. Their weapons appear to have been javelins/spears and a sword, although it is possible that at least some also used the *pilum*, though this is uncertain (see above).

Formed into small companies of troops – and ostensibly the origin of the Roman *maniple* – in the main they relied on flexibility, speed and a ferocious charge to break the enemy. The cavalry of the Samnites appears from all the evidence to have been armed similarly to the infantry, except that there is no evidence of them carrying a shield. Nevertheless, despite their light equipment, the sources describe the Samnite cavalry, like the infantry, charging the Roman cavalry on equal terms.

Location

Although there remains doubt about the location of the battle, possibly the only suitable place was the steep valley between Mount Tairano and Mount Vorrano. In the past this has been discounted since it did not have enough room for the vast numbers of troops usually associated with the battle. However, with the lower estimate outlined above, it would appear that fewer than 10,000 troops could be trapped within the valley (in modern times even a small to medium-sized park is large enough to be used as a venue for open-air rock festivals of similar or greater numbers), especially if the Samnites had enough warning to make the necessary preparations for blocking the return exit after the Romans had entered the valley.

Deployment

For the Romans, the term 'deployment' is meaningless for this battle. The army entered the valley in marching columns along the road and would only adopt a fighting stance once the trap was sprung. In the circumstances, a traditional battle line was impossible so the Romans would have 'deployed' as circumstances and terrain allowed: without knowing the specific location and deployment of the Samnites it is

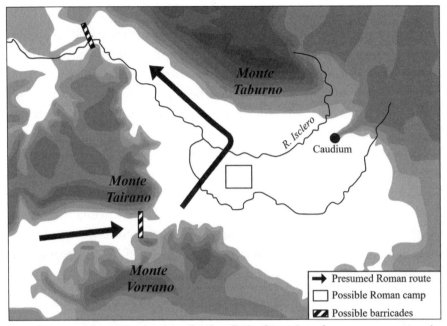

Possible location for the battle of the Caudine Forks. Since the information concerning the battle gives no specific details, only the possible location of the barriers is included. That the two exist but are not directly visible from each other explains how the Samnites were able to block both and trap the Romans. (The contours are greatly simplified).

impossible to assess the deployment of the Romans. However, one factor would appear certain: the confidence of the army and the arrogance of the commanders resulted in no troops being sent out to scout ahead of the marching army. This would come back to haunt them.

As just noted, the Samnites were not deployed for a normal 'set-piece' battle, so it is impossible to analyze their 'formations'. However, as it would appear that they had planned the ambush beforehand some assumptions can be made. One is that when they blocked the exit to the valley they used trees and rocks to do this. Consequently, they doubtless deployed a large number of men to protect the barricade and stop the Romans simply moving it out of the way. A second is that a large number were hidden near the entrance to the valley and were then ordered to block the Romans' return route. This probably included hidden wagons that were used to form the second barricade, carrying heavy material quickly into place before themselves being overturned to form part of the defensive wall. Again troops would be needed to man the barricade and prevent it simply being removed. With the Romans not using scouts ahead of their advance, the presence of loaded wagons would not be noticed.

Probably the majority of the Samnite force was positioned on the hills to prevent the Romans escaping across the hilltops. As a result, Pontius would have the advantage of being able to see every move the Romans made, so allowing him to redeploy his forces at threatened points. Apart from these assumptions, no detail of the battle survives in the extant sources.

The Battle

After the Romans had refused the Samnites' peace offers, the Roman Consuls Titus Veturius Calvinus and Spurius Postumius Albinus assembled their legions in Calatia (Le Galazze) and decided to take the war to the Samnite heartland. It is possible that they were attempting to knock the Caudini – one of the Samnite tribes – out of the war.[13] To do this they decided to take the route around the south of Mount Taburnus in the belief that there were no enemy forces in the region.[14] The claim by Livy (9.2) that they were attempting to relieve a (fictitious) Samnite siege of Luceria is obviously false, since the city was hostile to Rome until it was taken by the Romans in 315/4.[15] Livy's tale of the Samnite commander disguising ten men as shepherds to inform the Samnites of the siege is also discarded for the same reason.

With the narrative described by Livy discounted as repeating contemporary Roman propaganda, it would seem that the Samnites did not 'trick' the Roman commanders: instead, the Roman consuls were simply out-thought. The Samnite *Meddix* Pontius – described by Livy as 'their foremost soldier and commander' – had earlier that year captured Canusium and Gnaitha (unknown).[16] As Canusium was a long way away near the Adriatic coast, it would appear that the Roman commanders had good reason to believe that they were unopposed.

Possibly due to information that the Romans were gathering at Luceria, Pontius stationed his troops close to Caudium in the belief that the Romans would use the pass through the Caudine Forks. Pontius ordered 'a huge barricade of felled trees with great masses of rock piled against them' at the exit of the pass. He must also have prepared easily-deployed barricades to impede the return route once the Roman army had found their way forward blocked, probably by heavy obstacles mounted on carts and hidden from the advancing army that could be deployed with speed.

Consequently, when they reached the far end of the valley the Romans found their passage blocked. Contrary to the impression given by both the sources and modern historians who assume that the Roman army immediately retraced its steps, it is likely that the two consuls then held a brief conference to decide whether they should attempt to force the pass or turn back and exit from the valley. This delay allowed the Samnites to block the pass at the opposite end of the valley. Decision made, the Romans turned around and attempted to retreat. At this point they found that the Samnites had also blocked the rear exit.[17]

The Romans appear to have made several attempts to break out of the encirclement, almost certainly focused upon the two barricades, before they recognized that their endeavours were in vain. At this point they constructed a marching camp to defend themselves from attack and settled down for the night.[18] On the following day they again attempted to fight their way out of the valley, but failed to break out.[19] Defeated, they settled down to a siege, probably in the hope that either a relief force would be dispatched to save them, or that events elsewhere would force the recall of the Samnite army. As time passed and food became scarce they were soon aware that their hopes were unfounded.

Eventually the consuls entered into negotiations with Pontius. According to the sources, Pontius then sent messengers to his father asking what should be done. He was advised to either free the prisoners or kill them, with freedom being the preferred option. Pontius refused both choices, preferring to make his own decision.[20]

Yet there remained one problem. One factor which Livy may record accurately is that the consuls in the valley could not agree a formal treaty with Pontius since this would involve rituals that they were not allowed to perform.[21] Therefore, rather than settling a *foedus* (peace treaty), the consuls instead formulated a *sponsio* (promise).[22] Although informal in the strictest sense, the Roman Senate appears to have accepted the agreement.

The *sponsio* negotiated between the Roman consuls and Pontius appears to have been a straightforward agreement. In return for the release of the two trapped legions – which was a large proportion of the whole Roman army at this point in time – the Romans had to agree to halt the war and to surrender the colonies at Cales and Fregellae that had triggered the war.[23]

However, Pontius did enforce one particularly offensive provision in the *sponsio*: the entire Roman army was forced to cast aside their arms and armour before being made to 'pass under the yoke'. This was a traditional Italian method of humiliating an enemy force. The level of humiliation involved becomes clear due to the Roman army's response: 'When the result of this embassy was made known, such general lamentation suddenly arose, and such melancholy took possession of them, that had they been told that all were to die on the spot, they could not have felt deeper affliction.'[24] Similarly, when they heard the news the citizens of Rome went into mourning as if they had lost the entire army killed.[25]

The 'yoke' was made by fixing two spears upright into the ground with a third spear fixed horizontally across the top of the other two. The Roman army, wearing only their tunics, was made to walk through this contraption: a symbol of dishonour and defeat. With around 10,000 men in the Roman army, it is likely that several such 'yokes' were constructed.

Aftermath

According to Livy, once the army had returned to Rome the Senate renounced the agreement and the war instantly resumed, but Livy's description of events concerning the campaign of 321–320 'bristles with absurdities' and should not be seen as fact.[26] In fact, even Livy accepts that there was a peace following the defeat later in his narrative: an example of Livy's internal contradictions due to his reliance upon disparate sources.[27] In reality, the 'Caudine Peace' endured until 317, when war again erupted between Rome and the Samnites.

Although vanquished, the Romans could not live with the humiliation of the defeat at the Caudine Forks and took measures to strengthen their position against the Samnites. With the agreed peace holding, they expanded in central Italy by taking control of the Oufentina and the Falerna and attacking and defeating the Apulians and the Lucanians. Feeling themselves to be in a much stronger position and with at least part of their military reputation restored, Rome then renewed the war with the Samnites. However, they were defeated, especially at the Battle of Lautulae in 315. These defeats weakened Roman control and several of her allies defected and joined the Samnites, including the Etruscans.

Their timing was poor: according to recent research, the Romans had finally acknowledged the need for change and the inflexible battle lines, which were at a disadvantage in the hilly homeland of the Samnites, were abandoned. They appear to have begun to change their linear formations for the new *manipular* system – possibly imitating the Samnites' methods. In theory, the army was divided into groups of c.200 men, who were trained to fight effectively as small groups or to form into the more traditional lines for formal battles. If this theory is correct, there would still have been problems. The *principes*, armed with the *pilum*, may have adapted quickly to the new formation, but this formation was not as suitable to the *hastati*, armed with the *hasta*, who relied on cohesion to fight effectively. This hypothesis lends further weight to the changes in formation and tactics evolving over time rather than in a single moment, with the *principes* adopting and successfully adapting to the *manipular* formation before it was realized that the *hastati* also needed to change equipment and tactics.

Although the change is usually dated to c.311 BCE, it is possible that it began earlier and the use of unfamiliar tactics and deployments were responsible for the Roman defeat at the Battle of Lautulae. However, after this setback, and possibly using these reformed troops and tactics, the Romans managed to seize the initiative (for more on this debate, see Chapter 3). In 308 they defeated the Etruscans and in 304 they captured the Samnite 'capital' of Bovianum. Finally, the Second Samnite War was over.

Effects

Politically and mentally, the defeat continued to haunt the Romans. For example, in 197 BCE the consul Quintus Minucius allegedly extricated himself from a similar situation, spurred on by the memory of the disaster of the Caudine Forks.[28] Throughout Roman history the battle was ranked alongside the defeats at the Allia and the later Battle of Cannae as one of the most humiliating defeats the Romans ever suffered, handed out to them by the Samnites, the only tribal group in Italy feared by the Romans.

Certainty is impossible as changes in the army are not well documented, but it was probably after the defeat at the Caudine Forks that the Roman army was forced to adopt the more flexible tactics and formations of the Samnites. Although the dating is insecure, a change in the formation and deployment of the army explains the drastic change in fortunes of the Romans after the battle. With war again breaking out in 317, it is interesting to note that in the first exchanges the Romans were again defeated, possibly indicating a period of change where the army had not yet fully mastered the new organization. Yet in time things changed: in 308 the Etruscans were forced to sue for peace, and finally, in 304, the Samnites were in turn compelled to capitulate. With the majority of Central Italy now secured, the Romans could look further afield for new conquests.

Select Bibliography

Appian, *Samnite Wars*, 4.2–6 (App. Sam. 1.pos=28) http://www.perseus.tufts.edu/hopper/text?doc=Perseus%3Atext%3A1999.01.0230%3Atext%3DSam.%3Achapter%3D1%3Asection%3Dpos%3D28Cicero, *Cato Maior* http://penelope.uchicago.edu/Thayer/E/Roman/Texts/Cicero/Cato_Maior_de_Senectute/text*.html

Cicero, *De Officiis*, 3.109 [30] http://www.perseus.tufts.edu/hopper/text?doc=Perseus%3Atext%3A2007.01.0048%3Abook%3Dpos%3D3%3Asection%3D109

Cicero, *Cato Maior De Senectute*, 12 [41] http://penelope.uchicago.edu/Thayer/e/roman/texts/cicero/cato_maior_de_senectute/text*.html

Dio, *frg.*, 7.26: http://penelope.uchicago.edu/Thayer/E/Roman/Texts/Cassius_Dio/8*.html

Dionysius of Halicarnassus: http://penelope.uchicago.edu/Thayer/E/Roman/Texts/Dionysius_of_Halicarnassus/home.html

Eutropius, 2.9: http://www.tertullian.org/fathers/eutropius_breviarium_2_text.htm

Jerome, *De viris illustribus*: http://www.thelatinlibrary.com/lhomond.viris.html

Livy: http://www.gutenberg.org/files/19725/19725-h/19725-h.htm#h8

Plutarch, *Camillus*: http://penelope.uchicago.edu/Thayer/e/roman/texts/plutarch/lives/camillus*.html

Sallust, *Bellum Catilina* http://penelope.uchicago.edu/Thayer/e/roman/texts/sallust/bellum_catilinae*.html

Salmon, E.T., 'The Resumption of Hostilities after the Caudine Forks', *Transactions and Proceedings of the American Philological Association* (1956), pp.87, 98–108.

Salmon, E.T., *Samnium and the Samnites* (Cambridge, 2010)

Sextus Julius Frontinus, *Stratagemata*, pp.5, 16 http://penelope.uchicago.edu/Thayer/e/roman/texts/frontinus/strategemata/1*.html

Chapter Three

Pyrrhic Defeats: Pyrrhus of Epirus
The Battle of Heraclea, 280 BCE
The Battle of Asculum, 279 BCE

[Author's note: Although these were obviously two separate battles, the dates, the results and the impact are so closely tied together that I feel it is justifiable to combine them as a single entry.]

The Sources

Marcus Tullius Cicero was one of the greatest orators and writers of the Roman Republic. He wrote in the first century BCE, one of the most dramatic periods of Roman history. His *De Finibus Bonorum et Malorum* (*On the Ends of Good and Evil*) was a Socratic Dialogue and his *Tusculanae Disputationes/Tusculanae Quaestiones* (*Tusculan Disputations*) was an attempt to popularize Greek philosophy in Rome. Although neither work is historical in nature, they do include some details, especially the names of individuals, which can be added to the main accounts of the battles.

Dionysius of Halicarnassus lived and wrote in the first century BCE and the early first century CE. His *Antiquitatum Romanarum* (*Roman Antiquities*) runs from the beginnings of Rome to the First Punic War, and was an attempt to reconcile Greeks to Roman rule. As part of his aim, in the earlier part of the history Dionysius fakes a Greek origin for Rome, with the (obvious) result that much is distorted or simply false. However, as he comes nearer to his own time his work becomes more accurate and can thus be used, although the temporal distance between Dionysius and Pyrrhus still needs to be remembered.

The Greek historian and philosopher **Plutarch** wrote his *Lives of the Noble Greeks and Romans* (commonly known as *Parallel Lives*) late in the first century and/or early in the second century CE. The 'Lives' are arranged in pairs, and used to compare the 'common virtues or failings' of the two men covered. These 'biographies' include much information that is otherwise unknown, but the fact that Plutarch was writing with the specific aim of comparing individuals means that his information may be biased towards his intended purpose. Consequently, although useful, the 'Lives' needs to be used with care and not accepted at face value.

Paulus Orosius was a Christian priest and writer from the late fourth/early fifth centuries CE. His most important work as far as historians are concerned is the *Historiarum Adversum Paganos Libri VII* (*Seven Books of History Against the Pagans*), written after the Gothic Sack of Rome in 410 CE. Despite the fact that the work was written with a specific purpose – that the abandonment of the old gods and adoption of Christianity was not responsible for the Sack of Rome – it contains much that is otherwise unknown. Yet the distance in time between Orosius and Pyrrhus means that care is needed when using Orosius' work.

Joannes Zonaras was a Byzantine scholar of the twelfth century CE. Writing in Greek, his *Epitome Historiarum* (*Extracts of History*) contains details concerning the Pyrrhic War, but due to the many centuries between Zonaras and the third century BCE his work is obviously dependent upon earlier works. These earlier works are lost, so Zonaras may contain information that is otherwise unknown, but the accuracy of these fragments is uncertain.

There are many snippets of information in other sources – for example, in Polybius – and where necessary these are used to confirm the main sources, to add detail or to give an opposing viewpoint. Yet despite the fact that much is uncertain concerning the accuracy of the accounts and as there is no other option, when these are all used to correct/check each other a reasonable account emerges of the two battles and these are recounted below.

The Battle of Heraclea

Background

Following their success in the Second Samnite War, Rome was forced to fight a third war with the Samnites between 298 and 290 BCE. Their victory finally established Rome as the dominant force in Italy. The war

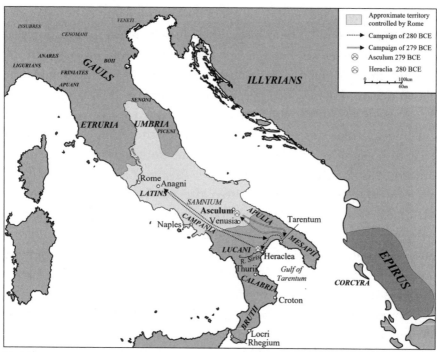

The Pyrrhic War.

also brought Rome into contact with the peoples and cities of southern Italy.

The city of Tarentum, founded in the eighth century BCE by colonists from the Greek city of Sparta, was one of the major cities in Magna Graecia ('Greater Greece': the many Greek settlements in southern Italy and Sicily). Although descendants of the feared Spartans, under pressure from the Italian tribes the Tarentines had earlier resorted to asking for military help, first from Archidamus III of Sparta (in Italy 342 BCE until his defeat and death in 338 BCE) and then from Alexander of Epirus (in Italy 334 BCE until his defeat and death in 331). During his time in Italy Alexander had defeated the Samnites and Lucanians in 332 and had agreed a treaty with Rome.

However, as Roman power continued to expand, Tarentum was again compelled to ask for aid, this time from Sparta as Tarentum was again at war with the Lucanians. The Spartan commander Cleonymus was sent with a mercenary army. Gaining support from both Tarentum and other Greek cities in Magna Graecia, Cleonymus expanded the allies' control in southern Italy before coming into contact with Rome and being driven back by Rome and her Italian allies.[1] Tarentum and Rome then concluded a treaty, acknowledging Tarentum's sphere of influence as being around the Gulf of Tarentum.

Frictions reappeared when, in the 280s, Rome responded to a request for help from Thurii, a Greek city on the Gulf of Tarentum and a rival of Tarentum. Despite the earlier treaty, Rome then entered into alliances with other Greek cities in the region, including Croton, Locri and Rhegium, further increasing the tension. Finally in 282, bad weather forced a Roman fleet to make landfall near Tarentum. In anger at this apparent breach of the treaty, the citizens attacked and killed the Roman commander and sank several ships.[2] Shortly afterwards Tarentum attacked Thurii, forcing the Roman garrison out. When the Romans sent ambassadors to Tarentum, they were mocked and humiliated.[3] In response, Rome declared war. As in previous wars, the Tarentines looked east for aid, this time to King Pyrrhus of Epirus. With the promise of massive Italian support, Pyrrhus agreed to lead an army to Italy. After forming alliances with some of the *Diadochi* (successors of Alexander) in the east, most notably Ptolemy II of Egypt, in order to ensure that Epirus would not be attacked in his absence, Pyrrhus shipped his troops across to Italy.

The focus on Pyrrhus – as here – has usually been on his exploits in Italy and Sicily. Yet it needs to be remembered that he was not simply a minor ruler who attempted to interfere in Italian politics. He was the *hegemon* ('head') of the Epirote League, and was a major character in the Wars of the Successors, the generals who had succeeded Alexander the Great: in fact, he had taken part in the Battle of Ipsus (301 BCE) as a supporter of Antigonus I Monophthalmus, whose defeat at the battle ended any chance of Alexander the Great's empire being ruled by one man.

Further battles and shifting alliances resulted in Pyrrhus sharing the rule of Macedonia with Lysimachus, one of the victors at Ipsus, from 288 until 284, when Lysimachus drove Pyrrhus back to Epirus.[4] Despite these difficulties and defeats, Pyrrhus had acquired a reputation as a gifted general. It was probably due in part to his reputation that under pressure from Rome, Tarentum turned to him for support. A further aspect may have been that Pyrrhus was actually indebted to Tarentum as, during the period of his joint rule of Macedonia, in 282 Tarentum had loaned Pyrrhus ships with which he retook the island of Corcyra. Stymied in

Greece and the East, Pyrrhus seized the chance of glory and conquest in the 'barbarian' West and prepared for war in Italy.

The Opposing Forces: Rome

In the forty-year gap between the Battle of the Caudine Forks and the Battle of Heraclea the Roman army had undergone reform. Any vestige of the linear formations used earlier had gone. Instead, the army was almost certainly now using the *manipular* system as described by Polybius.

Polybius states that a normal legion was by now composed of 4,200 infantry and 300 cavalry divided into smaller contingents for flexibility, although he also notes that in time of emergency the legions could be increased to c.5,000 men, or possibly even 6,000.[5]

The close-order infantry was divided into three lines. The front line was called the *hastati* and the second the *principes*. These two lines were organized in the same way. The lowest division was the century, which during Polybius' time was c.60 to 80 men strong, but possibly at this earlier date was still at the 100 which gave the sub-unit its name. Two centuries were combined to form a *maniple* ('handful'), and there were ten of these *maniples* in each of the first two lines. The third line, the *triarii*, was slightly different in that each of its *maniples* was composed of a single century. The net result was that the third line was much smaller than the first two. The line assigned to each man was determined by age. The *hastati* was composed of men up to 25 years of age, the *principes* those between 26 and 35, and the *triarii* men aged between 36 and 46.[6] These three lines then deployed in a formation known to modern authors as the *quincunx*, based upon the dots for the number five on a six-sided dice. In this, the *principes* of the second line were deployed to cover the gaps in the first line of the *hastati*, and the *triarii* in the third to cover those in the *hastati*. The exact manner in which this system worked is still a matter of debate.

For body protection, the majority of the infantry still wore a small pectoral, a piece of bronze armour that only covered the chest/upper stomach, but those who could afford it – especially the older men in the *triarii* – wore *lorica*, mail covering the whole body and with an extra layer across the shoulders to give added protection against downward slashes.[7]

Head protection consisted of bronze helmets. The Romans at this time appear to have used three main types of helmet: the *Montefortino*, the

Italo-Corinthian and various *Attic* types. The *Montefortino* covered the head but also had cheek guards; the *Italo-Corinthian* was a variant of the Greek Corinthian, but the Greek original had a face-guard whereas in the Italian version the 'face-guard' was ornamental and did not cover the face but the eye-holes were kept as an integral part; and the Attic helmets were similar to the Greek *Chalcidian* ones but lacked the latter's nose-guards. In all cases the main priority was a balance between protection and communication. Polybius states that the helmets were adorned with either black or purple plumes to increase the soldiers' apparent height.[8]

For their main protection the close-order infantry carried the *scutum*, a long oval shield that was convex and so gave excellent protection against contemporary enemies. In addition to its defensive duties, the boss of the *scutum* could be used offensively to punch at the enemy, knocking them off balance and making them easier targets for the sword.[9]

When it comes to the arms carried by the infantry, there is a problem with the sources. As noted in the description given in the earlier battles, it is known that at some point the first line of the Roman army adopted the *pilum*. In addition, it is known that at some point the second line also began using the *pilum*, but sadly these changes are not dated. In an attempt to synchronize the sources into a cohesive and sensible chronology, it has been assumed that at the Battle of the Caudine Forks the *principes* had adopted the *pilum*, but that the army was fighting in three distinct single lines.

As noted in the previous chapter, the reform is sometimes seen as being a rapid change introduced by a single man or in response to a single event and so datable to a single year. This would seem to be an impossibility, given the many factors surrounding the reform. The main objection is concerned with the revolutionary command and control system needed to make the new, multi-unit army function efficiently. Training and experience would be necessary for the tribunes, centurions and *optios* to understand how the new formation worked and how to react in different situations. It is more likely that this was a process of trial and error over several years rather than an instantaneous change that worked without any difficulties as described in the sources.

In accordance with the attempt to make sense of the changes, it is here postulated that, after the defeat at the Caudine Forks, during the Third Samnite War (298–290) the Romans had begun to experiment with a more flexible system, later known as the *quincunx*, a gradual implementation of changes brought about when fighting in the Apennines against the Samnites, where simple linear tactics would have been less effective.

Since it is being assumed that the changes were gradual, it is possible that when Pyrrhus landed in Italy the use of the *pilum* was still reserved only for the *principes*. On the other hand, it is likely that fighting in a more open style to correspond with the hills and mountains of the Apennines clearly demonstrated that the *hasta* (spear) was of limited use for offensive manoeuvres in broken terrain. As a consequence, it is here postulated that the change to the more flexible *quincunx* deployment corresponded with a change to the equipment being used, with the *hastati* finally being equipped with the *pilum*.

The question then remains as to why the *triarii* retained the *hasta*. As the *triarii* were the last line of defence should the first two lines be repulsed, the phrase 'the battle came to the *triarii*' was used by the Romans to signify a closely-fought battle where the third line actually came into play, their purpose being to act as a defensive wall behind which the other two lines could reform and return to the battle. In this context, their use of the spear to form a defensive wall remains consistent with the change in tactics.

In addition to the *pilum* or the *hasta*, the Roman infantry also had a *gladius* (short sword) and a *pugio* (dagger). In theory, the common tactic was for the *hastati* to advance to within c.15–30 yards, throw the *pilum* – which would hopefully throw the enemy line into confusion – draw the sword and engage in close-quarter combat. Once the *hastati* had tired, they would withdraw and the *principes* would use the same method to advance and take their place. Should the *principes* also be forced to withdraw, both the *hastati* and the *principes* could reform behind the *triarii*.

Although the theory works, it is unclear as to how this actually worked in battle, and has led to debate and controversy among modern military historians.

In front of the three lines went the *velites*, unarmoured light infantry. They were equipped with a light helmet, and a *parma* (a small round shield possibly named after the Etruscan city of the same name). Offensively they continued to carry the *hastae velitares* (light javelins, see Chapter 2) and a sword. Their purpose was to skirmish in front of the close-order infantry in an attempt to cause disorder in the enemy's ranks and to prevent the enemy's skirmishers from disrupting their own formations.

The few cavalry supplied by the Romans were provided by the richest men, able to provide a horse and full equipment, as described in earlier chapters. The Romans remained reliant upon the allies to supply the majority of the cavalry.

The Allies

Concrete, specific evidence is non-existent when it comes to the allies who fought alongside the Romans. It is usually assumed that by this stage the Latin allies were armed, equipped and fought in an identical way to the Romans. The other allies either fought in the same way or in their traditional manner, probably depending upon how long the alliance had been in place, with those allied for longer being more likely to adopt Roman methods.

Possibly supporting this theory, a bronze shield fragment found at Dodona and assumed to have been dedicated by Pyrrhus after one of his Italian battles is inscribed as follows:

'[KIN]G PYRRHU[S AND] / THE EPIROTES AND THE T[ARENTINES] / FROM THE ROMANS AND [THEIR] / ALLIES TO ZEUS NA[IOS]'

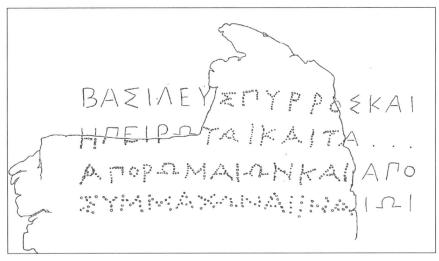

(Drawing after Carapanos), found at Dodona, preserved in the National Museum, Athens (EAM Kar. 514). Inscription (Syll 3923, SGDI 1368).

Although certainty is impossible, it would appear that the shield was dedicated after the Battle of Heraclea as only the Epirotes and Tarentines were present at this battle whereas other allies fought at the later Battle of Asculum and it would be expected for them to be mentioned if the shield was from this battle. As the Romans no longer used bronze shields, it would appear that the shield was taken from one of the allies, probably equipped with a bronze *hoplon*.

Consequently it is likely that at least some of Rome's allies fought as close-order troops equipped as traditional Greek hoplites, whereas some, even from the same allied contingent, may have fought as fast-moving javelin men specializing in charging the enemy or in skirmishing, or as a mix of both.

In one way, however, there remained one major factor: the Italian allies still supplied a greater number of cavalry: 900 as opposed to 300 per legion. These were equipped in a similar manner to the Roman cavalry, with the exception that many did not carry shields.

Numbers

No ancient source gives a plausible account of the battle and no numbers for the troops involved are included. Consequently it is necessary to resort to speculation. Such conjecture can be warped due to the similar outcomes of the two consecutive battles: Heraclea and Asculum. Although both were 'Pyrrhic defeats', at the second, the Battle of Heraclea, in the following year it is known that both consuls were present, so it is sometimes assumed that at both battles the Roman army must have contained four legions for the outcome to be so similar. However, there is no evidence that Laevinus led more than a single consular army. A clarification of the confusion will be discussed below.

In normal circumstances a consular army consisted of two Roman legions, each of c.4,200 men in the centre, flanked by two *alae* ('wings'), also each of c.4,200 men, of allies. The right flank was composed of the Roman cavalry and the left of the allied cavalry. In front went the *velites*, skirmishing with the enemy.[10]

Consequently, it is assumed here that Laevinus' army was composed of c.16,800 infantry and c.1,200 cavalry. The Roman legions would be deployed in the new *manipular* formation, with the *hastati* in front, the *principes* in the second rank and the *triarii* acting as a reserve. The allied legions would deploy in whichever formation was used by the allies.

The Opposing Forces: Pyrrhus

Prior to his crossing to Italy, Pyrrhus sent a man named Cineas with 3,000 infantry to Tarentum to prepare the groundwork for the war. This included the organizing of the large numbers of transports needed for the main army. According to Plutarch, this consisted of a main body of 20,000 infantry and 3,000 cavalry, along with 2,000 archers, 500 slingers and 20 elephants, giving a total of 25,500 men plus the elephants.[11] Rather than a mass outpouring of support by disgruntled Italian tribes, due to both the speed of events and fear of Roman arms and retribution, it would appear that Pyrrhus had to rely solely on a force of c.6,000 hoplites recruited from Tarentum, bringing his force up to c.31,500 men.

Sadly no indication is given of the proportions of specific troops in the main body, but with regard to the infantry it is likely that the main strike force was a large number of phalangites (close-order infantry armed with a *sarissa*, a long pike) possibly supported by an unknown number of *peltastai* (troops originally carrying the *pelta*, a small crescent-shaped shield) or *thureophoroi* (troops who had swapped the *pelta* for the *thureos*, a larger, oval shield; the date of the change is uncertain), both of which types by this date were capable of skirmishing with the enemy or of taking their place in the main battle line depending on circumstances.

For the cavalry, at this point it is likely that Pyrrhus was following Alexander the Great, riding at the head of his *agema*, shock cavalry armed with a two-handed lance who as a consequence did not carry a shield; these were the contemporary version of Alexander's *companions*. Under Alexander it had been the *companions* who had been the decisive arm, striking at the enemy's weak point while the enemy's main line was pinned by the phalanx. His successors, however, had slowly changed this, in part due to the influx of elephants from India. Now it was a combination of the phalanx and the elephants that made up the decisive force, being sent forward to force the enemy back until they broke in rout. The cavalry defended the phalanx's flanks, but when the enemy broke the cavalry would be unleashed in pursuit.

War elephants had impressed Alexander the Great during his invasion of India and they had become integral to the armies of his successors. They could be the large Indian species or the smaller Africans, depending on supplies. Pyrrhus was being supported by some of the eastern kings, so had access to the larger Indian elephant.

Alongside his 'native' troops Pyrrhus had arranged for both local and mercenary skirmishers to join the army. These made up the archers and slingers. Although the most efficient mercenaries were archers from Crete and slingers from the Balearic Islands, it is not certain whether such mercenaries were serving with Pyrrhus in the Italian campaign.

Pyrrhus was assured by the Tarentines that many peoples in Italy would join them when they landed, but in the beginning these peoples appear to have been reluctant to commit themselves without evidence of Pyrrhus' abilities as a commander. For the first battle Pyrrhus was only to receive new troops from the Tarentines.

Location

Hearing of Pyrrhus' imminent arrival in Italy, the Romans reacted with their usual speed. They raised eight legions, demanded the usual troops from their allies, and prepared for war. The eight legions were divided into four traditional 'consular armies', each of two Roman and two allied 'legions'. One army was sent to the north to ensure that the Etruscans would not consider an alliance with Pyrrhus, one to Venusia to similarly deter the Samnites, and one remained in Rome to protect the city.

The fourth was placed under the command of Publius Valerius Laevinus and was sent to the south. The aim was to place an army between the Tarentines and the Greek cities in Calabria to avoid these cities also joining the fight.

Pyrrhus' reaction to these moves was to gather his forces ready to face Laevinus. Possibly in the knowledge that delay would be a sign of weakness, but just as likely due to his aggressive and impulsive nature, Pyrrhus seized the initiative and marched towards Heraclea in order to meet the Romans. Near Heraclea Pyrrhus came into contact with Laevinus and set up his camp on the banks of the River Siris. Laevinus also set up his camp on the opposite side of the river. According to Plutarch, Pyrrhus went to observe the Romans and was surprised by 'their order, the appointment of the watches, their method and the general form of their encampment'. He allegedly said to his companion: 'This order…of the barbarians is not at all barbarian in character.' Consequently, he resolved to await the arrival of the promised allied Italian tribes.

Deployment

No details of the deployment survive, but taking into account the course of the battle it would appear that on the morning of the battle Laevinus formed his troops behind the river in the standard formation with the Roman legions in the centre, flanked by the allied *cohorts*, in turn flanked by the Roman cavalry on the right and the allied cavalry on the left.

In response, Pyrrhus sent a detachment of missile troops to cover the river and deter any attempt by the Romans to cross. Hoping that the deterrent would delay the Romans, Pyrrhus was determined to avoid battle until the promised reinforcements arrived. However, realizing that Pyrrhus was intent upon delay and so was not focusing upon defending the river, after a few hours Laevinus decided to seize the initiative and ordered an assault across the river. The battle had begun.

Course of the Battle

The description that follows is based primarily on Plutarch's *Life of Pyrrhus*. Although written several centuries after the events described, it is the only narrative that outlines the course of the battle in detail so is used here, although it should be remembered that Plutarch would have relied on earlier sources which are now lost and their reliability is therefore uncertain.

Advancing in front of the main body, the *velites* quickly engaged the opposing skirmishers, effectively pinning them in place while the cavalry found alternative crossing-points. Once across, the cavalry quickly routed the enemy light troops.

Pyrrhus was apparently surprised by the speed and efficiency of the attack. He ordered his main body to form into battle order while he advanced with 3,000 cavalry. Allegedly he was hoping to attack the Romans, assuming that as they crossed the river they would be disordered. Even though he was disappointed by the tight formations crossing the

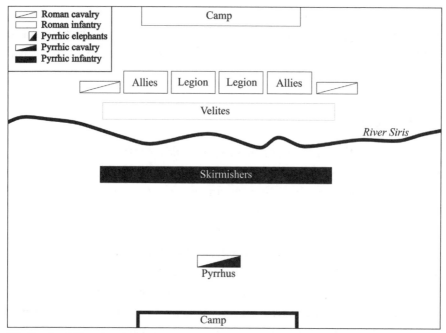

The Battle of Heraclea: deployment.

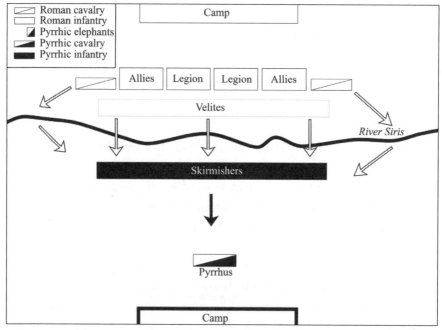

The Battle of Heraclea: 1st phase – Roman velites and cavalry defeat Pyrrhus' skirmishers.

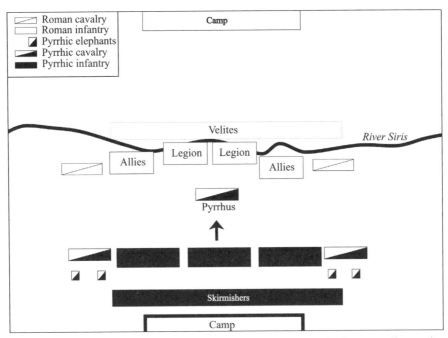

The Battle of Heraclea: 2nd phase – Pyrrhus' cavalry push back the Romans, allowing his main body to deploy.

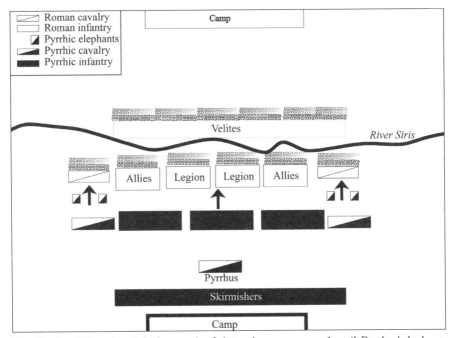

The Battle of Heraclea: 3rd phase – the fighting becomes general until Pyrrhus' elephants cause a Roman collapse.

river, he still decided to attack: the Epirote cavalry charged the Roman lines. Although he did not manage to break the Romans, the delay caused by his attack allowed the main body of infantry to form up and join the battle.

Early in the battle a Frentanian named Oplacus killed Pyrrhus' horse, but was in turn killed by Pyrrhus' companions.[12] Realizing that his conspicuous armour made him a target, Pyrrhus swapped it with his friend Megacles; a wise move as Megacles thus became the main target and was eventually killed.

Slowly, the Romans were pushed back to the river, but it was at this point that Megacles was killed. Assuming that Pyrrhus was dead, the Epirote troops lost heart and the jubilant Romans in turn began pressing forward. It was only when Pyrrhus rode around the field with his head bare, proving that he was still alive, that the battle lines once again stabilized.

Finally Pyrrhus committed his elephants, which he had held in reserve, against the Roman cavalry. Having never seen elephants, the Roman horses panicked and became disordered. Seeing them waver, Pyrrhus ordered the Thessalian cavalry to charge. The Roman cavalry broke, and with their flanks exposed, the main Roman body also broke in rout. The battle ended with the Epirote cavalry pursuing the fleeing Romans into the river and beyond. As a result of their experiences with the elephants the Romans came to call elephants *Luca bos*, 'Lucanian ox', due to the battle in Lucania.

Aftermath

According to Plutarch, the sources he used gave different numbers for the losses incurred by the two armies: Dionysius claimed almost 15,000 Romans and 13,000 Epirotes were killed, whereas Hieronymus stated only 6,000–7,000 Romans and 4,000 Epirotes. According to Pyrrhus' own figures, he lost 3,505 men.

The difference in numbers is easy to explain. Dionysius only records one battle against Pyrrhus and so is conflating the numbers of both Heraclea and Asculum. Consequently, it is here assumed that the lower numbers are more accurate, especially in view of the overall numbers of troops projected above, with the Romans losing 7,000 killed and 2,000 captured out of c.18,000, while the Epirotes lost 4,000 killed out of 31,000. Despite the fact that the Romans had lost half their army, they still had three more in existence. Pyrrhus had lost one-eighth of his army, including many of his best troops and – more importantly – his veteran officers and these were irreplaceable.

Losses notwithstanding, Pyrrhus' victory gave confidence to those in Italy unhappy with Roman dominance. Many (but not all) of the Samnites and Lucanians threw in their lot with Pyrrhus. As his army grew, Pyrrhus advanced to within 40 miles of Rome, but this was in the knowledge that, despite his new allies, Rome was able to field vast numbers of men.

Accordingly, Pyrrhus then attempted to achieve a diplomatic solution to the war. Cineas was sent to Rome, where he proposed the return of the men captured at Heraclea in return for an alliance with both Pyrrhus and the Tarentines. After a debate in the Senate, the proposal was rejected and Rome demanded that Pyrrhus leave Italy. On the other hand, a man named Fabricus was sent to negotiate the release of the prisoners and this may have ended successfully.[13] Later the Romans compared the humanity of Pyrrhus with the lack thereof in Hannibal.

In the meantime, Pyrrhus campaigned in southern Italy, advancing past Capua and Naples to threaten Rome itself, hoping to pressure the Romans into a negotiated treaty. Learning of their defeat, the Roman senate recalled Tiberius Coruncanius, the second consul of 280 (alongside Laevinus), who had been dispatched with an army to police Etruria. In addition, Decius Vibelius, the garrison commander of the Greek city of Rhegium, ordered the execution of those in the town who wanted to join Pyrrhus and took control of the town.[14]

As Pyrrhus reached the town of Anagni, c.37 miles from Rome, he found Coruncanius and a new consular army facing him. With the previous battle having been so close and knowing that there were two other Roman armies in Italy, Pyrrhus decided to avoid battle. Instead he returned to Tarentum, where he billeted the troops over the winter of 280–279.

When the campaign season of 279 began, and having already campaigned along the western side of the Apennines, he decided to advance along the east coast, hoping that there would be defections from tribes in the region still allied to Rome. Obviously, the Romans were aware of his moves and knew that they had to act before more of their allies deserted to Pyrrhus.

With the close nature of the Battle of Heraclea and knowing that Pyrrhus had been joined by new Italian allies, it was decided that a single consular army would not be enough to defeat him. Accordingly, both the consuls for 179, Publius Decius Mus and Publius Sulpicius Saverrio, were ordered to join their armies and advance to meet Pyrrhus. The opposing armies advanced towards each other and finally came in contact near the town of Asculum, modern-day Ascoli Satriano in Apulia.

*   *   *

The Battle of Asculum

The Opposing Forces: Rome

It is when analyzing the strength of the armies at Heraclea and Asculum that difficulties in interpretation have arisen. As noted above, there is no indication that the army under Laevinus consisted of more than one consular army, but the fact that the two battles had such similar outcomes and that at Asculum both consuls were present has resulted in Laevinus sometimes being allocated a double consular army in order to make the result understandable. However, as will be noted below, there is an explanation for the discrepancy.

Using the figures calculated for the single consular army at the Battle of Heraclea, simple maths gives a figure of c.40,000 infantry and 2,400 cavalry for the double-consular army fielded at Asculum, a figure supported to some degree by Frontinus, who suggested that both sides had c.40,000 men.[15] It is also possible that, due to the defeat in the previous year, Rome requested stronger reinforcements from the allies. In addition, and now aware of the use of elephants by Pyrrhus, the Romans attempted to devise means of nullifying the new terror-weapon. The devices used were 300 'anti-elephant wagons'.

According to Dionysius:

These wagons had upright beams on which were mounted movable transverse poles that could be swung round as quick as thought in any direction one might wish, and on the ends of the poles there were either tridents or sword-like spikes or scythes all of iron; or again they had cranes that hurled down heavy grappling-irons. Many of the poles had attached to them and projecting in front of the wagons fire-bearing grapnels wrapped in tow that had been liberally daubed with pitch, which men standing on the wagons were to set afire as soon as they came near the elephants and then rain blows with them upon the trunks and faces of the beasts. Furthermore, standing on the wagons, which were four-wheeled, were many also of the light-armed troops – bowmen, hurlers of stones and slingers who threw iron caltrops; and on the ground beside the wagons there were still more men.

For propulsion, it would appear that there was a harness at the rear to allow oxen to push them forward without as much threat to the animals from either missile fire or the elephants themselves.

According to the sources, the Roman army was supported by troops supplied by the Latins, the Campanians, the Sabines, the Umbrians, the Marsi, the Paeligni, the Volscians, the Marrucini, the Frentani and the Dauni.[16] Many of these tribes had only submitted during the Third Samnite War (298–290 BCE), but chose to remain allied to Rome, either through expectations of Roman victory or trust in Roman promises.

The Opposing Forces: Pyrrhus

Despite the losses he had suffered during the Battle of Heraclea, Pyrrhus' forces had actually grown during the following year due to the defection from Rome of many of the Italian tribes. According to the sources, he had the survivors of the first battle, which included his Epirotes, Aetolians, Acarnanians and Athamanians plus troops supplied by the Tarentines, but had now received reinforcements from the Bruttii, the Lucani and – yet again resisting Rome's rise – the Samnites. However, it should be noted that the affiliation of Italian tribes was not wholly towards one side or the other: some tribal groups were divided in their loyalties.

The fact that Pyrrhus had greatly increased the size of his army in Italy is of great importance, as it explains why, although a single consular army had been unable to defeat him in the first battle, a double-consular army still failed to defeat him in the second.

Numbers as given by the sources vary wildly, with Dionysius claiming that Pyrrhus had 70,000 foot, with Pyrrhus' initial troops supplying just 16,000 of them, whereas the Romans similarly fielded 70,000 with only about 20,000 of them being actual Romans. The cavalry of the two sides are depicted as being 8,000 for the Romans and slightly more for Pyrrhus, although Pyrrhus had 19 surviving elephants. As already noted, Frontinus suggests that both sides had c.40,000 men, and it is assumed here that the lower number given by Frontinus is much closer to the actual number than other exaggerated figures.

Deployment

The deployment is described in some detail by Dionysius, although there are some comments by other authors which in some respects contradict this, as will be shown.[17] The description given by Dionysius is used here, with notes where necessary to add detail or give alternative suggestions.

Due to there being two consular armies with four legions and four allied *alae*, the traditional deployment of the Roman army was impossible.

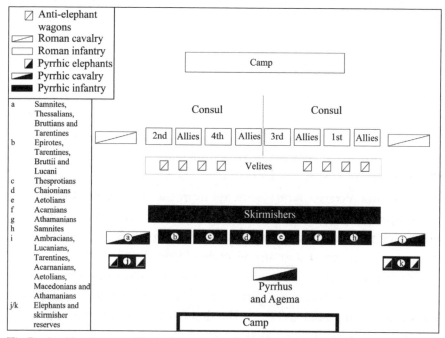

The Battle of Asculum: possible deployment. Due to the disparity of the sources, no description of the battle is possible.

Normally the legions would be numbered one to four, with one consul taking command of legions one and three, with the other consul commanding legions two and four. Consequently, the consuls appear to have decided to deploy the army as follows.

On the Roman right was the Second Legion. Usually seen as being a position of importance, it is likely that a Roman unit was placed here. Next to this was an *ala* of allies, as Dionysius states that the allies were interspersed with the legions. Then came the Fourth Legion, again followed by an *ala* of allies. This was the army of one of the consuls. The other consular army was deployed in a similar fashion, with the Third Legion followed by an allied *ala*, then the First Legion and finally the last allied *ala*.[18] Usually the Roman cavalry was placed on the right wing and the allied cavalry on the left, but this would result in the right flank, composed of only 600 cavalry, being vastly undermanned compared to the left wings' 1,800 horsemen. Consequently the cavalry was divided more equally between the two wings.

Although the description lacks clarity, it would appear that the *velites* were in front of the main body as usual, but intermingled with them were the 300 anti-elephant wagons: as the Romans did not know where the 19 elephants would be deployed and as the ox-propelled wagons would be slow to manoeuvre, they would have been deployed to cover the frontage of the army.

Opposite the Romans, Pyrrhus deployed his troops as follows. On his right flank, facing the Roman allies, Pyrrhus placed his Epirote pikemen with the Tarentines (who had white shields), the Bruttii and the Lucani. Although it is usually accepted that these three groups deployed separately, it is likely that this is not the case: according to Polybius, Pyrrhus deployed a *maniple* of Italians and a company of his own phalanx alternately in his battles against the Romans.[19] In the centre were the Thesprotians, the Chaonians, the Aetolians, the Acarnanians and the Athamanian mercenaries. Finally, on the left wing were the Samnites.

With regard to the cavalry, Pyrrhus deployed the Samnites, the Thessalians, the Bruttii and the Tarentine mercenaries on the right and on the left wing were the Ambracians, Lucanians, Tarentines, Acarnanians, Aetolians, Macedonians and Athamanians. He divided the skirmishing infantry and elephants in two and deployed them on raised ground behind the wings.

Finally Pyrrhus himself, along with his 2,000 *agema*, remained behind the main infantry line as a mobile reserve to support troops who were hard-pressed.

Frontinus has a different account of the deployment. Although he mirrors the positioning of the Roman troops, he claims that Pyrrhus deployed his 'poorest' troops, the Tarentines, in the centre and stationed the Samnites alongside the Epirotes on the right flank, with the Bruttians, Lucanians and Sallentines on the left. However, he does state that the elephants were held as reserves, and he suggests that the cavalry was also in a withdrawn position to support the main infantry force. However, Frontinus also claims that the outcome of the battle was a Roman victory, with the Romans only losing 5,000 men whereas Pyrrhus lost half his army.[20] Consequently it is assumed here that his source for the battle included some items that were accurate but that it was heavily biased towards Rome and that subsequently Pyrrhus' poor deployment is being used as a reason for his defeat; a defeat fitting the narrative of Frontinus' source rather than reflecting reality.

Course of the Battle

There are three main accounts of the battle, by Plutarch, Dionysius and Cassius Dio. Sadly, there are several discrepancies between the accounts that cannot easily be rectified.

Dionysius claims that the infantry advanced into contact as usual, but that the cavalry forces acted differently to each other, with the Roman cavalry resorting to a hand-to-hand stationary combat, with the Epirote cavalry attempting flanking and extravagant manoeuvres. With regard to the anti-elephant wagons, these apparently worked well until the Epirote supporting skirmishing troops attacked the wagons, forcing the crews to flee to the main infantry line.

Shortly after, the centre of Pyrrhus' line routed. Pyrrhus ordered part of the *agema* and cavalry from the right wing to reinforce the centre and halt the rout. To make matters worse, reinforcements from the Daunian city of Argyrippa then arrived and attacked the Pyrrhic camp. Pyrrhus' reaction was to dispatch the elephants and some cavalry to help defend the camp, but before they could arrive the camp was taken and set on fire. Seeing the approaching troops, the Daunians retired to a nearby hill where they could not be attacked by mounted troops, and instead the elephants were deployed against the Roman troops who had broken through the centre. They in turn retired to a nearby wooded hill where the elephants and cavalry could not easily attack them. Although this stopped the mounted Epirotes, the Roman forces came under attack from missile troops, who killed and wounded many. Seeing this, both commanders sent reinforcements and a new battle began for the hill.

As darkness fell the armies withdrew, but whereas the Romans retired to their own camp, Pyrrhus' army, with their camp destroyed, had to bivouac 'under the open sky', as a result of which many wounded men perished. Dionysius concludes with the veiled claim that the Romans won the battle.

Alternatively, Cassius Dio's version has the two armies facing each other for several days, with Decius taking the decision to 'devote himself', a practice in which the commander offers prayers to the gods before charging deep into the enemy lines; in effect, offering himself as a sacrifice to the gods in order to ensure victory. Interestingly, both his father and his grandfather had done the same at the Battles of Sentinum (295 BCE) and Vesuvius (340 BCE) respectively. When Pyrrhus sent messengers warning Decius that he knew of the proposal and that he would not succeed, the consuls responded that they did not need such a sacrifice as they were already confident of victory.

The two armies had deployed on opposite sides of a river, but Pyrrhus now gave the Romans permission to cross the river unmolested in order to have a 'fair fight', as he was confident that his elephants would secure victory. His confidence was to prove accurate: initially, the Romans forced the Greeks back until Pyrrhus committed his elephants. According to Dio, these were not deployed 'opposite their chariots' (possibly the anti-elephant wagons), but were used against the cavalry, who immediately routed through fear.

Dio also agrees with the attack upon the Epirote camp, but states that it was simply 'Apulians'. In response, Pyrrhus detached some of the infantry to counter the threat, but when his army saw the camp under attack they routed, giving the victory to Rome. Dio further writes that due to a lack of food and medical supplies the Epirotes then lost a large number of troops.

Both the above accounts suggest that the battle was fought over one day and that the Romans were victorious. Plutarch, however, gives a different version of events with slightly more detail. In this version, Pyrrhus was forced to fight the Romans on 'rough ground, near the swampy banks of a river, where his elephants and cavalry were of no service'. Forced to rely on the infantry, after a day's hard-fought battle the two armies separated as night fell.

On the following day, Pyrrhus outmanoeuvred the Romans, forcing them to fight on a more open plain between two areas of rough ground where his elephants and cavalry would be of more use. He then deployed troops to defend the irregular ground, and interspersed the archers and slingers with the elephants. It is worthwhile to show Plutarch's account of the battle in full:

> The Romans, who were unable on the level ground to practise the bush-fighting and skirmishing of the previous day, were compelled to attack the phalanx in front. They endeavoured to force their way through that hedge of spears before the elephants could come up, and showed marvellous courage in hacking at the spears with their swords, exposing themselves recklessly, careless of wounds or death. After a long struggle, it is said that they first gave way at the point where Pyrrhus was urging on his soldiers in person, though the defeat was chiefly due to the weight and crushing charge of the elephants. The Romans could not find any opportunity in this sort of battle for the display of their courage, but thought it their duty to stand aside and save themselves from a useless death, just as they would have done in the case of a wave of the sea or an earthquake coming upon them. In the flight to their camp, which was not far off, Hieronymus says that six thousand Romans perished, and that in Pyrrhus's commentaries his loss is stated at three thousand five hundred and five.

There is no certain explanation of the disparity in the accounts. The most likely is that the Roman sources used by Dionysius and Dio were aware that Decius had 'devoted himself', during which act he was killed.[21] Consequently the Romans 'must' have won, otherwise the sacrifice was in vain and the gods had obviously not listened to Decius' vows. This would explain why the battle was fought in one day, the day on which Decius was killed, and why a 'victory', however narrow, must have been the outcome.

In addition, the battle must have been a Roman victory as shortly after Pyrrhus left Italy, which was hardly likely had he won the battle.

On the other hand, Plutarch may have been correct in assigning two days to the battle with a draw on the first. He either did not know of Decius' sacrifice or, in order for his account to make sense to Roman readers, he was forced to ignore it. Accordingly, it is here assumed that Plutarch's account is probably the most accurate.

Approaching each other near Asculum, the two armies spent at least two days either jockeying for position or hoping that their opponent would make a mistake or attempting to win a minor skirmish in order to build morale ready for a major engagement.

The Romans appear to have won this initial phase as Pyrrhus was forced to fight near a river with woods and marshes restricting the ability of his cavalry and elephants to fight effectively. Consequently, and despite Decius' *devotio*, the first day ended in a stalemate, with losses about even.

On the second day, Pyrrhus demonstrated his military ability by outmanoeuvring the Romans – most likely by threatening to place his army behind them – and luring them away from their excellent defensive position. Instead, they were forced to fight on flat ground between two areas of rough going that was already occupied by Pyrrhus' troops. On this second day Pyrrhus used more traditional 'Successor' tactics by pinning the Roman infantry with his phalanx and allies before sending in his elephants to disrupt and destroy the enemy. The Romans finally broke, apparently losing 6,000 men in the battle. However, the infantry fighting had again been intense and Pyrrhus had also lost heavily, with 3,505 casualties. Most of these had been his veteran troops and officers, including many close friends and acquaintances. It was now that Pyrrhus allegedly stated 'If we are victorious in one more battle against the Romans, we shall be utterly ruined.'[22]

Aftermath

After Asculum, in 278 BCE Pyrrhus was invited by the Syracusans in Sicily to help restore freedom to the Greeks on the island, who were being defeated by the Carthaginians. Unsurprisingly, he decided to take them up on their offer. Driving the Carthaginians back to Lilybaeum, he demanded that his Greek allies supply him with ships and troops to lay siege to the city. When they refused, he returned to Italy and in 275 BCE he met the Romans in battle for a third time. At the Battle of Beneventum the Romans finally defeated Pyrrhus. Chastised, Pyrrhus returned home, fighting against the Macedonians and in Greece, during the latter conflict being killed in a battle on the streets of Argos.

Effects

It is difficult to assess the political and moral effect of the losses to Pyrrhus, mainly because shortly after their defeats they were able to overcome Pyrrhus at Beneventum. Yet the close nature of the defeats and the final victory may have had one lasting impact upon Roman commanders: the ability to beat the army of Alexander the Great that had conquered Persia and been victorious in all foreign wars appears to have given Rome's generals a sense of invincibility. Their arrogance after Beneventum seems to have made them overconfident; an approach that would cost Rome dearly in the next century.

Select Bibliography

Cassius Dio: https://www.gutenberg.org/files/18047/18047-h/18047-h.htm

Cicero, *De Finibus*, 2.61: https://penelope.uchicago.edu/Thayer/E/Roman/Texts/Cicero/de_Finibus/2*.html

Cicero, *Tusculan Disputations*, 1.39: https://www.gutenberg.org/files/14988/14988-h/14988-h.htm

Dionysius of Halicarnassus, *Roman Antiquities*, 20.1–3, 10–11:
  https://penelope.uchicago.edu/Thayer/E/Roman/Texts/Dionysius_of_Halicarnassus/20*.html
  https://archive.org/details/in.ernet.dli.2015.183525/page/n1/mode/2up

Frontinus, *Stratagemata*: https://penelope.uchicago.edu/Thayer/E/Roman/Texts/Frontinus/Strategemata/home.html

Horace, *Odes*: https://www.gutenberg.org/files/14020/14020-h/14020-h.htm

Livy, *Epistle*, 13, 14

Orosius, 4.1, 2: http://attalus.org/translate/orosius4A.html

Plutarch, *Pyrrhus*, 16–17, 21, 24: https://www.gutenberg.org/files/14114/14114-h/14114-h.htm

Zonaras, 8.3, 8.5.

Chapter Four

Hannibal: The Battle of Lake Trasimene, 217 BCE

[Author's note: It may be expected that the next battle covered would be that of Cannae, given its reputation as possibly the greatest defeat ever suffered by Rome. However, the fact that it has been covered by most historians concerned with Republican Rome means that it has been decided instead to focus upon the earlier and much less covered defeat at Trasimene.]

The Sources

As with the earlier battles, the main sources for the Battle of Lake Trasimene were written later and in this case the detailed descriptions that survive are by **Polybius** (3.75.1–8, 77.1–78.7) and Livy (21.57–63, 22.1–8). As already noted, the Greek historian Polybius is acknowledged as being a historian of the highest calibre, one who attempted to report events accurately. The main difference between this battle and those covered in earlier chapters is that Polybius is now writing a lot nearer to the actual event, but he is still writing long after the battle and is reliant mainly upon Roman sources, which due to their nature are liable to be biased in one way or another. This is especially true of his accounts of the Scipio family: Polybius was the tutor of Scipio Aemilianus, (adopted) great-grandson of the Scipio who took part in this battle. However, due to his being much closer in time it is usually acknowledged that his account is likely to be accurate in many details.

The other source is **Livy**. Unlike Polybius, he is writing centuries after the battle, but he is still reliant upon written and oral histories, including Polybius. However, the intervening years may have allowed Roman historians and families a longer period in which history could be distorted to fit current political and military prejudices. Despite this, he can sometimes be used to correct or confirm the details given by Polybius and other fragmentary sources.

Background

The First Punic War (264–241 BCE) between Rome and Carthage had ended in Roman victory with the signing of the Treaty of Lutatius. Carthage was to pay reparations and cede control of her territories in Sicily to Rome.

For the Carthaginians, this was a disaster: not only were they defeated and practically bankrupt, their reliance upon mercenaries was now to backfire as they could not pay the 20,000 troops they had hired for the war. The result was the 'Mercenary' or 'Truceless' War (241–237 BCE). After initial defeats, a general named Hamilcar Barca finally defeated the mercenaries.

With expansion eastwards halted by Rome, Barca decided to expand Carthaginian control in Hispania in order to restore Carthage's fortunes. Crossing to the peninsula, he took control of many of Hispania's silver mines, as well as Hispanic manpower and agricultural resources. When he died he was succeeded in Hispania by his son Hasdrubal, and in 226 BCE a treaty was agreed with Rome specifying the River Ebro as the northern limit of Carthaginian influence/southern extent of Roman influence in Hispania. Unfortunately, sometime after this Rome made a separate

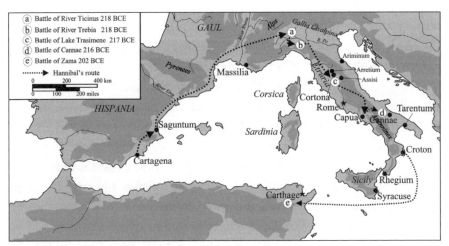

Hannibal and the Second Punic War.

treaty with the city of Saguntum, far to the south of the Ebro. When Hasdrubal died in 221 BCE he passed on control of Carthaginian territory in Hispania to his son Hannibal, who also inherited Hasdrubal's hatred of Rome.

Supremely confident in his own military ability, Hannibal was determined to further restore the fortunes of Carthage and humiliate Rome. In 219 BCE he besieged, captured and sacked Saguntum before Rome could intervene. In response, Rome declared war: the Second Punic War had begun.

Determined to seize the initiative, in late spring 218 Hannibal led his army north. In three separate columns, he crossed the River Ebro. As speed was of the essence, he accepted high casualties by taking towns he encountered by direct assault. Leaving his brother Hanno in northern Hispania with a small army, in late summer/early autumn Hannibal crossed the Pyrenees into Gaul. Possibly known to Hannibal, he was helped by the fact that Rome was at war with the Gauls in northern Italy, which delayed their response to Hannibal's advances in northern Hispania.

Once in Gaul, Hannibal defeated the Allobroges as they attempted to block his army. At around the same time a Roman fleet carrying a Roman army to Hispania made landfall at Massilia (Marseilles) and its commander, a man named Scipio, was shocked to learn that Hannibal and an army was upstream on the River Rhône. Failing to catch Hannibal's forces, Scipio dispatched the main army on its way to Hispania, but himself returned to Italy.

In a feat that is still celebrated, Hannibal crossed the Alps, defeating attempts to stop him by the natives, and after a journey of between 15 and 28 days (the sources are confused about the duration of the crossing) entered Italy with 6,000 cavalry and 20,000 infantry (12,000 Libyans and 8,000 Spanish) and a number of elephants. The Romans had planned an invasion of Africa, but Hannibal's unexpected arrival cancelled the invasion.

The Battle of Ticinus

The local Gallic tribes were either hostile or suspicious of Hannibal's intentions and he was forced to assault the main city of the Taurini. Shortly afterwards, however, he achieved his first success against Rome.

Scipio had landed back in Italy and taken control of the army facing the Gauls/Alps. Scipio led a strong force of cavalry and *velites* (skirmishing infantry) in a reconnaissance mission to determine the Carthaginians' strength. Hannibal sent out troops to oppose them and what is known as the Battle of Ticinus took place. Although none of the main armies took part, the encounter was seen as a defeat for Rome: Scipio himself was wounded and was allegedly only saved by the intervention of his son, also named Scipio. With this victory Hannibal's reputation soared and several Gallic tribes joined his cause, with his army correspondingly growing in size.

The Battle of the Trebia

If the victory at Ticinus was really only a large skirmish, in late December 218 BCE Hannibal won a definite victory over a Roman army. The Roman army in Sicily, originally intended to invade Africa, was recalled and sent to face Hannibal. Its commander was a man named Sempronius Longus. Closing with the Carthaginians, Longus sent out a strong force of light troops that managed to gain the upper hand in a full day's fighting. Encouraged, Longus was determined to face Hannibal in battle.

It is here that a word of caution is needed: the story as told by Polybius and his successors depicts Longus as an impetuous commander who refused to accept Scipio's advice not to offer battle. However, Polybius was a close associate of Scipio Aemilianus, a member of the Scipionic family. Consequently it is possible that Polybius is simply repeating the Scipios' claims that they were not responsible in any way for the defeat rather than strict fact.

Setting his brother Mago in ambush, Hannibal sent his Numidian cavalry to lure the Romans out for battle. Longus responded, his troops crossing the River Trebia and forming to face the Carthaginians. However, they had fewer cavalry than Hannibal and their cavalry broke and fled, leaving the infantry surrounded, a factor exacerbated when Mago emerged from ambush and attacked them in the rear. With their cavalry protection removed, the flanks of the Roman infantry also gave way, but 10,000 men in the centre – including Longus – routed the Libyans and Gauls opposite them and escaped. The result of the battle was that even more Gauls then joined Hannibal's army. Sadly for Hannibal, over the ensuing winter all but one of his elephants died.

At Rome, despite the defeat, it was noted that the main Roman infantry line had succeeded and so morale, although damaged, was not yet fatally wounded. New recruits were mustered until Rome had eleven legions in the field and fresh troops from Rome's allies were also enrolled. Despite the threat from Hannibal, it was still possible that troops from Africa and Hispania could be deployed elsewhere, so men were sent to Sardinia and Sicily and garrisons were sent to cities in Italy, especially the recently defeated Tarentum. A new fleet of sixty ships was also ordered, and Hiero of Syracuse sent 500 Cretan archers and 1,000 other light troops.

Thanks to Hannibal's obvious superiority in cavalry, the plains in the Po valley were thought to be poor terrain on which to face Hannibal, so the Romans decided to remain in the mountainous terrain to the south where their infantry was superior. Consequently one consul, Flaminius, took up station at Arretium (Arezzo) to guard the western Apennines with his consular army (now standardized at two Roman legions plus two allied legions), while the other consul, Servilius, took up station at Ariminum (Rimini) to guard the eastern Apennines. Three of the remaining legions were retained at Rome to defend the city, while the others were deployed to face the Carthaginians elsewhere.

In the meantime, Hannibal wintered in northern Italy. In a major propaganda campaign, he treated his Roman prisoners badly but freed his Italian prisoners without ransom, telling them that he had not come to make war on them but to free them from Roman oppression. This may have influenced some Roman allies to change sides, but it compared unfavourably with the earlier actions of Pyrrhus and so hardened the attitude in Rome, stiffening opposition to Hannibal.

With the coming of spring, Hannibal decided to invade Etruria. Polybius gives his order of march:

> He placed the Libyans and Iberians and all his best soldiers in the van, and the baggage within their lines…. Behind this vanguard he placed the Celts, and in the rear of all the cavalry. He entrusted the command of the rear-guard to his brother Mago, that he might see to the security of all, and especially to guard against the cowardice and impatience of hard labour which characterised the Celts; in order that, if the difficulty of the route should induce them to turn back,

he might intercept them by means of the cavalry and force them to proceed.

Polybius, 3.79.

Crossing the Apennines, the army entered the marshes around the mouth of the Arno. Hannibal had discovered that the marshes were shallow, but

In point of fact, the Iberians and Libyans, having great powers of endurance and being habituated to such fatigues, and also because when they marched through the marshes were fresh and untrodden, accomplished their march with a moderate amount of distress: but the Celts advanced with great difficulty, because the marshes were now disturbed and trodden into a deep morass: and being quite unaccustomed to such painful labours, they bore the fatigue with anger and impatience; but were hindered from turning back by the cavalry in their rear. All, however, suffered grievously, especially from the impossibility of getting sleep on a continuous march of four days and three nights through a route which was under water: but none suffered so much, or lost so many men, as the Celts. Most of his beasts of burden also slipping in the mud fell and perished, and could then only do the men one service: they sat upon their dead bodies, and piling up baggage upon them so as to stand out above the water, they managed to get a snatch of sleep for a short portion of the night. Another misfortune was that a considerable number of the horses lost their hoofs by the prolonged march through the bog. Hannibal himself was with difficulty and much suffering got across riding on the only elephant left alive, enduring great agony from a severe attack of ophthalmia, by which he eventually lost the sight of one eye, because the time and the difficulties of the situation did not admit of his waiting or applying any treatment to it.

Polybius, 3.79.

After a brief rest, they continued south, ravaging the countryside as they went.

The destruction of 'home' territory was a great disgrace which, coupled with Hannibal's treatment of Roman prisoners, resulted in outrage among the Senate. As Hannibal had chosen the western route,

Flaminius set out in pursuit with his army. As they marched it took time for the Carthaginians to cause damage, so Flaminius began to catch up with Hannibal. Possibly aware that bad luck could allow the Romans to attack his rear, passing close to Cortona Hannibal found himself nearing Lake Trasimene. Here the road passed through a narrow opening between the hills and the lake, and then spread out into a wider stretch of land, with hills on one side and the lake on the other. In addition, in the mornings a mist could rise off the lake, reducing visibility drastically. With the Romans closing, Hannibal realized that the area was the ideal place to set an ambush on a vast scale.

Hannibal marched his men along the banks of the lake, setting up his camp on a hill at the far end. When Flaminius reached the lake he also set up his camp. Towards dawn, Hannibal deployed his men in position and awaited the coming of day.

The Opposing Forces: Rome

By the date of the Battle of Lake Trasimene the normal legion of the Roman army was composed of 4,200 infantry and 300 cavalry, although in time of emergency the legions could be increased to c.5,000 men, or possibly even 6,000.[1]

The close-order infantry was divided into three lines: the *hastati*, the *principes* and the *triarii*. Without doubt the legion now deployed in the *quincunx* formation, with the *hastati* in front, the *principes* of the second line deployed to cover the gaps in the first line of the *hastati* and the *triarii* in the third to cover those in the *hastati*. As already stated, the exact manner in which this system worked is still a matter of debate.

In front of the three lines went the *velites*, unarmoured light infantry skirmishing in front of the close-order infantry in an attempt to cause disorder in the enemy's ranks and to prevent the opposing skirmishers from disrupting their own formations.

The few cavalry supplied by the Romans were still provided by the richest men, able to provide a horse and full equipment. It is most likely that, although the infantry had undergone major reform, in the deployment and equipment of the cavalry little had changed in the previous century.

The Allies

Alongside the Roman troops was an equal number of allied infantry, and it is likely that by this later date a greater proportion of the troops who had earlier fought in their traditional manner had converted to Roman equipment and tactics. However, the allies continued to supply the majority of the Roman army's cavalry, still 900 as opposed to 300 Romans per legion. The weakness of the Romans' cavalry arm was likely the main cause of the defeats at the battles of the Ticinus and the Trebia.

Consequently, Flaminius' army was apparently composed of the two Roman legions (c.10,000 men including the *velites*), two allied legions (also of c.10,000 men), plus 1,000 archers, 1,000 light troops supplied by Hiero of Syracuse and around 3,500 cavalry. It would appear that in the period between the Battle of Asculum and the invasion of Hannibal the Roman army had finalized the reforms, becoming accustomed to the new system of deployment and combat required by the shift to the *manipular* system.

The Opposing Forces: Hannibal

The army of Hannibal was one of the most diverse ever fielded against Rome. His native close-order infantry was composed of troops similar to Greek hoplites fighting in a *phalanx* formation, with long spears and swords for offensive work, protected by body armour of various sorts and a large shield, probably similar to the Greek *hoplon*. Alongside these were a number of javelin-armed skirmishers, similar to the *velites* of the Roman army. The Carthaginian cavalry would appear to be similar in equipment and tactics to their Roman opponents. However, Hannibal had larger numbers of these available than Rome.

The greatest difference between Hannibal's army and the majority of other armies in antiquity was the variety of troops he was able to deploy in Italy. To supplement his native Carthaginians, Hannibal was able to rely upon an alliance with the Numidians to supply him with a number of troops; certainly skirmishing light horsemen, but also some skirmishing light infantry, again similar to the *velites*.

When he had campaigned in Hispania Hannibal had also gained the loyalty and service of some of the Hispanic tribes. These had agreed to supply him with troops for his upcoming campaign in Italy. The infantry was of two main types. These were troops more suited either to close combat or to skirmishing. The majority of close-combat troops, known as *scutarii* (shield men), carried an oval *scutum* which gave them their name and were otherwise equipped similarly to the poorer Romans, with either no armour or some form of a bronze pectoral. The more affluent, especially tribal leaders, may have worn a mail shirt as well as a bronze helmet of Greek, Corinthian or Montefortino pattern. For the rest, probably a leather helmet: Strabo describes a sinew helmet worn by the Lusitanians. The skirmishers, known as *caetrati* after the *caetra*, the small, light shield they carried, were to function in the same way as their opponents the *velites*, otherwise equipped in the same way as the poorer *scutarii*.

Although Hispanic infantry had a good reputation, it was nothing when compared to that of the cavalry. For example, Strabo states that 'They ride double on horseback, though in the time of battle one of the two fights on foot.'[2] This, plus their nimbleness and speed, made the Iberian cavalry respected; although the Numidian cavalry have retained a reputation for their skill that survives even to the present day, Livy claims that the Hispanic cavalry were 'their equals in speed and their superiors in strength and daring'.[3] In addition, Livy also states that during the war 'Numidian cavalry ranged far and wide, and Celtiberians and Lusitanians were doing so wherever the ground proved too difficult for the Numidians.'[4] The Hispanic cavalry were well respected. There were two distinct cavalry types. The first was the 'shock' cavalry, trained to fight in close combat, wearing helmets, bronze pectorals (and possibly mail for the wealthy) and mainly carrying a *scutum*.[5] The second were skirmishing cavalry with lighter armour and the *caetra* shield.

The main strength of the Gauls lay in their infantry. These warriors remained feared thanks to the earlier Sack of Rome. In the intervening period, the Gauls had undergone a change in attitude. Although still attacking with great ferocity, the majority no longer fought naked. At the Battle of Telamon in 225 BC, the (mercenary) Gaesati had still fought naked – allegedly due to vanity and bravado but also the belief that the brambles in the area could catch in their clothes and impede the use of their weapons – whereas the Insubres and the Boii had retained their breeches and light cloaks.[6]

On the other hand, Polybius describes the Gauls as fighting naked at the later Battle of Cannae.[7] Although these descriptions may have been *topoi* (standard methods of describing 'barbarian' warriors), it would appear that it may have been relatively accurate. Obviously the richer Gauls, especially the chieftains and military leaders, would have been protected by armour, most likely the mail shirts that the Gauls are believed to have introduced to Italy. These men at least would also have worn bronze helmets. However, the majority appear to have relied upon manoeuvrability and a large *scutum* to avoid wounds, relying upon a long 'slashing' sword for offensive duties. In addition, it would appear that Gallic warriors could decide to fight either naked or without shirts, depending upon circumstances (weather, terrain and opponents).

The mounted arm of the Gallic army still consisted of chariots and cavalry. Propertius describes the chieftain Virdomarus (Vidimarius): 'He boasted he was born of the Rhine itself, agile at throwing Gallic javelins from unswerving chariot-wheels. Hurling them, he advanced, in striped breeches, in front of the host.'[8] Even as late as 110 BCE, a Roman coin could depict a Gallic chieftain as riding in a chariot, but it may be that as time passed chariots became more a symbol of extremely high prestige, resulting in them slowly declining in numbers. The only difference between the Gallic cavalry at Trasimene and that of the earlier period may have been that a greater proportion wore armour thanks to the increase in wealth brought about by extended trade with Rome and other regions.

Both the Hispanic and Gallic infantry had the traditional 'barbarian' reputation for attacking fiercely at the first onset but then, if they did not break the enemy, of being brittle and quickly collapsing into rout. Although, as usual, possibly a *topos*, the description of non-Roman troops in battle does, to some extent, vindicate the description. This is most likely due to a lack of training: troops trained to hold formation and fight in a specific manner may have had more stamina than troops relying on individual prowess, so those lacking group cohesion may have been more likely to become disheartened when the battle becomes long and wearying.

In addition to these main troops, Hannibal also employed mercenaries. On the whole these tended to be specialist types he did not have in his home-grown forces; for example, slingers from the Balearic Islands.

It is impossible to assess the number of men Hannibal had at his disposal. It is known that when he had fought at the Trebia he had had around 31,000 infantry and 11,000 cavalry. Later at Cannae he would fight with 40,000 infantry and 10,000 cavalry. Consequently, due to the losses incurred here, it is believed that his army here was larger. However, as he was to be supplemented by disaffected Roman allies throughout his time in Italy, assessing the numbers accurately is impossible. However, if it is assumed that he had around 40,000 infantry and 10,000 cavalry then it is likely that the number is not far off.

Location

The road that both Hannibal and Flaminius were following passes through a narrow opening between the hills and the northern shores of the lake before entering a wider area of flatter ground, exiting to the east of the lake where the hills again came near to the lake. The lake itself is large and today has a maximum depth of 6 metres. However, at the time of the battle it was larger (it is now drained by several man-made canals) and so both the 'passes' and the wider plain were narrower than they are today, plus the depth of the lake would have been slightly greater as well.

Deployment

Over the previous days Flaminius had come close to Hannibal, and was by then only around twelve hours behind the Carthaginians. However, he had a problem: the Carthaginians' superiority in cavalry meant that any scouts he sent out were liable to be attacked and killed before they could report. As a consequence, Flaminius did not send out scouts and appears to have deployed his troops into a formation that could easily be transformed into battle array, as suggested by the fact that his army was trapped in a small space: if he had been in marching columns, the longer line would have resulted in at least some of his army not entering the pass between the lake and the hills. This assumption is supported to some degree by the course of the battle. It is probable that he expected to meet the Carthaginians deployed on the hills at the far end of the pass.

On his part, Polybius writes that Hannibal deployed the Spanish and African infantry on the left, probably with the African infantry nearest

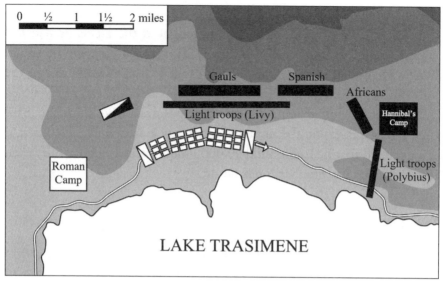

Hannibal sets his ambush and the Roman troops begin their march, expecting to face the enemy at the far end of the pass.

to his camp. In the darkness, he positioned the cavalry near the Roman camp, with the intention of using them to cut the Romans off from any chance of a retreat. The Gauls were stationed in the centre, with the light troops and the Balearic slingers positioned to the far side of his own camp, although Livy suggests that the light troops and the slingers were in the centre with the Gauls.

Course of the Battle

Having deployed his troops into a formation from which they could easily be ready for battle, so shortening the length of the Roman line, Flaminius set out to find Hannibal. Entering the pass between the lake and the hills, Flaminius found himself blinded by the mist rising from the lake.

It is often noted that Flaminius did not send out scouts, despite knowing that Hannibal liked to set ambushes, but there are two mitigating factors here. One is that by his deployment Flaminius was expecting to meet the enemy in battle at the far end of the lake. The other is that there had never before been any attempt to ambush an entire army using an entire army. Neither Flaminius nor any other Roman general would have expected or been prepared for what happened next.

Marching along the lake, at the far end the Roman vanguard finally contacted the African and Spanish troops and began to deploy into battle formation. At this point Hannibal ordered the army to attack, no doubt with a pre-arranged sounding of horns as the troops further round the hills would probably not have seen any visual signal.

Although the vanguard could see the enemy, the majority of the Roman troops, still enveloped in mist, would then have heard the sound of horns and shouts from all along the flank and to their rear as the Carthaginians launched their attack. Not knowing what was happening and with the sounds being distorted by the mist, it was impossible for the majority of the army to form a fighting front. Except for the vanguard, the confusion and disorientation ensured that the Romans were unable to fight back effectively. In some places the Romans were able to form groups that could stand together and defend themselves, but in others they were slaughtered or attempted to flee, either being stopped by Carthaginian forces, especially the cavalry as they tried to retreat the way they had come, or being drowned in the lake.

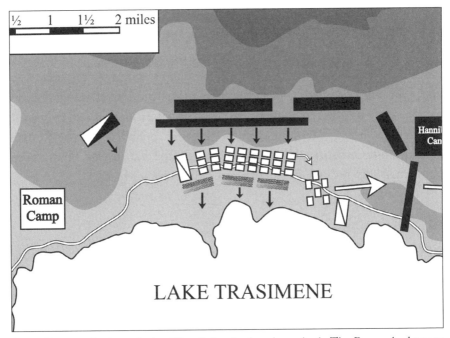

As the Romams begin to deploy, Hannibal unleashes the ambush. The Roman lead troops break out of the trap, the remainder are trapped against the lake and cut down.

The events at the head of the Roman army were very different. Able to deploy properly, the vanguard of around 6,000 men were able to break through the enemy ranks ahead of them and so escape the ambush. Surprised at being able to break through the enemy so easily, it was only when they reached a hill and were able to look back that they realized why they had faced only a small proportion of Hannibal's army.

As the mist slowly cleared they saw that the bulk of the Carthaginian forces had surrounded their comrades on the lakeside and there was no chance of the rest of the Roman army escaping from the trap. With the circumstances as they were, it would have been pointless for them to attempt to return to the battle so they retreated to an unnamed village.

In the meantime, the fighting continued on the shore of the lake. With his troops in disorder and pressed back to the lake, Flaminius was also caught in the melee. According to Polybius, he quickly fell into despair at the disaster. Livy, however, writes that Flaminius did his best to organize a defence and attempted to retrieve the situation. Certainty is impossible in this matter, but it is notable that after the battle Hannibal attempted to find Flaminius' body in order to give it an honourable burial, hardly likely unless Flaminius had died honourably. Whatever the case, the fighting around Flaminius was fierce thanks to his visible apparel, and Livy claims that he was killed by an Insubrian (one of the Gallic tribes) named Ducarius, allegedly being specifically targeted thanks to Flaminius' actions during the latter's campaigns against the Insubres in 223. Although trapped against the lake and so finding it impossible to form a viable fighting line due to the crush, the fighting was still to last for two or three hours, a testament to the fighting capabilities of the Roman army despite its untenable position. When the battle was finally over, Rome had suffered one of the greatest defeats in her history.

Aftermath

At least 15,000 Romans and Italians are said to have died at the Battle of Lake Trasimene, not including the many that died later from their wounds.[9] The troops in the vanguard who had broken through the Carthaginian lines retreated to an unnamed Etruscan town where they were surrounded by Marharbal, a commander sent by Hannibal, with Spaniards and javelin-throwers, and surrendered on condition that they received good treatment. Hannibal later told them that Marharbal did not have the authority to offer such terms. Contrary to some popular opinion, many Roman troops escaped from the battle – not surprising as their escape would be helped by the confusion and the mist – and fled into Etruria.

The Carthaginians lost between 1,500 (Polybius) and 2,500 (Livy) men, but these were mainly Gallic troops who had attacked the centre of the Roman line. Again, more men were to die later from their wounds, but more importantly for Hannibal he had lost thirty of his senior officers, a loss that would take time to replace.

Overall, Hannibal is said to have taken captive around 15,000 Roman and Italian prisoners at the battle. As usual the Roman captives were treated badly, being given starvation rations and very little water, whereas Rome's Italian allies were released in the hope of seducing the allied tribes to defect from Rome and join Hannibal.

Furthermore Servilius, the other Roman consul, having learned of Hannibal's route of attack, set out to join his colleague. As it would take time for him to reach Etruria, he sent a man named Gaius Centennius with 4,000 cavalry in the hope that they could reinforce Flaminius. Hannibal heard of their approach and immediately took action. He directed Marharbal with cavalry and skirmishers to attack Centennius. Shortly after Trasimene, in a second battle near Assisi, half the Roman cavalry were killed and the rest surrounded and taken prisoner.[10] The loss of so many cavalrymen and their mounts was a major blow to the Romans, who were already deficient in cavalry when compared to Hannibal. After Trasimene, the public in Rome had become demoralized but the Senate had remained calm. However, when news arrived of this second defeat, even the Senate became alarmed.

As Hannibal was now between Rome and Servilius, there was no consul in the city to take charge. Instead, with the situation seemingly desperate and with Rome open to assault from the victorious Hannibal, the Senate appointed a dictator, Quintus Fabius Maximus. He immediately adopted a new strategy, reasoning that Hannibal would find it difficult to get new recruits from Africa and that it would be better to wear Hannibal's forces down while using Rome's superior manpower reserves to reconquer those areas that had defected. The strategy was to prove so successful that from then on it was to be known as the Fabian Strategy.

Sadly for Rome, his methods were not universally appreciated and in 216 the new consuls were of a more traditional mindset. Determined to defeat Hannibal once and for all, they advanced to meet the invader. The result was the even more disastrous Battle of Cannae in which their army was virtually annihilated. Only after this battle did the Roman system of alliances begin to degrade. Yet this was never to reach a level that would threaten Rome's existence. Hannibal's campaign slowly fizzled out until he was forced to return to Africa to defend Carthage itself from a Roman invasion and was defeated at the Battle of Zama.

Effects

The defeats at Ticinus, Trebia, Trasimene and Cannae ensured that Hannibal lived long in the memory of Romans. Consequently Rome would retain a distrust and fear of Carthage, which was only expunged by the complete defeat and destruction of the city in the Third Punic War (149–146 BCE), although the city was later rebuilt during the reign of Augustus (r.27 BCE–14 CE).

Rome was never again to suffer such ignominious defeats in such a short period of time to one commander. The main significance of the defeats was that the Roman psyche became convinced that, although Rome could suffer defeats, perseverance would bring eventual victory. Nevertheless, Rome continued to be haunted by the memory of Hannibal, the man who had inflicted the greatest and most humiliating series of defeats they ever suffered.

Select Bibliography

Livy: https://www.gutenberg.org/ebooks/19725
Polybius: https://www.gutenberg.org/ebooks/44125
Propertius, *Elegies*, 4.10.46–7: https://www.poetryintranslation.com/PITBR/Latin/Prophome.php
Strabo, *Geography*, 3.4.18: https://penelope.uchicago.edu/Thayer/E/Roman/Texts/Strabo/home.html

Chapter Five

The Gallic and Germanic Tribes: The Battle of Arausio, 6 October 105 BCE

The Sources

There are several sources for events before, during and after the battle, but surprisingly the actual details of the battle are nowhere delineated and neither is there a reliable description of the combatants. In some ways this is surprising as two of the sources were actually alive during the battle. The main difficulty here is that the scale of the defeat meant that, following Roman tradition, the loss was ascribed to the failures of individuals plus the astronomical numbers faced by the Roman army.

Although he had died prior to the battle, the works of **Sallust** (c.86–c.35 BCE) are important for analyzing events prior to it. As he was alive during the period he describes, it is assumed that, in the main, he was accurate in his description of events. However, it should be remembered that he was a politician and so his works are biased towards his friends and against his enemies.

For the period of the battle itself, the main source is **Livy** (c.60 BCE–c.15 CE), who was around 50 years old at the time of the battle. However, the description is to be found in the *Periochae*, a later summary of Livy's work. Consequently the abridgement of the *Periochae* may have resulted in some details being lost.

As well as writing a history, **Velleius Paterculus** (c.19 BC–c.30 AD) was a soldier and senator, so theoretically should be a good source for military events. Sadly, though, his style is highly rhetorical so omits many of the details necessary for military history.

The main work of **Plutarch** (46 CE–after 119 CE) concerning this period is his *Life of Marius*. Although he was writing of events within the living memory of contemporaries, there are two major caveats concerning his work. One is that Plutarch's aim was not to write 'history', but to compare equivalent personalities of Greek and Roman history to show the impact of 'character' on history. Consequently his works are not concerned with historical accuracy and hence follow Roman literary traditions when it comes to defeat in battle and the assessment of the enemies of Rome so they cannot be accepted at face value.

Although writing later, **Granius Licinianus** (second century CE) includes details in his work that have either been lost or are not included by others. Sadly, however, his aim was not to write an accurate 'history', but in many respects to focus upon 'anecdotes' and items he found interesting. This, coupled with the fact that his work only survives in fragments, means that he needs to be used with caution.

Cassius Dio (c.155–c.235 CE) is a well-respected historian, although it is noted that he is sometimes unreliable, or perhaps he was too reliant on inaccurate sources for the period prior to his lifetime. However, his work includes many of the details used below for the battle – despite the acknowledged problems – mainly because he is the only source to describe such details.

Finally, writing long after the event, **Orosius** (c.380–c.420 CE) wrote the *Historiarum Adversum Paganos Libri VII* (*Seven Books of History Against the Pagans*) which, as the title suggests, was intended to compare 'pagan' history with the new times under Christianity. Consequently it was not intended as an 'accurate' history in the modern sense, but was more an attempt to prove that the conversion of Rome to Christianity was not the cause of recent calamities, especially the Sack of Rome by the Goths in 410. As a result, although his work contains much material that is otherwise not recorded, it needs to be used with caution as it has a definite aim and therefore a definite bias.

Background

It is sometimes pictured that after the defeat of Hannibal in the Second Punic War the Roman army waged successful wars on all fronts, quickly conquering the whole of the coasts surrounding the Mediterranean basin. Although to some extent this is true, the sweeping generalization that implies an all-conquering Roman army is not quite correct.

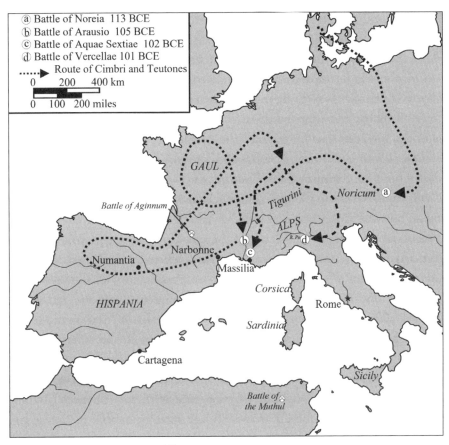

The migration of the Cimbri and Teutones.

With a large part of Hispania secure and with northern Italy finally becoming part of the Roman state, Rome began to expand into southern Gaul, in part to support their allies, the city of Marseilles, but also to secure a land route to the armies in Hispania. Slowly the Romans established themselves across the Alps, founding Narbonne (118 BCE) and establishing the province of Gallia Narbonensis.

However, during this period there were upheavals further north, the main instigators being the Teutones and the Cimbri. These tribes first came into contact with Rome when they plundered Noricum on the far side of the Alps in 113 BCE. Envoys were sent by the consul in the area, Gnaeus Papirius Carbo, explaining that the tribes in Noricum were friends of Rome. The Teutones apologized for their actions, stating that they were ignorant of these things, and began to withdraw. Despite this,

Carbo attacked them and was defeated at the Battle of Noreia (Neumarkt). Rather than following up their victory with an invasion of Italy across the Alps, the Teutones and the Cimbri instead headed towards Gaul.

Once in Gaul, the Cimbri sent envoys to Rome asking that they be allotted territory for settlement. The Senate refused, and one of the consuls for 109 BCE instead attacked them in southern Gaul. He was defeated and later (in 104 BCE) sent for trial for the defeat, but was acquitted.

The movements of the Cimbri and Teutones had caused disturbances throughout the region and the Tigurini, a Helvetian tribe, had also entered Gaul. In 107 BCE the Consul Lucius Cassius Longus had set out to find them, but was ambushed and killed at the Battle of Aginnum (Agen). In a scene reminiscent of the Battle of the Caudine Forks, the Romans were pursued to their camp and forced to surrender: the survivors were sent under the yoke.

These repeated defeats finally stirred Rome into serious action. In 105 BCE Gnaeus Mallius Maximus, a *novus homo* (a 'new man', not a member of the aristocracy) was elected as one of the new consuls and sent to Gaul to face the threat. Already in Gaul was the proconsul Quintus Servilius Caepio. Sadly for Rome, Caepio was an aristocrat of the old school and refused to cooperate with the 'upstart' Mallius. Theoretically the combined armies should have been able to defeat the Cimbri and Teutones, but the disconnect between the commanders was to prove crucial.

Once in Gaul, Mallius sent his legate Marcus Aurelius Scaurus to establish a forward camp ahead of the main body. When the Cimbri and Teutones advanced they had little difficulty in overrunning the camp, defeating the troops and capturing Scaurus. According to tradition, Scaurus advised the Cimbri not to attack Rome and was killed for his insolence.[1]

The defeat was a foreshadowing of things to come, but the detaching of a small body of troops may indicate that Mallius was not a competent general: to send cavalry forward as scouts was one thing, but to order them to construct a camp was another, although it should be noted that the construction of an overnight camp was a common practice for Roman troops so this may simply have been bad luck rather than poor judgement on Mallius' part.

The Opposing Forces: Rome

The greatest difficulty in assessing the Roman army at the Battle of Arausio is the controversy surrounding the so-called 'Marian Reforms', commonly dated to 107 BCE, two years before the Battle of Arausio. Marius was a Roman general who was the main mover of events around the time of the battle. Born in 157 BCE, he was a 'new man' (*novus homo*), meaning that his family was not a member of the aristocracy, the 'old men'. By 134 he was serving in Numantia (North Africa) and later he served in the war against Jugurtha, where his actions during the Battle of the Muthul (109 BCE) saved the army from destruction. After this he was elected consul in 107 BCE, but as he was not given an army, he called for volunteers. In this way he allowed the *Capite Censi* (citizens who did not fulfil the property requirement for service in the army) to enlist. After this the property requirement was eventually dropped.[2]

The need to enlist the poor in opposition to the Senate's wishes was not the only reason for Marius' decision. Sadly over the preceding centuries of warfare the manpower of Rome had become depleted, mainly due to the fact that except in dire circumstances – as during the Hannibalic War – entry into the legions was limited by financial status. Over the intervening time the rich in Rome had acquired great wealth, but with a corresponding fall in the wealth of the masses, meaning that fewer men possessed the lowest limit of wealth to enter the army. Consequently, with the need for new conscripts, Marius was allowed to recruit men who were otherwise ineligible. After (eventually) defeating and capturing Jugurtha, Marius returned to Rome. From this point onwards there was no means-testing of recruits prior to their enlistment into the army.

The enlisting of the poor and subsequent perceived changes in the nature and equipment of the army have since been ascribed solely to Marius, hence the term 'Marian Reforms'. However, it is likely that some of the changes were already taking place before Marius took control of the army. For example, and the main exception, is that archaeological study of Roman marching camps in Hispania point towards there being a change from the *manipular* organization to that of the *cohort* in the mid-second century BCE, with the *cohort* being assessed as being between 320 and 480 men, equating to fourth century *maniples*.[3] This suggests that at this early stage the commanders in Hispania had accepted that the *quincunx* formation was not suitable for fighting the different strategic and tactical methods of the enemies then being encountered.

Certainty is impossible, but it would seem likely that these new formations were an amalgamation of the *hastati* and the *principes*, armed with the *pilum*. If so, then this would mean that each legion had five of these *pilum*-armed *cohorts*. However, incorporating the spear-armed *triarii* into these formations would have caused complications. Therefore it may have been that the *triarii* were still the separate elite, last-stand troops.

To mirror the new amalgamated *maniples* of the front two lines, it is also theoretically possible that the *triarii* were also combined into larger units. Their ten smaller *maniples* may have been combined into five units of two *maniples* each. Although postulation, this hypothesis has the benefit of there being a total of ten *cohorts* per legion, a feature that became the norm for later legions.

Due to the limits of the evidence, it is unknown whether the change to a *cohort*-based army – whether the mixed *cohort/triarii* army as may have been the case in Hispania or the new, total conversion to a *cohort* system equipped solely with the *pilum* – was universal by the last decade of the second century BC. In reality, the Roman ten-*cohort* legion as perceived by many historians may not yet have come into effect by the time of the Battle of Arausio.

Some see Marius as instantly changing all Roman armies. This is extremely unlikely, as many armies had been in existence for a long time and were stationed away from Italy. To implement a change on the scale needed was going to take time, especially in implementing the corresponding modifications needed in the command structure of the new army. Consequently it is likely that by the time of Arausio the conversion was incomplete. This analysis suggests that at Arausio the army was based on a mixture of *cohorts* for shock attack and *triarii* for last defence, as was proving successful in Hispania.

Whatever the case, the equipment of the troops would have been the same as previously, with those who could afford to purchasing superior defences, and with the offensive *cohorts* equipped with the *pilum*; the defensive *triarii* may have retained the *hasta* if, as postulated, the legion was not yet reformed.

On the other hand, if the legions had indeed been reformed, each legion was now formed of 10 *cohorts*, 9 of which were composed of 6 *centuriae* ('centuries') of 80 men each (6 x 80, giving 480 men per *cohort*). The 'first' *cohort*, however, consisted of only 5 'centuries', but these were double the size of the other centuries (5 x 160 men, giving 800 men in the *cohort*). The centurion of the first century of the first *cohort* was the *primus pilus*, the senior centurion for the legion. This would give a total of 5,120 men in the legion, plus numerous affiliated personnel.

The recruitment of the poor would have a further significant impact on the Roman army. In theory, though not in practice, Roman men were expected to leave their farms and serve in the army for a single campaign season before returning home. However, as the Empire expanded and campaigns became protracted, this expectation ceased to exist in reality. As a consequence, the farmers were unable to maintain their land and so it was bought by the aristocracy, increasing their wealth but also inflating the numbers of the poor. The change to a 'professional' army allowed for the enlistment of men without attachment to land for a longer period of service, originally for sixteen years.

There was one further impact incurred by the recruitment of the poor into the legions. Earlier, soldiers had equipped themselves out of their own pocket prior to service, but the poor could not afford this. Consequently, with the change the state had to provide the equipment for the troops and so began a level of centralization and standardization that had not existed before.

Alongside this provision of equipment, over the preceding century the *triarii* had become something of an anachronism: although the phrase 'the battle came to the *triarii*' was used to denote a hard-fought battle, the number of times the Romans had snatched victory from the jaws of defeat thanks to the spear-equipped *triarii* had diminished almost to extinction. As a result, the *triarii* were, at some indeterminate time, phased out. The legions were then uniformly equipped with the *pilum*. The veterans, instead of being at the rear, were now the main troops in the first *cohort*, placed in the front line of battle. The recruits, in the higher numbered legions, were used as the reserve, in which place they could gain experience of battle.

In one way, however, the Romans retained one feature of the earlier legions: the three-line battle formation, now known as the *triplex acies* (triple line), was still in use, although in dire straits they could field a *duplex acies* (double line) or even a *simplex acies* (single line).

Almost certainly after the Battle of Arausio but possibly before, Marius may have imposed some new practices. The main one was the order that legionaries were to carry their own supplies rather than relying on a slow and cumbersome baggage train, although a smaller train remained necessary for major campaigns due to the need to carry extra food, supplies and equipment. The obligation to carry a lot of equipment and supplies resulted in the legionaries becoming known as 'Marius' Mules'.

When it comes to the number of Roman troops at the battle, there are problems with the figures commonly accepted and as given in the sources. According to standard Roman practice, each consul would be given command of two Roman legions, plus two allied legions of equal strength to the Roman. Consequently, and assuming that the legions were of the new, slightly enlarged format, that would mean approximately 10,000 Romans (2 x 5,120 men) plus 10,000 allies for a total of 20,000 men per consul. Therefore at the battle the Roman army would have a strength somewhere in the region of 40,000 men plus cavalry.

On the other hand, the Romans could field double-strength armies in times of emergency, and from the numbers given in the sources that would appear to be the case here. Each consul had 4 Roman legions (20,000 men) and 4 allied legions (20,000 men) for a total of 80,000 troops plus associated cavalry. If accurate, this was a vast number of troops and would be difficult for the generals to control. The animosity between the two commanders would ensure that things would be even worse than they should have been.

The Opposing Forces: the Cimbri-Teutones

When it comes to assessing the nature and style of warfare practised by the Cimbri and Teutones there is a main hurdle to overcome, which is whether the two tribes were 'Gauls' or 'Germans'. Although some believe them to have been northern Gallic tribes, others see them as being Germanic.[4] Both Germans and Gauls fought in roughly the same manner, relying on a devastating infantry charge to break the enemy's line, but if this failed they tended to be brittle and crumble into defeat. On the other hand, it may be that the German tribes fielded fewer mounted troops than the Gauls due to their comparative poverty and thus having fewer warriors being able to afford to raise and keep horses. However, as the two tribes appear to have existed on the borders between 'Gallia' and 'Germania' prior to their migration, it is here assumed that any differences were minimal and that the confusion over whether they were Gallic or German is caused by the fact that they were on the boundary between the two 'cultures' and so had aspects of both in their society. However, the fact that at least some of the population believed them to be Gauls would have reinforced the *metus Gallicus* ('fear of the Gauls') that had been in Roman hearts since the Sack of Rome after the Battle of the Allia.[5]

When it comes to the size of the army, if there are problems with accepting the numbers given for the Roman army at face value, with respect to the Cimbri and Teutones the numbers are astronomical. For example, Plutarch claims that the combined force consisted of 'Three hundred thousand armed fighting men…and much larger hordes of women and children were said to accompany them.'[6] This would give a total migration of over half a million men, women and children wandering around Gaul and Hispania. The logistics of supporting this number of people on an exodus means that this figure has to be treated with extreme caution. With such large and improbable numbers, it must be acknowledged that it is impossible to gauge how many people were moving with the tribes and how many warriors the combined tribes could actually field.

It is noted in the sources that the Cimbri and Teutones were willing to attack the Roman army when it was divided (see below), which suggests that they believed themselves of at least equal strength to one of the armies but perhaps not both. In that case, if the Roman forces were of c.40,000 men per consular army, then the Cimbri and Teutones may have numbered between c.30,000 and 50,000 men (with perhaps the real number being towards the lower estimate), explaining their willingness to attack one army but their desire to avoid facing both.

It is unclear how the two tribes were equipped or the proportion of cavalry they fielded. Most Roman descriptions of 'barbarian' warriors depict infantry charging wildly with their swords waving high in the air. However, as swords – and armour – were expensive, it is likely that the majority of the infantry were equipped with a spear and shield and dressed solely in tunics and trousers.

The cavalry, being the aristocracy, were more likely to have armour, but even here there would be no unity in the quality or style of equipment as financial considerations would be the main criteria. As to the proportion of cavalry to infantry, no clue is given in the sources so it is necessary to resort to speculation. As an example, at the Battle of Telamon in 225 BCE the Gallic army reportedly consisted of 50,000 infantry and 20,000 cavalry. This gives a ratio of 5:2, so if the Cimbri and Teutones numbered 40,000 warriors (the equivalent of one of the two Roman consular armies), then the foot would have numbered around 28,500 with the cavalry around 11,500. Although extremely speculative, this at least gives some idea of the numbers that may have been involved.

Despite not knowing the numbers and proportions of the tribal forces, it is clear that in one way they had a major advantage over the Romans: unlike the Roman commanders, Boiorix of the Cimbri and Teutobod of the Teutones were willing and able to cooperate militarily.

Location

The Cimbri-Teutones had ravaged large areas of Gaul, but now seemed to be heading for Italy. Mallius, with responsibility for Roman Gaul, decided to halt the advance by blocking the crossings of the River Rhône in the region of Arausio (Orange, in the Vaucluse department in the Provence-Alpes-Côte d'Azur region of France). The Rhône is renowned for its fierce currents, but in late summer the water level can fall, leaving shallows allowing passage. Mallius appears to have stationed his camp opposite one such crossing where the Cimbri-Teutones could cross the river without the need for a bridge.

Deployment

As noted above, the main difficulty faced by the Roman army was the disconnect between Servilius Caepio and Mallius. Caepio had been consul in the previous year, but the need to face opponents on several fronts meant that he was maintained as proconsul in command of the army in Cisalpine Gaul in northern Italy. As an aristocrat and ex-consul he felt that he was above Mallius who, although now one of the two consuls for

105 BCE, he saw as a 'new man' and an upstart. His jealousy was to play a major part in the upcoming campaign:

> Servilius became the cause of many evils to the army by reason of his jealousy of his colleague; for, though he had in general equal authority, his rank was naturally diminished by the fact that the other was consul. After the death of Scaurus, Mallius had sent for Servilius; but the latter replied that each of them ought to guard his own province. Then, suspecting that Mallius might gain some success by himself, he grew jealous of him, fearing that he might secure the glory alone, and went to him; yet he neither encamped in the same place nor entered into any common plan, but took up a position between Mallius and the Cimbri, with the evident intention of being the first to join battle and so of winning all the glory of the war.
>
> *Cassius Dio, 27, 91.1–2.*

The refusal of Servilius is mirrored in the writings of Granius Licinianus, but there is the possibility that, as they are both writing much later, they are using the same source and so giving the same information:

> The ex-consul M. Aurelius Scaurus was thrown from his horse and captured. When they [the Cimbri] summoned him to a council, he neither did nor said anything which was unworthy of a Roman, who had held such great honours. Because of this he was killed, although he could have escaped; he refused their request to act as their leader, out of shame that he should survive after the loss of his army.
>
> The consul Mallius was alarmed by this victory of the Cimbri, and sent a letter begging Caepio to join forces with him and confront the Gauls with a large combined army; but Caepio refused. Caepio crossed the Rhône and boasted to his soldiers that he would bring help to the frightened consul; but he did not even want to discuss with him how to conduct the war, and he disdained to listen to the envoys whom the senate sent, asking the generals to co-operate and jointly to protect the state.
>
> *Granius Licinianus, 33L 11.25*

Obviously these passages could easily simply be stating Roman propaganda that the defeat was due to individual Romans rather than barbarian superiority. However, as this is the main thrust of the sources it is necessary to accept it, albeit with reservations.

Dio goes on to state that, immediately prior to the battle, things could still have turned out well for Rome:

> Even thus they inspired their enemies with dread at the outset, as long as their quarrel was concealed, to such an extent that they were brought to desire peace; but when the Cimbri made overtures to Mallius, as consul, Servilius became indignant that they had not directed their embassy to him, gave them no conciliatory reply, and actually came near slaying the envoys. The soldiers forced Servilius to go to Mallius and consult with him about the situation. But far from reaching an accord, they became as a result of the meeting even more hostile than before; for they fell into strife and abuse, and parted in a disgraceful fashion.
>
> *Cassius Dio, 27, 91.3–4.*

This discord was not concealed from the barbarians by a simple factor. The consul Mallius had arrived on the scene first and camped behind the

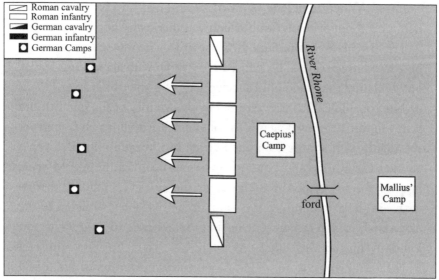

Battle of Arausio, Caepio deploys and begins his attack on the German camps.

Rhône. Upon his arrival, Caepio had crossed the river to place his camp between that of the Cimbri/Teutones and that of Mallius.

His placement so confused later historians that Orosius assumed that the Rhône was actually the boundary between their commands.[7] In this description, it would seem that Caepio wanted to ensure that he would play a part in the expected defeat of the enemy and so gain at least equal plaudits with Mallius. In addition, according to Licinianus, when

> The Cimbri sent envoys to arrange a peace and to ask for land and for corn to sow…he dismissed them so brusquely that they attacked the next day. His camp was situated not far away from Mallius' camp, but he could not be persuaded, though he was so close, to join together their armies.
>
> *Granius Licinianus, 33L 11.25.*

What happened next is nowhere described in detail in the sources, so it is necessary to resort to speculation.

The first question to be decided is on which side of the Rhône were the consuls and the opposition. Mallius, the consul with responsibility for the region, was undoubtedly aiming to defend Italy from attack: the memory of Hannibal crossing the Alps was still strong in the Roman imagination. Consequently he almost certainly deployed on the eastern side of the river, meaning that if the Cimbri-Teutones were intent upon crossing the river to move on Italy, he was in an excellent defensive position to prevent this.

Supporting this supposition is the fact that Granius Licinianus describes that 'Caepio crossed the Rhône and boasted to his soldiers that he would bring help to the frightened consul.'[8] As he was travelling from Cisalpine Gaul, had Mallius been on the west bank of the Rhône Caepio would not have needed to cross the river. In this way he took up 'a position between Mallius and the Cimbri'.[9]

Having thus established that Mallius was on the right (east) bank and Caepio on the left (west) bank, it is also safe to state that the camps of the Cimbri and Teutones were also on the left (west) bank. However, due to the size of their forces and the fact that there were several different tribal groupings involved, it is also safe to say that the Cimbri-Teutones had more than one encampment, though sadly this is not detailed in the extant sources.

Moving on to the battle itself, the sources all agree, without giving details, that Caepio was defeated and his camp overrun. It is hard to believe that a well-protected and manned Roman camp could be overrun with ease by any enemy. Consequently it is probably safe to assume that Caepio, after dismissing the envoys, realized that should Mallius agree a treaty with the enemy there would be no chance of battle. Consequently, and in spite of Mallius being the senior commander, Caepio decided that the best way to win glory for himself was to defeat the enemy before Mallius could join the fray.

Therefore it is likely that on the morning of the battle Caepio deployed his army and advanced against the Cimbri-Teutones. Doubtless upon hearing the calls to arms in the nearby camp, Mallius also ordered his army to form up outside his own camp.

Course of the Battle

Even when heavily outnumbered, the Roman army was usually capable of putting up stiff resistance, even of winning. The fact that Caepio's army was destroyed suggests that something other than a straightforward battle was fought. It is feasible – though impossible to prove – that Caepio launched his men against the enemy's camps and that these, being near to each other and

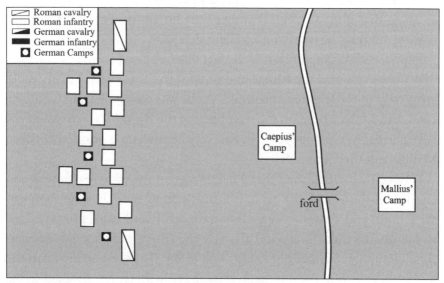

Battle of Arausio, the attack fragments against the German camps.

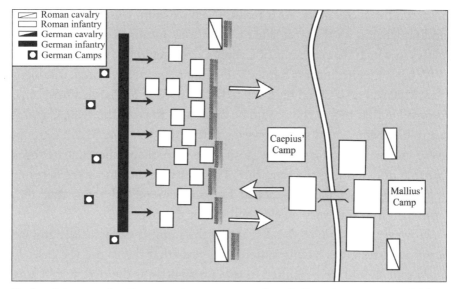

Battle of Arausio, the German tribes counter-attack and Caepio's troops route. Mallius attempts to deploy his troops and cross the river.

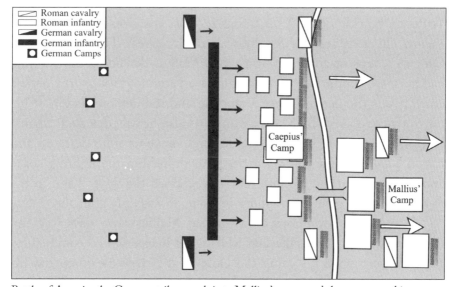

Battle of Arausio, the German tribes crash into Mallius' troops and they are routed in turn.

so self-supporting, caused a disruption in the usual disciplined formation of the troops. Consequently they were too dispersed when the counterattack came and so were unable to defend themselves, being attacked from all sides and hemmed in by the enemy's camps.[10] Not only was Caepio's army decimated, but the remnants that made it back to the camp were too few to defend it successfully. As a result, Caepio's camp was also overrun. In addition, being on the west side of the Rhône meant that there were few places in which the remnants of Caepio's army could find safety.

What happened next is harder to decipher. As already noted, it is likely that Mallius had ordered his army to form up ready for battle. However, it is possible that before they could be organized to cross the river, Caepio's army had been wiped out. However, if this was the case Mallius' troops were still in a good defensive position and perhaps should have been capable of defending the river line. The fact that they too were defeated may suggest that Caepio's defeat had so demoralized them that they crumbled into rout very quickly and so lost the river line.

However, the scale of the defeat and the number of losses the Roman army are attested as having suffered suggests that this is not the case: an early rout should have resulted in fewer casualties as the river would have hindered pursuit. Therefore it is probably safe to assume that Mallius' army also engaged the enemy in combat.

This in turn suggests that Mallius, seeing Caepio attacking the Cimbri-Teutones, quickly ordered his troops to cross the river and engage the enemy. This may account for the scale of the defeat. The rapid rout of Caepio's troops means that, rather than Mallius defending the river, he had to cross it in the face of opposition in an attempt to support Caepio's army. It was the need to force a crossing and the demoralization of his forces that explains why Mallius' army was also heavily defeated. Unable to cross the river in strength, the leading elements were defeated and forced back onto the following troops, compressing the fighting space and meaning that the Cimbri-Teutones retained the upper hand in the fighting. Finally giving way under pressure, it was only after the enemy had forced them back from the river that Mallius' army gave way and turned to rout. It is possible that Mallius, an inexperienced commander, had also positioned his camp too close to the river, meaning that his routing troops did not have an easy line of escape, which contributed to the scale of the defeat. The fact that the Cimbri/Teutones had crossed the river in the fighting prior to the rout of Mallius' army also helps to explain why the pursuit was so effective and hence why the number of Roman casualties was so high.

Although, given the poor quality of the sources other outlines of the battle are feasible, this description not only explains why Caepio was so intent upon attacking the enemy, it also clarifies why the armies of both Caepio and Mallius were so heavily defeated. The attack on the enemy's camps gives a reason why Caepio's forces were defeated, and the need to cross the river in the face of enemy opposition explains why Mallius' troops were routed with such loss.

None of the sources give any indication of the losses suffered by the Cimbri/Teutones at the battle, instead focusing solely on the casualties suffered by Rome and her allies, which were undoubtedly heavy. Publius Rutilius Rufus, the consular colleague to Mallius, reportedly claimed 70,000 soldiers and 40,000 camp followers killed and captured. Orosius, writing centuries after the event, notes that the contemporary writer Antias, whose work is lost, claimed that 'eighty thousand of the Romans and their allies were slaughtered in that disaster and that forty thousand servants and camp followers were killed. Of the entire army it is said that only ten men survived.'[11]

Aftermath

Although these numbers are of dubious accuracy and may be more representative of Roman distress at the defeat, the scale of the loss is undeniable. Mallius' sons were killed and, as they had been with Mallius on the east bank of the river, this clearly demonstrates that Mallius' forces suffered heavy losses. Both Mallius and Caepio escaped from the battle, but both were later prosecuted for their roles in the defeat. Although Caepio was blamed by all for the loss, Mallius was also judged to be at fault and both men were exiled from Rome for their actions.

In Rome the loss was devastating to morale. In response, and discarding earlier laws preventing anyone from being appointed as consul a second time until after a gap of ten years from his first consulship, Gaius Marius was assigned as senior consul after a gap of only three years. Furthermore, while the Cimbri-Teutones remained at large, for a further four successive years Marius was repeatedly appointed as consul. These continuous consulships paved the way for later Roman commanders – most notably Julius Caesar and Pompey (among others) – to command large armies on campaigns lasting several years, resulting in the troops becoming more loyal to their commander than to the abstract concept of the Roman Republic.

The scale of the defeat is on a par with those inflicted earlier by Hannibal, and as such it should be as well reported as these earlier reverses. Yet although Hannibal is well-remembered to this day, both ancient and modern historians have tended to neglect the Battle of Arausio. The reason for this is unclear, but is most likely simply due to the fact that Hannibal's victories were due to his superior generalship and were also a 'clash of civilizations', whereas the victory of the Cimbri-Teutones was due mainly to the failings of the Roman commanders and the victors are not seen as 'civilized' and therefore the battle was based simply upon luck and poor Roman generalship and not upon skill.

In addition, the victors did not invade Italy and so pose a direct threat to Rome. Instead, the Teutones remained in Gaul and the Cimbri invaded Hispania, where they were defeated in battle by the native Hispanics. Returning to Gaul, the Cimbri once again joined the Teutones and planned to invade Italy, dividing their forces for the purpose of crossing the Alps. In 102 BCE the Teutones were defeated at the Battle of Aquae Sextiae by Marius, but at the same time Catulus – the second consul – was forced to withdraw in front of the Cimbri at the Battle of Athesis. Finally, in the following year (101 BCE) Marius – then in his fifth consulship – defeated the Cimbri at the Battle of Vercellae and the threat was finally over.

Effects

Although often overlooked by historians except as a footnote, the Battle of Arausio was to be a major catalyst in the formation of the Roman Empire. The defeat by the Cimbri-Teutones, tribes sometimes associated with the 'Gauls' rather than the 'Germans', helped to reinforce the *metus Gallicus* (Gallic fear) suffered by the Romans ever since the Battle of the Allia and the Sack of Rome. This doubtless influenced the Senate and people of Rome to change the law forbidding Roman leaders from accepting a second consulship until at least ten years after their first. The successive consulships of Marius paved the way for those of men such as Sulla, Pompey and Julius Caesar, which ended in the accession to power of the first Roman Emperor Octavian/Augustus. Without the defeat, this sequence of events may never have happened, or at least taken a different form with different individuals at different dates.

The second change that the defeat helped to create was the permanent and legal transformation of the Roman army from an 'amateur' army composed of 'citizen-famers' (although by this date the designation of 'amateur' and 'citizen-farmer' was no longer really applicable) to a permanent, professional and highly-trained army with professional logistical support capable of defeating every enemy it encountered. However, as will be shown, the fact that the army could defeat every enemy did not mean that it did.

Select Bibliography

Cassius Dio: https://penelope.uchicago.edu/Thayer/E/Roman/Texts/Cassius_Dio/22-29*.html

Granius Licinianus, 33L 11.25: http://www.attalus.org/translate/granius.html#book33

Orosius, 5.15.25; 5.16.1–7: http://attalus.org/info/orosius.html

Plutarch: https://penelope.uchicago.edu/Thayer/E/Roman/Texts/Plutarch/Lives/home.html

Sallust, *Bellum Jugurthinum* (*The War with Jugurtha*) 86.2: https://penelope.uchicago.edu/Thayer/E/Roman/Texts/Sallust/Bellum_Jugurthinum/3*.html#ref159

Velleius Paterculus, 2.12.2: https://penelope.uchicago.edu/Thayer/E/Roman/Texts/Velleius_Paterculus/home.html

Chapter Six

The Persian Menace:
The Battle of Carrhae, 53 BCE[1]

The Sources

There are two sources for the Battle of Carrhae, one of the greatest defeats the Roman army ever suffered. The main source is **Plutarch** (46 CE–at least 119 CE). One of his *Lives* is that of Crassus, the Roman commander at the battle. The greatest difficulty when using Plutarch as a source is the need to remember that he is not a historian in the modern sense. Rather than attempting to cut through the bias and prejudices of his sources, Plutarch was contrasting the careers of important individuals, specifically the character of the individuals concerned. As a consequence, all his writings are biased due to the requirement to fulfil the purpose of the text. However, in this case Plutarch's account of the battle is the only detailed description, so it must be used.

The other source is **Cassius Dio** (c.155–c.235 CE). Dio was writing around two centuries after the battle and so was reliant upon earlier sources. Although Dio aimed to write an accurate history, his intention was to write a book for popular consumption rather than for the political elite. As a consequence, and despite the fact that recent works have attempted to demonstrate his accuracy and improve his reputation, his work still needs to be used with caution rather than being accepted at face value. However, in some cases this is impossible as he is the only source available. In this case the content can be used to supplement the account given by Plutarch.

Background

Following the defeat at Arausio, Roman politics had changed into a system dominated by successful generals, the most prominent being Marius, who had finally managed to defeat the Teutones at the Battle of

Aquae Sextiae (Aix-en-Provence, 102 BCE) and the Cimbri at the Battle of Vercellae (101 BCE), and later Sulla, the successful commander during, among others, the Social War (91–88 BCE) and the First Mithridatic War (89–85 BCE).

After the retirement and death of Sulla (d.78 BCE), political life in Rome once again became turbulent and deadly. Eventually, in 60 BCE the three most prominent individuals in the Republic joined forces and formed the First Triumvirate. The three men were Gnaeus Pompeius Magnus, the most prominent military commander of the time who had finally conquered and settled most of what would become the Eastern half of the Roman Empire; Julius Caesar, a politician who represented the plebeians and a general who had recently won military victories in Hispania; and Marcus Licinius Crassus, a member of a prominent senatorial family and by 60 BCE allegedly the richest man in Rome.

The political result was that Pompey managed to pass measures rewarding his troops for their long service (measures that had previously been blocked by the Senate) and Caesar was awarded a military command that resulted in his dramatic conquest of Gaul (58–50 BCE). Consequently Caesar began to rival Pompey for military reputation, leaving Crassus as the only one of the three whose reputation was by this time founded solely on his wealth. In Republican Rome, wealth was not the ultimate sign of power and influence: it was military glory. Although he had won a victory at the Battle of the Colline Gate in 82 BCE and defeated Spartacus in 71 BCE, this was almost twenty years earlier. Furthermore, the Battle of the Colline Gate had been part of a civil war and Spartacus had been 'merely' a barbarian gladiator. Neither of these was the equivalent of the foreign conquests of Pompey and Caesar.

In order to raise himself to the prestigious levels of his two partners, Crassus needed military victories over external enemies. However, as Pompey had settled the East and Caesar was fighting an ongoing campaign in Gaul, Crassus' military options were limited. The only region open to a new major campaign was further to the east than Pompey had managed. With this in mind, as part of the triumvirate Crassus managed to secure for himself control of the province of Syria for a period of five years, similar to that of Caesar whose region of control was Gaul. Crassus' aim was to go to war with the Parthian Empire and so gain military glory to match that of his partners.

There are other potential reasons for Crassus' desire to invade Parthia. Obviously he expected to gain incredible wealth, both for himself and the Republic. In addition, his son, Publius Crassus, had served with distinction in Gaul under Caesar and had a very promising political career. A successful campaign in the East would promote Publius in the public eye and help further his career.

Yet possibly the main reason for Crassus' decision to invade Parthia was that he did not expect much in the way of opposition. Firstly, earlier Roman armies had usually been successful in the East, especially when they had defeated the armies of Pontus under Tigranes the Great, who in turn had defeated the Parthians. Consequently the Parthians were seen as an easy opponent to defeat.

Secondly, the Parthians were undergoing a period of crisis. Civil war had erupted in 57 BCE after Phraates III had been assassinated and his sons had then fought each other for the throne. Orodes II had won and made his defeated brother Mithridates king of Media in the hope of ending the war. However, the war had restarted and Mithridates had fled to Roman territory. The Roman proconsul in Syria, Aulus Gabinius, set out alongside Mithridates to regain the throne, but then turned back to support Ptolemy XII of Egypt: Egypt was seen as far more important to Rome than Parthia. Despite losing Roman support, Mithridates succeeded in regaining the throne.

In 54 BCE the civil war appears to have restarted. Crassus, as the successor to Gabinius, also attempted to ally himself with Mithridates. This may have been a new attempt to establish a Roman puppet on the throne of Parthia, but may also have been an attempt by Crassus to establish a *casus belli*: there was a large opposition in Rome to Crassus' proposed war in the East.

According to the sources, after Crassus arrived in the East he quickly crossed the Euphrates, defeated the Parthian satrap Silaces in battle near Ichnae and captured many towns, mainly those that had been founded and/or were mainly populated by Greeks and Macedonians during Alexander the Great's campaigns.[2] The only town that resisted was Zenodotium/Zenodotia, which was captured and sacked.[3] Crassus placed garrisons in the cities, which deployments allegedly reduced his force by 7,000 infantry and 1,000 cavalry, before retiring to winter quarters in Syria.

Once in Syria he waited for the arrival of his son Publius from Gaul, where Publius had been serving under Caesar, with an additional 1,000

Gallic cavalry.[4] Dio castigated Crassus for his decision to retire to Syria, stating that 'He certainly would have subdued also the other regions this side of the Tigris, if he had followed up the advantage of his own quiet attack and the barbarians' panic consistently in all respects, and also if he had wintered where he was, keeping strict watch of affairs.'[5] By beginning the war with a very limited campaign, Crassus lost the element of surprise and gave the Parthians advanced warning that a major invasion was imminent in the following year. Taking advantage of the delay, Orodes' *Spahbad* Surena (Rustaham Suren, head of the House of Suren) defeated and executed Mithridates in 54 BCE.

Having gathered his forces and fresh supplies and following his son's arrival, in 53 BCE Crassus crossed the Euphrates at Zeugma with a substantial army of seven legions. His intention was apparently to march on the Parthian 'capital' of Ctesiphon (on Parthian 'capitals', see below). What happened next is not altogether clear as we only have Roman sources for the campaign, mainly Plutarch and Cassius Dio.

Artavasdes, king of Armenia and ally of Rome, advised Crassus to take a route through the mountainous and hilly regions of Armenia – where the Roman infantry had the advantage over mounted troops – and so

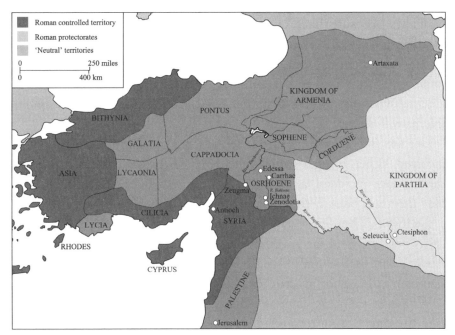

The East and Carrhae.

avoid the desert where the terrain was more suited to cavalry warfare. As an incentive, Artavasdes offered Crassus reinforcements of 16,000 cavalry and 30,000 infantry should he travel through Armenia.[6] Obviously in some respects Artavasdes had an ulterior motive, as having the combined forces in Armenia would ensure that Armenia was safe from a Parthian counterattack, a distinct possibility now that the Parthians had had time to assess the situation and formulate their own strategy. However, Artavasdes' advice was sound: the Roman legions were far more vulnerable away from the hills and mountains of Armenia.

According to the Roman sources this was not the only advice being given to Crassus. Allegedly Abgar of Edessa, king of Osrhoene, was working for the Parthians and treacherously exhorted Crassus to follow the direct route, as taken earlier by Alexander the Great, through Mesopotamia and so across the desert. The Roman sources claim that the aim of this 'treachery' was to lure Crassus into the path of the Parthian army. This may be true, but perhaps should be seen as unlikely. As evidenced by later events, the Parthian strategy was to pin Crassus with an army only a fraction the strength of Crassus' force. Consequently, if Abgar did indeed convince Crassus to advance across Mesopotamia, this was after the Parthians' decision to invade Armenia. If so, the aim would have been to ensure that Crassus did not enter Armenia and so nullify the Parthians' plans rather than put him in the way of danger. It may also have simply been to ensure that Crassus was always under observation: as the route was within his own kingdom, Abgar could quickly advise Surena of Crassus' whereabouts. On the other hand, later events possibly disprove this, as will be seen below.

Despite the statements in the sources, no treachery need have been involved. When Roman armies were defeated the usual excuses given by the Romans included, among others, treachery. It was easier to believe that they had been betrayed rather than that they had been beaten in a 'fair fight'. The defeat at Carrhae was not a 'fair fight': the Romans vastly outnumbered the Parthian victors. Consequently it is possible that Abgar's part in the affair was fabricated after the war, which saw both Armenia and Osrhoene unambiguously transferred to the Parthian orbit.

Whatever the case, Crassus refused Artavasdes' offer and decided to take the direct route through Mesopotamia, apparently aiming to gain glory by being able to recite the number of cities he had captured during the campaign. He may also have been influenced by the fact that his route followed that of Alexander, the man seen as the pinnacle of military glory, though this is not specifically mentioned by the sources.

Dio claims that Crassus' strategy was to march to Seleucia, a 'Greek' city which he hoped would support him, and from there he would advance to Ctesiphon.[7] It would appear that Crassus believed that capturing the city would result in the Parthians immediately surrendering. In some respects this was a mistaken assumption. The Parthians indeed had important centres where the Parthian court could gather, but there were several such cities, including Ctesiphon, Ecbatana, Hecatompylos, Susa, Mithradatkirt/Nisa, Asaak and Rhages, depending upon where the ruler most needed to be within the Empire for either defensive or offensive purposes. Consequently, if Crassus hoped that taking Ctesiphon would end the war, he was almost certainly wrong, but circumstances would ensure that the capital was never in danger.

In response, and as noted above, Orodes decided not to face the Romans first, instead taking most of his army, and especially those troops capable of operating in rough terrain, in an invasion of Armenia. His aim appears to have been to defeat Artavasdes and force him to abandon his alliance with Rome. In this he was to succeed, but this is not the main narrative of events by the Roman sources.

To face the massive Roman offensive Orodes gave the *Spahbad* Surena a much smaller force. Only a quarter the strength of the Roman invasion, this was doubtless not deemed strong enough to defeat the Romans, but was ordered to delay them while Orodes conquered Armenia. It may be that Orodes was planning a lightning campaign against Armenia with the intention of then turning south, cutting Crassus' communications with Rome and threatening his rear. This is impossible to prove, as events would mean that he would not need to face the Roman army.

The Invasion

The precise chronology of events is uncertain; however, taking into account travel times the following may be a reasonably accurate account of the campaign. Early in 53 BCE an embassy arrived from the Parthians, asking why the Romans had declared war and suggesting peace terms.[8] At about the same time or shortly after, men who had been in the garrisons in Mesopotamia returned, describing the great strength and military capabilities of the Parthians. According to Plutarch the Roman troops became discouraged as they had earlier believed that the campaign would be easy.[9] Fearing that these reports, plus (allegedly) unfavourable omens, would cause troop morale to drop to dangerous levels, some of the officers thought that Crassus ought to call a halt and reconsider the whole undertaking. Among these was 'Cassius the quaestor' (none other than Caius Cassius Longinus, afterwards one of the assassins of Caesar).[10]

Crassus refused to listen, and once his son had arrived and his preparations were complete, he invaded Parthia, starting from the city of Zeugma. He had the advantage both in numbers – although he wouldn't have known this yet – and in the fact that some of the cities on the border had already been taken and, despite the return of troops with the news as noted above, these appear to have remained in Roman hands. Therefore at first his advance would have been rapid, augmented by extra supplies from the captured cities.

As already noted Orodes ignored Crassus' attack and instead invaded Armenia. Artavasdes' worst fears were confirmed: without Roman support he faced defeat. As the Parthian army advanced into Armenia, ravaging the countryside, he sent messengers to Crassus asking for support.[11] According to Plutarch Crassus was angry with Artavasdes, although the reason for his annoyance is not clear.[12] In return, Artavasdes was almost certainly angry with Crassus for failing to support him.

Not long after the invasion, Artavasdes was forced to sue for peace and had no choice but to surrender and agree to the marriage of his sister to the son of Orodes, thereby securing his change of allegiance from Rome to Parthia. The decision was doubtless helped by Crassus' refusal to send him troops. It is sometimes thought that Crassus knew of the surrender and chose to carry on with his invasion regardless, but this is unlikely: he obviously knew of the invasion but the time taken for Orodes to complete the conquest of Armenia plus the time needed for the negotiations concerning the Armenian surrender and the betrothal of Artavasdes' daughter would have lasted for quite some time. Crassus doubtless saw Orodes' invasion as a useful diversion of the Parthians' main army away from his own invasion, and therefore believed that the absence of the main Parthian army would actually help him complete his conquest.

Crassus' confidence then appeared to have been justified, because as the army advanced his scouts returned and reported that they had come upon the tracks of many horses that had apparently wheeled about and fled from pursuit. Despite this good news, Cassius the quaestor apparently advised Crassus not to advance in a rash manner, but to allow the troops to rest and recover in one of the captured cities while the scouts gathered more information. He also counselled that the army advance along the river, as in that way the army could be supplied from the supply transports.[13]

Although the claim by Plutarch concerning Cassius' advice may be accurate, it is impossible to be certain: Plutarch's aim was to compare Roman individuals with Greek counterparts. In this case, Crassus was to be compared to Nicias, an Athenian general who had been one of the commanders of the disastrous Athenian expedition in Sicily (415–413 BCE). Plutarch needed to portray Crassus in a poor light, and suggesting that he refused advice that would have proved to be beneficial may simply have been one way of achieving his aim.

Again according to Plutarch, it is at this point that Abgar intervened and advised that Crassus leave the Euphrates and head across the desert.[14] This is commonly interpreted as an enormous mistake and is therefore seen as another of the failings of Crassus' generalship, but this assumption may be an error.

Crassus may have been aware that the standard route into the Parthian kingdom, which he had used in the previous year, followed the Euphrates. In the earlier campaign he had fought a battle near Ichnae against a Parthian blocking force. By heading across the desert and following the River Balissus instead of the Euphrates he was probably convinced that he would surprise any Parthian army adopting the usual defensive positions further south and so gain a major advantage.

In addition, during his conquest of Persia three centuries earlier, Alexander the Great had also taken the route across the desert. Probably influenced as much by the possibility of following in Alexander's footsteps as from listening to advice from Abgar (if this report is indeed accurate), Crassus pressed on with the invasion, leaving the Euphrates and heading across the desert.

According to Plutarch it was now that messengers arrived from Artavasdes, notifying Crassus that Orodes had invaded Armenia and advising that Crassus change course and join the Armenians.[15] With the main Parthian army in Armenia Crassus may have seen speed as one of the main means of achieving victory, and so became determined to reach Ctesiphon as quickly as possible, another possible factor in his decision to cross the desert.

Ignoring any conflicting advice and possibly convinced that with the main Parthian army in Armenia his own campaign would be much easier, Crassus and his men marched on. Finally, Crassus' scouts returned with reports that a Parthian army was in the vicinity. Knowing this was only a small part of the Parthian army, Crassus decided to attack. Although it is alleged by Dio that Crassus was convinced by Abgar to attack the Surena, as he heavily outnumbered the Parthian army, as noted earlier this is almost certainly a *topos* aiming to excuse the coming Roman defeat: there can be little doubt that Crassus needed no encouragement to attack the small Parthian force.[16]

At first Crassus acceded to his junior commanders' wishes, especially those of Cassius, who recommended that the army deploy with the infantry in a long line and the cavalry on the wings, a deployment intended to avoid having the enemy outflanking the Romans and probably with the idea of encircling the enemy's flanks; this was a possibility as the Parthians were heavily outnumbered.[17] However, shortly afterwards Crassus changed his mind and ordered the troops to form a hollow square with twelve *cohorts* on each side, each supported by cavalry. Cassius was given command of one of the wings and the other was given to Publius, Crassus' son.[18] The new deployment was much more secure in defence, but was far less manoeuvrable in attack and a lot slower in movement. Despite their reduced pace, shortly afterwards they reached the River Balissus and were able to replenish their water supplies.

Now that the large Roman army and the small Parthian force were within striking range of each other, the stage was set for the Battle of Carrhae.

The Opposing Forces: Rome

More than fifty years since the Battle of Arausio, the Marian system, with the *cohort* as the basis of the Roman legion, was now well established. All the legionaries were equipped with a metal helmet, a ring mail cuirass and an oval *scutum* (shield) for defence, and with a pair of *pila* and a *gladius* (sword) for offensive duties. Trained to throw the two *pila* effectively and fight as a unit with the *gladius*, the Roman legionary was now approaching the peak of efficiency.

For his campaign Crassus amassed seven legions, and as this was a planned major assault it is probable that the legions were brought up to or near full strength. Consequently it is likely that Crassus led around 35,000 Roman infantry in the invasion.

One major change that had happened concerning the army was that at the start of the first century BCE tensions had increased between Rome and those of her Italian allies who had been denied full citizenship. In the Social War (91–87 BCE), Rome and the Italians had fought a vicious conflict which, although it had ended in a Roman victory, also gave the Italian tribes the full citizenship they wanted. These new citizens were now enrolled into Rome's legions rather than fighting alongside Rome.

As a consequence, Rome was now using non-Italians to supplement their armed forces, especially with regard to cavalry and specialist troops such as archers. Alongside the legions, Crassus had 4,000 light infantry and 4,000 cavalry. The latter included 1,000 Gallic cavalry brought by his son Publius from Gaul during the winter of 54–53 BCE.[19] This brought the total to around 39,000 infantry and 4,000 cavalry. It had been further supplemented by around 6,000 cavalry supplied by Artavasdes, king of Armenia, although whether these had remained with the Roman army following the Parthian invasion of Armenia is unclear. Undoubtedly these would have left after the surrender of Artavasdes, but as this is undated the timing is uncertain.

The Opposing Forces: Parthia

The Parthian army of this period was, despite Roman beliefs in 'barbarian' deficiencies, a well-organized force which, although not professional like the Romans, was still of high quality.

Whereas the Roman army was formed around an infantry core, the Parthian army was a cavalry-based force. The majority of the army was composed of skilled, lightly-armed horse archers. With little in the way of defensive equipment, for the offensive they were armed only with bows and swords. Despite their apparent weakness, in reality their compound bow outranged most Roman missile weapons and was capable of penetrating even legionary armour.[20] These troops were capable of firing arrows accurately and of performing complicated manoeuvres, including riding close to an enemy and then away again while constantly peppering the enemy with arrows (the 'Parthian Shot'). These hit-and-run tactics made the Parthian horse archers a formidable enemy, but by themselves they found it difficult to decisively defeat a determined foe.

As a consequence, to support the horse archers the Parthians had developed a shock force of *cataphracts*, heavily-armed cavalry in which the rider was protected by strong iron armour and the horse by armour of iron or bronze, although in some cases the horse would probably have had leather or quilted armour to save cost and weight. Offensively they carried a lance and a bow. The spear was of unusual thickness and length, and despite some modern authorities' claim that using a lance without stirrups was not effective, they are attested as being able to 'pierce through two men at once'.[21]

The main tactic of the Parthian army was to send the horse archers to harass the enemy and locate or create gaps or weak points in an enemy's deployment, which could then be exploited by a furious charge of the heavily-armed *cataphracts* to break the enemy's line. With the line broken, the horse archers would then be free to flow through the gap and wreak havoc on the enemy from both sides.

Alongside the cavalry, the Parthians did have access to infantry, both indigenous and supplied by allies and subject nations. However, despite the immediate threat from the Roman army, Orodes II had decided that his first task would be to punish the Armenian King Artavasdes for his role in supporting the invasion, as well as to ensure that there would be no secondary invasion from Armenia. He had set out for Armenia with the main Parthian force, including all the infantry, with the aim of defeating Artavasdes and then returning to face the Romans after they had entered Parthia.

In accordance with this strategy, he had ordered the *spahbad* (army commander) Surena to monitor and harass the Roman invasion with an army composed solely of mounted troops, around 1,000 *cataphracts* and 9,000 horse archers. Plutarch claims that Surena also had a personal baggage train of 1,000 camels, but it is probable that this was the baggage train for the army with the camels carrying, among other things, a vast number of arrows for the horse archers.[22]

Location

Located in the kingdom of Osrhoene, ruled by the Abgar named in the sources as the 'traitor', Carrhae (Harran) was a settlement located not far from the capital city of Edessa, close to the River Balissus. The region is, on the whole, level ground with occasional hills. This is superb terrain suited to a cavalry army, with little in the way of impassable features and a minimum that could be used to give cover to an enemy, important for an army reliant largely upon horse archers. This was almost the worst possible terrain for the Roman army.

Deployment

According to Plutarch, Crassus gave the men permission to have something to eat and to drink water from the river, but ignored his officers' advice to make a camp for the night. Instead he ordered the troops to eat while standing in formation. Even before they had all finished eating, Crassus ordered them to advance towards the Parthian army.[23] Despite outnumbering the Parthians by around four to one, Crassus remained wary of the mobility of the Parthian army and so retained the square formation he had used on the march.

Almost certainly hoping to tempt the Romans into a rash attack, Surena had drawn up his force in at least two lines. His horse archers were placed at the front, and his *cataphracts* in the rear with their armour covered by 'robes and skins' so as not to alert the Romans to their presence. As a consequence, when the Romans sighted the Parthians they were surprised by the apparent weakness of the army facing them.[24]

The Battle

They were even more surprised a short time later when the Parthians facing them raised their battle cry and began beating their battle drums. At the same time the *cataphracts* dropped the cloths covering their armour and revealed their presence before advancing towards the Romans with the aim of charging and breaking through the Roman formations.[25] However, they were dissuaded by the fact that the Romans had continued their advance in the hollow-square formation and the Parthians quickly realized that a charge would simply end with them being left embedded deep within the Roman army and very vulnerable to the infantry pressed on every side.

Instead, Surena ordered the *cataphracts* to withdraw a short distance and his horse archers to surround the Romans and bombard them from a distance with as many arrows as possible; the archers rarely missed a target due to the density of the Roman formation. Proving his worth as a general, Surena had already foreseen the possibility that his army would struggle to defeat the Romans simply by close combat and had ensured that his army would not run out of arrows by commanding that extra supplies of ammunition be brought to his army by camel train.[26]

As the rain of arrows continued, Crassus attempted to seize the initiative by ordering his missile troops to leave the safety of the legionary square and counter the horse archers' rain of arrows. Unfortunately for the sallying troops, the horse archers, who had been firing blindly into the mass of legionaries, then shifted to aim shots at them. They quickly broke and returned to the shelter of the square, in doing so demonstrating both that the Parthians were going to be hard to defeat, but also proving that Roman armour was not a guarantee of safety against the powerful Parthian bows.[27] Numerous additional sorties only proved that the Parthians would not allow the Romans to come to close quarters, instead avoiding combat and using the 'Parthian shot' to inflict casualties even as they evaded the Roman attacks.[28]

Realizing that the Parthians were being resupplied by the camel train and so would not run out of arrows, Crassus ordered his son Publius to take the 1,000 cavalry from Gaul and some additional horsemen together with 500 archers and 8 *cohorts* of legionaries (c.3,500–4,000 men) to attack the Parthians and force them to come to close quarters rather than standing off and shooting. The opposing Parthians quickly took to their heels.

Encouraged by the enemy's apparent flight, Publius and his force pursued them until they had gone some distance from the main Roman body. At this point the Parthians wheeled around again and faced the Romans with the *cataphracts* advancing to pin them, while the horse archers surrounded them and shot them down.[29]

In desperation, Publius and his Gallic cavalry charged the *cataphracts*, but despite their bravery their assault was repulsed by the well-armed and armoured *cataphracts*. Publius had been severely wounded in the charge and the remnants of the force retired to a nearby hill where they prepared to defend themselves. Unfortunately the hill simply allowed the Parthians to shoot at all the Romans, not just the front ranks. Realizing their cause was hopeless, shortly before the final Parthian assault Publius and some of the other commanders committed suicide rather than risk being captured. The Parthian charge swept over the hill and destroyed the Romans, taking only 500 men prisoner from the c.5,000 men who had made the assault.[30]

In the meantime, the withdrawal of Parthian troops to face Publius' advance and defence on the hill had lessened the pressure on Crassus' main body. He took advantage of the respite to deploy his army in defensive array on sloping ground. Learning that Publius was in danger, Crassus ordered the army forward, but due to the defensive nature of the deployment the advance was too late: having destroyed Publius' detachment, the Parthian army returned to the attack, with Publius' head paraded upon a spear. The knowledge of Publius' defeat and death destroyed the morale of the main body of Romans.[31]

Plutarch claims that at this point Crassus gave a speech to raise the troops' morale, but also notes that the speech had little effect.[32] Instead the slaughter continued, with the horse archers devastating the Romans with arrows and the *cataphracts* repelling any attempts to break out. The *cataphracts* also ensured that the Roman army remained in close formation, providing tempting targets for the archers, a plight described tellingly by Dio.[33]

At this point Dio alleges that the allied Osrhoene troops under Abgar attacked the Romans in the rear, completing the betrayal of Crassus begun by his advice to cross the desert.[34] There are two problems with this claim. One is that no other Roman source mentions this attack. The second is that, after the battle, Parthia gained control of the region and Orodes deposed Abgar. As Orodes' action is not what would be expected in the treatment of a successful ally, the betrayal is therefore discounted here.

Finally darkness put a halt to the slaughter. The Parthians withdrew and made camp, while the Romans simply stopped where they were.[35] During the night Crassus' officers eventually convinced him to withdraw, leaving behind the majority of the wounded. Caring for the few wounded who could manage to follow them and constantly disordered and disorientated by false alarms of Parthian attack, the main body made its disjointed way towards Carrhae.[36] A commander named Ignatius took his own troop of 300 cavalry ahead and informed Coponius, the commander of the garrison, that there had been a battle before riding off to Zeugma.[37] In response, Coponius armed his men and went out to escort the survivors to the city.[38]

When morning came the Parthians attacked and killed the wounded that had been left behind – allegedly around 4,000 men – before picking off any stragglers they could find. This included c.2,000 men and their legate Vargonteius who had become lost during the night. These were all killed except twenty men who were allowed to escape thanks to the Parthians respecting their extreme bravery.[39]

Believing that Crassus had escaped, Surena advanced to Carrhae. When Surena learned that Crassus was in the city, he proposed a truce, offering them safe conduct out of Mesopotamia in return for peace. Cassius accepted and a time was organized for formal negotiations to take place.[40]

Rather than entering talks, Surena led his men to lay siege to the city, demanding the surrender of Crassus and Cassius. Deciding to escape rather than surrender, the remaining troops then fragmented, leaving the city by night.[41] Cassius went with Crassus, but fearing treachery returned to Carrhae before leading 500 cavalry to safety in Syria.[42] Around 5,000 men led by a man named Octavius managed to reach the hill country around Sinnaca and build a camp before sunrise.[43]

As noted, Crassus led some of his men out, but Cassius returned to Carrhae with some of the troops. Crassus was left with 4 *cohorts* of legionaries (around 2,000 men) and a few cavalry. Allegedly led astray by a guide named Andromachus, when day came Crassus was surrounded by the Parthians on a hill about a mile and a half away from Octavius. As his position was on lower ground and was connected with Octavius' position by a long ridge, Octavius saw that Crassus was in difficulty.[44] Octavius and his men attacked the Parthians in the rear and rescued Crassus.[45]

Seeing that his troops were now battle-weary and probably running out of arrows, Surena again offered Crassus a truce. What happened next according to both Plutarch and Dio was that during the ensuing talks fighting erupted and Crassus and Octavius were both killed.[46] Of the remaining troops, some surrendered to the Parthians and were taken into captivity, but the majority scattered during the night. On the following day the Parthians mounted a pursuit, killing the majority of these, with only a few escaping.

The Battle of Carrhae was over. Much to the dismay of the Romans, it was found that during the course of the battle and the 'mopping-up' operations afterwards the Parthians had captured three legionary eagles. It was only during the later reign of Augustus that these were recovered, through diplomacy rather than war.

The chronology as given by Plutarch suggests that it was only after news of the battle reached the Armenian king Artavasdes that he accepted a peace treaty with Parthia, including the marriage of his sister to Orodes' son.[47] Although certainty is impossible, this probably makes more sense than the commonly-accepted theory that Artavasdes surrendered very quickly. Not only would it explain why Crassus was not worried about Orodes attacking his rear, but also it is more likely that Artavasdes would attempt to survive until Crassus had, as expected, defeated the Parthians and Orodes was forced to retire. None of the inhabitants of Parthia, Armenia or Rome expected Surena to win.

Aftermath

Roman expansion in the East had suffered a severe setback. Orodes soon retook all the lost cities east of the Euphrates.[48] However, a brief invasion of Syria was quickly repulsed by Cassius, who had taken control of the region following the death of Crassus.[49]

The defeat of a major Roman army by such a small force was a major embarrassment for Rome. To add insult to injury, the loss of three legionary standards was a humiliation that would not be eased until much later, when the Roman general Octavian had finally taken control as the first emperor of Rome with the title Augustus.

Effects

The opening of the conflict between Rome and Parthia, and especially the fact that Crassus had simply gone to war without a pretext, resulted in friction between the two powers that continued with only a few breaks throughout the existence of the Parthian Empire and was continued with their successors the Sasanids. The net result was that the Roman

Empire was obliged to station large forces on the eastern frontier to defend against a prospective Parthian/Sasanid attack. This only ended with the Islamic conquest of Sasanid Persia in the seventh century, a feat only made possible by a catastrophic war between the Sasanids and the East Roman (Byzantine) Empire, which made both empires so weak that large areas of the Byzantine Empire were conquered while the Sasanids were almost completely destroyed.

Internally, the most obvious immediate effect of the defeat was the collapse of the First Triumvirate: without Crassus as a mediator, 'Caesar's power now inspired the envy of Pompey, while Pompey's eminence was offensive to Caesar; Pompey could not brook an equal or Caesar a superior.'[50] The Republic reverted to fractious politics and civil war, which only ended after yet another internal conflict won by Caesar's heir Octavianus, who became the first Roman emperor with the title Augustus. Had Crassus not been defeated and killed, the history of the Roman Republic could easily have been very different.

Select Bibliography

Cassius Dio, 40.20: http://penelope.uchicago.edu/Thayer/E/Roman/Texts/Cassius_Dio/home.html

Plutarch, *Crassus*: https://penelope.uchicago.edu/Thayer/E/Roman/Texts/Plutarch/Lives/Crassus*.html

Chapter Seven

The German Wall: The Battle of the Teutoburger Wald, 9 CE

The Sources

There are four main sources for this battle. Nearest in time to the event is **Velleius Paterculus**. Born sometime in the late first century BCE and living until at least 30 CE, his history of Rome spanned from the end of the Trojan War until 30 CE. His work is generally accepted as accurate, if uninspired. As he was around 30 years old at the time of the battle, it is possible that he had access to first-hand accounts, so his information will not have been changed by distortion over the years. On the other hand, it is likely that it is still liable to bias due to inherent beliefs prevalent in Rome and the need to adhere to the standard *topoi* of the day. As a consequence, Paterculus' motives and style need to be taken into account.

The second author is **Publius Cornelius Tacitus**. Born in the middle of the first century CE and living until around 120 CE, Tacitus was a historian and politician, and his reputation as one of the greatest historians of Rome remains intact to this day. Whenever possible Tacitus' account will be used, supported by the other authors when they are seen as being independent and not reliant upon Tacitus himself.

The third source is **Cassius Dio** (c.155–c.235 CE). As noted in the previous chapter, Dio was writing around two centuries after the battle and so was reliant upon earlier sources. Dio's work is traditionally seen as being of relatively poor quality, and although there have been attempts recently to improve his standing, his work still needs to be used with caution rather than being accepted at face value.

The final source is 'Florus'. Although this history was written either at the end of the first century CE or early in the second, it is placed last here for a simple reason: the actual identity of the author is uncertain. One option is that he was Julius Florus, an ancient Roman poet and orator. A second is that he was Lucius Annaeus Florus, also attested as a Roman historian. The third, and the one accepted by the majority of historians, is **Publius Annius Florus**. All three appear to have lived at around the same time, between c.70 and c.140 CE. Although there is debate concerning which one is the historian whose work still exists, it is possible that the sources concerning 'Florus' were confused and that either two or all three could in fact be the same man.

Whether he was one of these men or not is realistically unimportant. What is important is that the work is, for the most part, an epitome of Livy. As a consequence, it is useful as it epitomizes some of the lost sections of Livy. However, it includes mistakes either in geographical details or in the chronology, in this echoing Livy's own work. Consequently, it needs to be used with caution.

Background

By the time Julius Caesar was assassinated in 44 BCE he claimed to have conquered the whole of Gaul, although there was still resistance to Roman rule in some areas. His campaigns had placed the boundary of the Roman Empire on the River Rhine. He had also written extensively on his campaigns and as a result the Roman perception was that Gaul and the Celts occupied the lands on the near side of the Rhine, but that the far bank was occupied by Germanic tribes. Although this is now seen as being extremely simplified, in the Roman mindset the Germans were generally associated with the Cimbri and Teutones who had inflicted the earlier defeat at Arausio.

As with most frontiers, these 'German' tribes were sometimes hostile and raided into Gaul. The most damaging of these invasions came when the local governor, Marcus Lollius, was defeated by the Sugambri, which in itself caused problems, but to add to the disgrace *Legio V Alaudae* ('Fifth Legion, the Larks') lost its eagle, the worst possible disgrace for a Roman legion. It was obvious that the defeat needed avenging.

Although it is usually assumed that the Romans were aware of other rivers to the east that ran parallel to the Rhine, especially the Amisia (Ems), the Aller, the Visurgis (Weser) and the Albis (Elbe), and that a campaign to reach any of these rivers could shorten the frontier in the north, this is reliant more upon modern assumptions than historical sources.

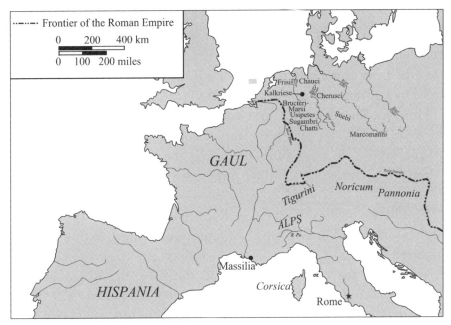

The Teutoburger Wald campaign.

Augustus had been emperor since 27 BCE, and it was he who decided that the Empire should take revenge upon the Germanic tribes. In 12 BCE he ordered his stepson Nero Claudius Drusus to begin the campaign to take the frontier into Germania. Between 12 and 9 BCE Drusus campaigned across the Rhine, using multiple forts and sometimes alliances with the Frisii among others, and a fleet in the North Sea to defeat the Sugambri, the Usipetes, the Bructeri, the Chauci, the Chatti, the Suebi (a conglomeration of smaller tribes including the Marcomanni) and the Cherusci. The campaigns were a great success, since as early as the first campaign it would seem that the eagle standard of *Legio V Alaudae* was recovered: a coin showing a 'Germanic' submitting a standard was minted in either 12 or 11 BCE.

Having crossed the Weser and advanced as far east as the Elbe and having been acclaimed *imperator* ('victorious commander', not 'emperor'), Drusus began a withdrawal to the Rhine at the end of the campaign season of 9 BCE. During the withdrawal his horse fell on him, breaking his leg. Shortly after, due to complications from the break, he died. Both he and his descendants were granted the name *Germanicus* by a grateful Senate.

Tiberius was given command of the German campaigns as Drusus' successor. He was so successful that he was able to settle 40,000 Suebi and Sugambri on the west bank of the Rhine, so pacifying the region that the area as far as the Elbe was seen as a Roman province, though not yet ruled by a governor or subject to taxation.

However, Roman politics then interfered. In 6 BCE Tiberius was forced to retire to Rhodes and command devolved upon Lucius Domitius Ahenobarbus. He went further, crossing the Elbe, and his successor Marcus Vinicius spent a further three years campaigning to eliminate resistance.

Finally, the political situation in Rome changed and in 4 CE Tiberius again took control in Germania. As resistance declined, in 6 CE Tiberius gathered his forces for a campaign against the Marcomanni under Maroboduus, the only region between the Elbe, the Rhine and the Danube that had yet to be conquered. The proposed war was halted by a revolt in Pannonia, which lasted until 9 CE: Tiberius was sent to put down the revolt.

Since Tiberius was then restoring order in Pannonia, command in Germania was allocated to a man named Publius Quinctilius Varus, who was well connected socially but had little experience as a military commander. Sadly for Rome, one of his most senior advisers was a man named Arminius who, although granted Roman citizenship for his service in the Roman *auxilia*, was a chief of the Cherusci. The Cherusci was one of the tribes that had been defeated by Drusus. What followed is covered in some detail by Cassius Dio and, although his work is open to question on the details, as it is the most comprehensive it is used here when possible.

According to Dio, it was Varus who began the process that led to his own defeat:

> But when Quinctilius Varus became governor of the province of Germany, and in the discharge of his official duties was administering the affairs of these peoples also, he strove to change them more rapidly. Besides issuing orders to them as if they were actually slaves of the Romans, he exacted money as he would from subject nations.
>
> *Cassius Dio, 56.18.3.*

Despite the obvious conclusion that this passage is rhetorical, aimed to demonstrate that from the start Varus made mistakes, it is possible that it is true: there was a long-standing tradition of the Roman aristocracy being arrogant and treating natives of 'conquered' provinces badly and so fomenting revolt, the most obvious comparison being that of Boudicca of the Iceni. Dio continues:

> Now they did not openly revolt, since they saw that there were many Roman troops near the Rhine and many within their own borders; instead, they received Varus, pretending that they would do all he demanded of them, and thus they drew him far away from the Rhine into the land of the Cherusci, toward the Visurgis (Weser), and there by behaving in a most peaceful and friendly manner led him to believe that they would live submissively without the presence of soldiers.
>
> Consequently, he did not keep his legions together, as was proper in a hostile country, but distributed many of the soldiers to helpless communities, which asked for them for the alleged purpose of guarding various points, arresting robbers, or escorting provision trains. Among those deepest in the conspiracy and leaders of the plot and of the war were Arminius and Segimerus, who were his [Varus'] constant companions and often shared his mess. He accordingly became confident, and expecting no harm, not only refused to believe all those who suspected what was going on and advised him to be on his guard, but actually rebuked them for being needlessly excited and slandering his friends. Then there came an uprising, first on the part of those who lived at a distance from him, deliberately so arranged, in order that Varus should march against them and so be more easily overpowered while proceeding through what was supposed to be friendly country, instead of putting himself on his guard as he would do in case all became hostile to him at once. And so it came to pass.
>
> *Cassius Dio, 56.18.4–19.4.*

Dio here states clearly that some among Varus' advisors were wary of the Germanic leaders, although these men had served in Rome's army and Arminius was even accorded equestrian status for his services. Paterculus gives more details although, as already noted, the accuracy of his account cannot be verified and so must be treated with caution:

This was disclosed to Varus through Segestes, a loyal man of that race [Cherusci] and of illustrious name, who also demanded that the conspirators be put in chains. But fate now dominated the plans of Varus and had blindfolded the eyes of his mind. ... And so Quinctilius refused to believe the story, and insisted upon judging the apparent friendship of the Germans toward him by the standard of his merit. And, after this first warning, there was no time left for a second.

Velleius Paterculus, Roman History, 2.118.4.

Returning to Dio, Arminius and Segestes then put their plan into action:

They escorted him as he set out, and then begged to be excused from further attendance, in order, as they claimed, to assemble their allied forces, after which they would quietly come to his aid. Then they took charge of their troops, which were already in waiting somewhere, and after the men in each community had put to death the detachments of soldiers for which they had previously asked, they came upon Varus in the midst of forests by this time almost impenetrable. And there, at the very moment of revealing themselves as enemies instead of subjects, they wrought great and dire havoc.

Cassius Dio, 56.19.4–5.

Apparently Arminius and his colleagues excused themselves from the march and set out to organize the ambush. Dio claims that the detachments that had been sent to garrison specific areas at the inhabitants' request were now butchered, but it is likely that this only happened after the beginning of the battle, and possibly even after the Roman defeat had been widely reported: the concept that all the tribes involved acted perfectly in unison is perhaps unlikely.

Whether the massacres are accurately reported or not, the Battle of the Teutoburger Wald had begun.

The Opposing Forces: Rome

By the turn of the millennium the reforms to the army instituted by Marius and then Augustus had come to full fruition and, despite a few tweaks here and there, this was the army that would last until the reforms started by Diocletian in the late third century.

The legions were now based upon the *cohort* system as seen earlier, but the army was now supported by troops supplied by non-citizens and allies. These *auxilia* ('helpers') appear to have been based roughly on the figures given below, but it should be remembered that, except for specific major campaigns, these formations would be below strength due to accident, disease, detachment for other duties or difficulty in receiving recruits due to deployment area or other units being given priority. It was the *auxilia* that supplied the cavalry and the specialist infantry such as archers, not included in the legionary system.

With regard to the cavalry, this was composed of two main types of unit: the more common *Ala Quingenaria* ('Wing of 500') consisting of 16 *turmae* ('troops'), each composed of 30 or 32 men – the number is disputed[1] – giving a total of 480 or 512 troopers; and the less common *Ala Milliaria* ('Wing of 1,000') which, disappointingly, only contained 24 *turmae*, giving a total of 720 or 768 cavalrymen.

The infantry was also composed of two main types: the more common *cohors quingenaria* ('cohort of 500') which consisted of 6 *centuriae* ('hundreds'), each of 80 men, for a total of 480; and the less common *cohors milliaria* ('cohort of 1,000') with 10 *centuriae* of 80 men, for a total of 800 infantrymen.

In between these two main divisions were the *equitata* ('Ridings'), a combination of infantry and cavalry in one unit. As can probably be guessed, there were two types: the *cohors equitata quingenaria* ('Riding cohort of 500'), which had 6 *centuriae* of infantry (480 men) plus 4 *turmae* of cavalry (120/128 cavalrymen) for a total of 600/608 men, and the *cohors equitata milliaria* ('Riding cohort of 1,000'), which had 10 *centuriae* of infantry (800 men) plus 8 *turmae* of cavalry (240/256 cavalrymen) for a total of 1,040/1,056 men.

Alongside these regular troops, it was possible for Rome to hire specialist mercenaries or to be supplied with troops by allied kingdoms. However, for this campaign in Germany it would appear that the Roman force was only composed of standard units so these do not need to be discussed here.

The troops taken by Varus for the campaign against Maroboduus consisted of three legions (XVII, XVIII and XVIIII), six auxiliary *cohorts* and three cavalry *alae*.[2] This would give a total of around 20,000 men, which was deemed easily sufficient for what was, effectively, seen as a 'mopping-up' operation.

The Opposing Forces: Germans

There were six main tribes associated with the battle by the Roman sources. The central core was the Cherusci of Arminius, but there were also elements of the Bructeri, the Marsi, the Sugambri, the Chauci and the Chatti. It is unlikely that all members of these tribes took part, with the possible exception of the Cherusci, and it is also possible that small numbers of other tribes took part but that these are not mentioned by Roman historians.

Although it would be easy to suggest that the warriors of these tribes were all dressed and armed the same, this may be in error. It is likely that different tribes wore slightly different fashions and may have carried distinctive weapons or had different shield patterns to indicate their tribal affiliations.

On the other hand, the similarities may have outweighed the differences. For defensive purposes, the warriors would all have carried a shield, possibly of distinctive shape or size for each tribe, but this is unknown. Normally armour and helmets may have been restricted to the aristocracy due to the comparative poverty of the mass of warriors; however, an unknown proportion of the Germanic soldiers had been serving alongside Arminius within the Roman army and so may have retained the use of their Roman armour and weapons, making them much more effective as soldiers.

For the offensive, the majority would have carried a spear, the most common being the style known as the *framea*, one with a long shaft and iron head which Tacitus equates to the *hasta*, the long thrusting spear used by earlier Roman armies. For close work, the warriors would probably have carried a sword and/or a dagger.

Only rich members of the aristocracy would have been able to afford the luxury of horses for riding and warfare as the cost of maintaining these animals and of keeping a trained staff to care for them would have been beyond the means of all but a few. As a result, the armies involved would only have had a limited number of cavalry, but the nature of the terrain at the Battle of the Teutoburger Wald meant that these would not have been of any great use.

As for numbers, there are no indications in the sources as to the size of the tribal force at the battle, nor is it possible to guess: the nature of the battle means that only a few thousand troops could have been responsible for the outcome, but also that the Romans could have been outnumbered, as will be seen below. Consequently no estimate will be given here: there is simply no way of assessing the numbers involved.

Location

Until recently the location of the battle has been totally unknown. Tacitus calls the battle the *saltus Teutoburgiensis* (usually translated as 'Wooded Area'/'Wilderness'/'Forest' of Teutoburg, but possibly more accurately as 'Teutoburg Pass'; see below).[3] The Teutoburg Forest is an extremely large area and any specific location was open to speculation. However, since 1988 official archaeological excavations have taken place at Kalkriese near Osnabrück, between the Weser and the Rhine, which clearly show that this was the site where many casualties were inflicted on the Romans by the Germanic allies. However, although it is now usually stated that the battle took place here, this is not strictly correct. The 'battle' took place over a very large area, although it is safe to say that Kalkriese was the site of a major confrontation within the battle.

Deployment

Due to the nature of the battle, no actual deployment was possible for much of the conflict, although in a few places the Roman army may have been able to adopt a more regular formation. As they were in effect conducting an ambush on a large scale, it is doubtful that the Germanic tribesmen adopted any traditional form of deployment. Where either force was capable of adopting such a deployment, this will be covered in the text.

The Battle

Varus and his legions continued their advance into Germanic territory. The terrain was causing major problems:

The mountains had an uneven surface broken by ravines, and the trees grew close together and very high. Hence the Romans, even before the enemy assailed them, were having a hard time of it felling trees, building roads, and bridging places that required it. They had with them many wagons and many beasts of burden as in time of peace; moreover, not a few women and children and a large retinue of servants were following them – one more reason for their advancing in scattered groups. Meanwhile a violent rain and wind came up that separated them still further, while the ground, that had become slippery around the roots and logs, made walking very treacherous for them, and the tops of the trees kept breaking off and falling down, causing much confusion.

Cassius Dio, 56.20.1–3.

The information given by Dio is of questionable value in some cases. Here, the statement that the Roman marching columns contained women and children as well as servants ties in with other statements which suggest that Varus was not expecting heavy opposition, but was simply bent on driving roads through the 'conquered' lands to allow for a swift Romanization of the region. Varus was only expecting to fight deeper into unexplored territory. On the other hand, the 'violent rain and wind' may be a Roman *topos*, giving both bad omens and a further excuse for the upcoming defeat. Dio continues:

While the Romans were in such difficulties, the barbarians suddenly surrounded them on all sides at once, coming through the densest thickets, as they were acquainted with the paths. At first they hurled their volleys from a distance; then, as no one defended himself and many were wounded, they approached closer to them. For the Romans were not proceeding in any regular order, but were mixed in helter-skelter with the wagons and the unarmed, and so, being unable to form readily anywhere in a body, and being fewer at every point than their assailants, they suffered greatly and could offer no resistance at all.

Cassius Dio, 56.20.4–5.

The Servian Wall at Termini Station.
(*Salvatore Falco, June 2005, CC1*)

Marble bust of Pyrrhus of Epirus.

Fresco from Poseidonia/Paestum purporting to show the 'Italian phalanx'.

Samnite warriors, frieze from Nola dated to the fourth century BCE.

The probable battlefield at Lake Trasimene. (*Tom Bennett, Creative Commons Attribution Share Alike, 3.0*)

War elephants crossing a river.

Marble bust, reputedly of Hannibal originally found at Capua.

A Roman coin issued during the Second Punic War (218–201 BCE) showing (obverse) Mars, and (reverse) a Roman cavalryman of the period wearing a plumed helmet and carrying the small cavalry shield (*parma equestris*).

The Altar of Domitius Ahenobarbus, Louvre (end of the second century BCE).

A terracotta statuette of a (Germanic) warrior carrying an oval shield, c.second century CE. (*Ashmolean Museum, Carole Raddato, Flickr, Creative Commons*)

A graffiti from private houses at Dura-Europos, early third century CE. (*After M. Rostovzeff, Caravan Cities, figs 2-3*)

A Parthian *cataphract* during a hunt.

A Parthian horse archer.

A reconstruction of the wall at Kalkriese that halted the Roman retreat.

The 'Grande Ludovisi sarcophagus' showing a battle scene between Roman soldiers and Germans, perhaps including Hostilian, the son of Emperor Decius. (*Proconnesus, marble Roman artwork, c.251–252 CE*)

Sculpture at Naqš-i Rustam showing the triumphant Shapur I and the defeated Roman emperors Valerian and Philip Arabicus. (*Diego Delso, delso.photo, License CC-BY-SA*)

Part of the Persian inscription at Naqš-i Rustam.

The walls of Amida/Diyarbakir. (*Marco Prins, CC0 1 0 Universal*)

A marble bust of the emperor Julian.
(*Jona Lendering, CC0 1.0 Universal*)

Statue of Theodosius I (r.379–395), the last emperor to effectively rule the whole of the Roman Empire. (*Wikimedia Commons*)

Cape Bon, the scene of the last combined expedition from the Eastern and Western Empires to reconquer Africa from Gaiseric.

This description has formed the basis of the majority of accounts of the battle. The main thrust is usually that the 'barbarians' now surrounded the entire Roman army and threw their javelins at the Roman marching columns. This is extremely unlikely. The number of Roman troops involved, the baggage train and the dependants and servants stretched out along narrow forest tracks has been estimated at between 9 and 12.5 miles long (c. 15–20 kilometres). To suggest that the tribesmen were able to spread their attack along a column this length and in terrain this dense is questionable. It is far more likely that they aimed their attacks at either vulnerable areas of the column, especially the baggage train and where there were masses of civilians unprotected by troops, and/or at the head and tail of the column where they could cause the most confusion and terror:

> Accordingly, they [the Romans] encamped on the spot, after securing a suitable place, so far as that was possible on a wooded mountain; and afterwards they either burned or abandoned most of their wagons and everything else that was not absolutely necessary to them. The next day they advanced in a little better order, and even reached open country, though they did not get off without loss.
>
> *Cassius Dio, 56.21.1.*

It would seem that Varus ordered a camp, but more possibly a simple defensive structure to be constructed into which he gathered all the survivors that he could. The fact that he was able to ensure the safety of a large number of troops and dependants implies that the barbarian assault was more fragmented than is usually claimed.

> Upon setting out from there they plunged into the woods again, where they defended themselves against their assailants, but suffered their heaviest losses while doing so. For since they had to form their lines in a narrow space, in order that the cavalry and infantry together might run down the enemy, they collided frequently with one another and with the trees.
>
> *Cassius Dio, 56.21.2.*

This passage, more than any other, portrays more clearly the problems faced by the Romans while trying to escape from the trap. They had advanced deep into enemy territory along narrow paths through the forest, and although there were areas where the trees thinned and allowed them to deploy in a more ordered fashion, the tribesmen knew this would happen so attacked mainly where the terrain closed in and prevented the Romans from using their training to advantage.

> They were still advancing when the fourth day dawned, and again a heavy downpour and violent wind assailed them, preventing them from going forward and even from standing securely, and moreover depriving them of the use of their weapons. For they could not handle their bows or their javelins with any success, nor, for that matter, their shields, which were thoroughly soaked. Their opponents, on the other hand, being for the most part lightly equipped, and able to approach and retire freely, suffered less from the storm. Furthermore, the enemy's forces had greatly increased, as many of those who had at first wavered joined them, largely in the hope of plunder, and thus they could more easily encircle and strike down the Romans, whose ranks were now thinned, many having perished in the earlier fighting. Varus, therefore, and all the more prominent officers, fearing that they should either be captured alive or be killed by their bitterest foes (for they had already been wounded), made bold to do a thing that was terrible yet unavoidable: they took their own lives.
>
> *Cassius Dio, 56.21.3–5.*

The detail by Dio that the battle extended over four days reinforces the concept that the tribesmen only attacked when the terrain was in their favour. The further information that the weather again took a turn for the worse and so hindered the troops from either using their *pila* (which were in any case of limited utility in close terrain) or their shields due to the slipperiness caused by the excessive rainfall gives a further excuse for the defeat, but may actually be an accurate detail.

Of more importance, Dio writes that many of the tribes were at first unwilling to join with the 'rebellion', which implies that it was only now that many of the detachments sent out earlier were overrun. This would make more sense in the context of Germanic politics than an instant agreement to join and fight as proposed earlier by Dio. The death of Varus caused despondency in the remaining troops:

> When news of this had spread, none of the rest, even if he had any strength left, defended himself any longer. Some imitated their leader, and others, casting aside their arms, allowed anybody who pleased to slay them; for to flee was impossible, however much one might desire to do so. Every man, therefore, and every horse was cut down without fear of resistance.
>
> *Cassius Dio, 56.22 1–2.*

Kalkriese

More details of the final stand of the Romans may have been unearthed – literally – at Kalkriese. Following the first tentative explorations in the 1980s, succeeding excavations have revealed remains from a strip of land almost 15 miles long by 1 mile deep. This would have been around one day's march for the Roman army along paved roads, so is probably the result of at least two days' march along forest paths by a column hemmed in by the terrain.

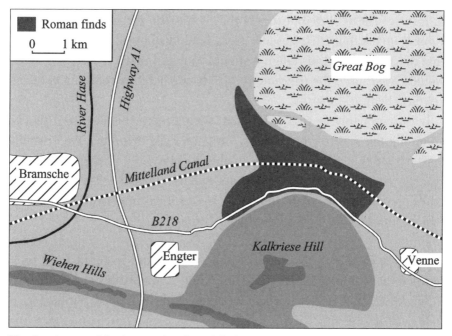

The distribution of the dense archaeological finds near Kalkriese.

Towards the western end of this strip lies a narrow piece of land between the *Schmittenhöhel Kalkrieser* Berg (Mount Kalkriese) and a large bog. It is the location of this 'pass' that has resulted in modern authors translating *saltus Teutoburgiensis* as the 'Teutoburg Pass' rather than the more traditional 'Teutoburg Forest'. It is here that an important discovery was made.

This was a rampart, obviously built by the tribesmen as part of the continuing efforts to annihilate the Roman army. It was 4ft high and 12ft thick, with passages to allow the hidden tribesmen to emerge and attack the Roman army. This rampart blocked the Roman route, but also provided cover for the tribesmen, especially at the start of this part of the conflict.

Due to the method of its construction, it is assumed that it was erected following the instructions of either Arminius himself or another individual who had served in the Roman army. This assumption has been made due to the fact that the wall 'zigzagged', an unusual design for the Germanic tribesmen, meaning that attacks by the Roman troops were both compressed and also open to attack from different sides. Furthermore, the passages allowed the tribesmen to attack the Romans in the flank and to retreat to safety if that became necessary. The number of artefacts found in front of the wall demonstrates that it was the focus of a determined Roman attack, but their absence from behind the wall is possibly proof that the attack failed, although it should be noted that a successful assault would have caused the tribesmen to fall back, therefore resulting in fewer artefacts behind the wall.

It was probably at this point that, with passage blocked and finally accepting the scale of the disaster, Varus took his own life.[4] Yet it would appear that the tribesmen were unable to block the passage of all the Roman troops as one column appears to have escaped to the south-west while another broke out to the north-west. One of these was the cavalry which, commanded by the legate Vala Numonius:

Left the infantry unprotected by the cavalry and in flight tried to reach the Rhine with his squadrons of horse. But fortune avenged his act, for he did not survive those whom he had abandoned, but died in the act of deserting them.

Velleius Paterculus, 2.119.4.

Despite this, the majority of the Roman army was finally trapped. Not all the commanders killed themselves: the prefect Eggius died leading his men in an attempt to break out. Some men escaped and joined the garrison at Aliso (see below), but the vast majority of the army was either killed or captured. After a conflict lasting for at least four days, the battle was finally over.

Aftermath

Taking into account the number of troops led by Varus and the few that escaped, Roman losses at the battle are assessed as being between 15,000 and 19,500. According to Tacitus, captured officers were sacrificed by the Germanic tribes during religious ceremonies held to celebrate the victory. Other individuals were ransomed, but many were sold into slavery.[5]

All the many detachments sent into Germania as garrisons were destroyed, with the exception of that at Aliso. Here the troops managed to resist a siege and, when rumours spread of an advancing relief force caused the Germans to relax the siege, the survivors broke out and the majority managed to reach the advancing army, which was led by Varus' nephew, Lucius Nonius Asprenas.[6] The resistance of the Roman garrisons, especially that at Aliso, plus the arrival of reinforcements under Tiberius, ensured that Arminius was unable to lead his victorious armies across the Rhine and into Gaul. Despite the protection of Gaul, the defeat had tremendous implications for Rome, not least with regard to a loss of prestige.

In Rome, after hearing the news Augustus was allegedly unable to sleep and wandered the corridors of the palace shouting '*Quinctili Vare, legiones redde!*' ('Quinctilius Varus, give me back my legions!').[7] As this was impossible, Augustus ordered a levy to replace the lost troops. After this he ordered Tiberius to avenge the defeat and restore the reputation of the Empire. Tiberius campaigned in Germania between 10 and 12 CE but, possibly aware that Tiberius was an experienced commander and in the knowledge that a second ambush was impossible, Arminius refused to face him in battle.

In 14 CE the Emperor Augustus died and the legions in Germania mutinied. Taking their chance, the tribesmen across the frontier crossed the Rhine and raided Gaul. Thankfully for Gaul, the mutiny was short-lived, and in the same year Germanicus, the adopted son of Tiberius, the new emperor, crossed the Rhine, defeated the Marsi and raided the territory of the Bructeri, the Tubantes and the Usipetes.

Over the next two years (14–16 CE), Germanicus campaigned in Germania. His forces recovered the lost eagle of the XVIIII legion and another of the lost eagles, but from which legion is not recorded. During one campaign he located the site of the Teutoburg defeat, burying some of the dead that remained on the site. He also fought a battle against Arminius at the *Pontes Longi* ('long causeways'), although this ended in a draw rather than a victory.

Finally, in 16 CE, Germanicus fought Arminius at the Battle of Idistaviso (Battle of the River Weser) and defeated him. He then defeated the Marsi and forced their ruler to reveal the location of the second lost eagle. Having buried (some of) the dead of Teutoburg, having recovered two of the three lost eagles and having defeated Arminius, Tiberius recalled him to Rome. Tiberius had decided that Roman prestige had been restored, but there was never again to be an attempt to reach the Elbe or conquer 'Germania'. Instead the Empire was to create two provinces: Upper and Lower Germany.

Effects

More than most, this defeat had repercussions, both in the immediate aftermath and the long-term history of the region. Obviously the defeat had a major impact on Rome. The Empire had lost approximately one-tenth of its legions in a single battle. Unlike other legions that had been defeated, legions XVII, XVIII and XVIIII were never re-established and the numbers were never used again.

More importantly, in the long term it meant that the Germans across the border were never imbued with Roman culture or language, unlike the Gauls, nor were the majority converted to Catholic Christianity until after the Empire had fallen. The result was that there was a hostile force across the Rhine that would forever be wanting to cross into the agricultural areas of Gaul and Italy. Almost 400 years later this lack of a victory over Germania would come back to haunt Rome as its frontiers in Gaul slowly eroded in the face of barbarian ingressions.

In the even longer term, the Rhine thus became a boundary between the Latin/Romance culture of Gaul/France and the German/Germanic culture of Germania/Germany. Had Varus been victorious, or rather had Arminius failed in his large-scale ambush, a large part of what is now Germany would have been included in the Empire, as a result of which there would have been a completely different series of events concerning the end of the Western Roman Empire. The least controversial result may have been that the Germans could now be speaking a Romance language. The history of Europe would have been very different.

Select Bibliography

Cassius Dio: https://archive.org/details/diocassiusromanh5660cass/page/n5/mode/2up

Florus: https://penelope.uchicago.edu/Thayer/E/Roman/Texts/Florus/Epitome/home.html

esp: https://penelope.uchicago.edu/Thayer/E/Roman/Texts/Florus/Epitome/2H*.html#XXX

Tacitus, *Annales*: https://archive.org/details/cu31924071188753/page/74/mode/2up

Velleius Paterculus: https://penelope.uchicago.edu/Thayer/E/Roman/Texts/Velleius_Paterculus/2D*.html

* * *

Kalkriese Excavations: https://www.kalkriese-varusschlacht.de/en/the-park/the-rampart/#:~:text=The%20rampart%20is%20one%20of%20the%20most%20important,sods%20not%20long%20before%20the%20Roman%20soldiers%20arrived

Chapter Eight

The Gothic Threat:
The Battle of Abritus, 251 CE

Sources

The Battle of Abritus was fought in 251 CE at the apex of the 'Third Century Crisis', during which period the Empire came close to extinction and can be seen as the point at which the Empire could either fall or resurrect itself in a new form. Thirty-three years later the Emperor Diocletian would choose the latter course. The battle was fought in a confused and disjointed period, and sadly the sources follow the national trend in being confused, disjointed and often contradictory.

There are two writers whose work has survived in large part, plus a few whose work is fragmentary and several others whose coverage is so brief as to be of little use in analyzing the battle. Both of the extant sources are 'Greek' in origin, being written in the sixth century in the Eastern Empire. Obviously this means that both were composed much later than events and so relied upon lost works for their information. Consequently it is impossible to state with confidence that they are accurate.

The one with the most detail and hence the one that will form the core of the description is that of **Zosimus**. Writing at some point around the turn of the sixth century, Zosimus was a pagan and was extremely critical of Christianity. Due to the late date of composition, the accuracy of the description is unclear, but due to the paucity of sources it must be used in order to give an idea of how the battle unfolded.

The other major source was **Jordanes**, a Roman of possible Gothic descent who wrote a *History of Rome* and a *History of the Goths*. His work is valuable as, along with **Isidore of Seville**, he was one of only two writers who attempted to write a history of the early Goths. Sadly, his bias towards the Goths and the fact that his work was much later than the events described mean that he must be used with caution.

Of possible equal importance to the above is the account written by **Publius Herennius Dexippus**. Written by a contemporary, this work would be of great value if it was complete, but sadly the text is so fragmented that modern authorities are still debating whether it is a chronicle or a history. It should probably supersede Jordanes who was writing much later, but due to its fragmentary condition it is difficult to analyze in detail.

Other sources, for example **Sextus Aurelius Victor**, may give some details, but these are usually either fragmentary or so brief as to be of little use in detailing events of the battle or simply repeat the information included in the sources already listed. Where these are utilized, their usefulness will be assessed within the text.

Background

Following two centuries of stability, in 235 CE the last of the Severan Dynasty, Alexander Severus, was assassinated. He was replaced by Maximinus Thrax ('the Thracian'), who over the ensuing few years instituted payments of 'subsidies' to the Sasanids, the Goths and various other frontier tribes; the need to pay the Goths may have been due to their alleged sack of Histria in 238, although this is uncertain. Maximinus was assassinated in turn by his own troops, also in 238. In his place the troops elevated Gordian III (r.238–244 CE), who was killed by his successor Philip Arabicus ('the Arab'), who reigned from 244 to 249 CE. During Philip's reign a man named Trajan Decius was sent to Moesia to put down a rebellion, after which he was proclaimed emperor by his troops. Advancing into Italy, he defeated and killed Philip near Verona and so became the new emperor, quickly promoting his son Herennius Etruscus to the post of *Caesar* ('junior emperor') in 250. He was later to be raised to co-*Augustus* in May 251.

Also in 250, Decius issued an edict aimed at ensuring the loyalty of the empire and ensuring his own survival. The edict ordered everyone to perform a sacrifice to the Roman gods, and those who did not were to be imprisoned or executed. The main result of the 'Decian Persecution' was that later, Christian writers held Decius in contempt and castigated his rule, since Christians were the main religious community to suffer. Consequently the works of Christian writers concerning Decius need to be analyzed carefully and their contents cross-referenced in order to ensure their veracity.

Decius inherited an empire with problems: there was an ongoing war with Sasanid Persia, plus a major plague as well as continuing discontent within the empire. In addition, not only had Philip cancelled the traditional payments of subsidies to the Sasanids, which was the reason for the ongoing war, but had also stopped payments to the frontier tribes on the northern borders, including the Goths.

What happened next is shrouded in confusion as the different accounts give different details and appear to give a different chronology. Wherever possible, the date will be assessed according to the contemporary account of Dexippus although, as noted, the fragmentary nature of this means that assessing its minutiae is difficult.

With the 'persecution' starting and with Decius attempting to secure his rule in Rome, in 250 CE there was a major incursion of barbarian

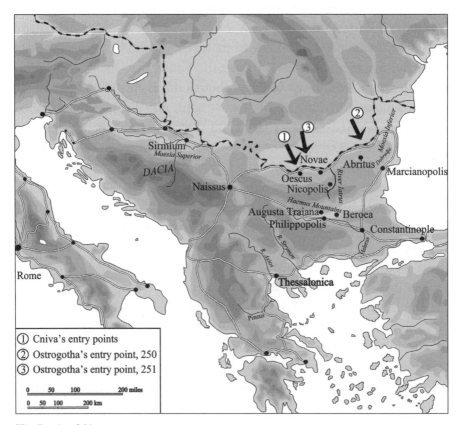

The Battle of Abritus.

tribes across the Danube led by men named Cniva and Ostrogotha/ Ostrogouthos. Although traditionally described as a 'Gothic' invasion, in reality it was composed of a core of Goths supplemented by Carpi, Bastarnae, Taifali and Vandals.

In 250, Cniva separated his force into two groups. While one division crossed the border on the Lower Danube and invaded Moesia Inferior in the region of the Dobrudja, Cniva and his division, allegedly 70,000 men, advanced through the province of trans-Danubian Dacia to cross the Danube near Oescus. Moving along the river, his group reached the fort of Novae, where the senatorial governor of Moesia, Trebonianus Gallus, and his army opposed them. Gallus could not defeat the Goths, but managed to defend Novae. Afterwards Cniva's army continued its progress to the southern parts of the province, along the River Iatrus (Jantra/Yantra) towards the Haemus Mountains. The territory surrounding Nicopolis ad Istrum, a town on the northern slopes of the Haemus, was plundered and the town besieged. However, before the siege could succeed, Decius himself arrived with the main army and forced the Goths to abandon the siege: the Goths withdrew into the mountains, apparently without there being any fighting between the armies.

Thwarted, Cniva refused battle but was forced to retire northwards, closely followed by Decius. Near the city of Augusta Traiana the Roman army was halted by Decius to rest and recover from their fast marches. Cniva, who was obviously a capable military leader, appears to have been maintaining a watch on the pursuing Romans and these scouts reported that Decius had stopped. Quickly reversing direction, Cniva's forces fell upon the Roman camp. Taken by surprise, the Roman army was scattered, allegedly suffering heavy casualties in the defeat; Decius escaped the defeat 'with a few survivors'.[1]

At least this is the account given by Jordanes, who places the defeat at Beroea. A new-found excerpt from Dexippus' account has recently been translated, which states that Decius made his camp at 'Amisos' with 80,000 men. However, as will be shown, although 'Amisos' was in the region of Beroea, the new camp may relate to Decius' movements in the following year.[2]

Heavily defeated, Decius retreated to Moesia, joining the remnants of his army to that of Gallus, who had earlier forced Cniva to retire from Novae. In the meantime, Cniva spent some time collecting the supplies and equipment left by the Romans after the battle. Having lost troops and also prestige, Decius took time to recruit further troops from Oescus before preparing to face Cniva again.

In the meantime, the Carpi and associated tribes, perhaps under Ostrogotha, headed towards Marcianopolis. Despite the lack of external aid, the inhabitants of Marcianopolis were able to resist Ostrogotha's attack.

Sadly, as usual for this period of Roman history, the chronology is confused. Events as portrayed by the sources are dated simply to 250–251, but with no mention of either winter or Cniva's army returning home. It is here assumed that after defeating Decius and gathering the loot from the battlefield, Cniva returned home. If this is accurate, Ostrogotha would also have returned home after the failed siege of Marcianopolis.

If this analysis is accurate, in early 251 Cniva invaded again. Knowing that Decius and Gallus were in the vicinity of Novae, it is here assumed that Cniva took a different invasion route, this time heading for the city of Philippopolis. It would appear that Ostrogotha also joined the invasion and, given later events, it is possible that he was deployed to guard the flank of Cniva's march, positioned between the latter's line of advance and Novae.

In late spring 250 CE Cniva arrived at Philippopolis and placed it under siege. The garrison commander, Titus Julius Priscus, was declared emperor by his Thracian garrison and agreed a treaty in which the city would be surrendered to Cniva but the citizens spared. As soon as they had entered the city, the Goths broke the agreement and sacked the city. Priscus disappears from history.

After the sack of Philippopolis, Cniva began the return journey to the Danube. Informed of the attack and sack of Philippopolis, Decius appears to have decided that 'though disappointed in his failure to relieve Philippopolis, [he planned] at least to prevent the Goths from taking their Thracian captives back across the Danube.'[3]

At this point the sources again disagree. Ostrogotha/Ostrogouthos disappears from Jordanes' account, but in that of Dexippus he takes part in the upcoming battle. Due to Jordanes' temporal distance from events, it is probable that Dexippus is more accurate in having Ostrogotha present for the next episode.

Knowing that Cniva was intent upon returning home and that his most direct route was back through the same region, Decius marched his new army back towards Beroea in order to intercept the Goths. The Goths themselves were a large army but were divided. According to the little information given concerning events, it would appear that Ostrogotha was in the region with one force, and that on the return journey from Philippopolis, laden with booty and prisoners, Cniva had divided his army into two columns to ease movement. As Decius advanced, his forces met those of Ostrogotha and the Battle of Abritus was about to begin.

Location

Excavations and the work of metal detectorists have located large numbers of Roman coins from the reigns of Gordian III to Decius in an area known as Poleto ('the Field') in the valley of the River Beli Lom, a tributary of the Rusenski Lom, a river in north-eastern Bulgaria which in turn flows into the Danube. This site, c.9.3 miles (15km) north-west of Abritus, would appear to be the site of the final engagement.

The Opposing Forces: Rome

The sources give an estimate of the Roman forces as around 80,000 men. If, as earlier, there was an approximately equal division between the legions and the *auxilia*, this would mean 40,000 legionaries. This in turn would equal around seven to eight legions, depending upon whether the legions were at full strength, equal to approximately one-quarter of the whole Roman army.

An analysis of the legionary deployment at this time would suggest that for the campaign Decius had access to the three local legions, namely *Legio XIV Gemina* (usually stationed at Carnuntum), *Legio IV Flavia Felix* (Sigidunum) and *Legio VII Claudia* (Viminacium), plus local *auxilia* and possibly *vexillationes* (see below) of the Praetorian Guard.[4] In addition, Decius may still have had close control of detachments of troops from the Danube frontier that had acclaimed him emperor and helped him defeat Philip in 249.

Even assuming that the three legions were at full strength, rather than *vexillationes*, this would only give a total of c.20,000 legionaries plus an equal number of *auxilia* plus other associated troops. Add in the possible additional units, then Decius was leading somewhere in the region of

50,000 troops at the Battle of Abritus. However, many of these units had been fighting both external and internal enemies in recent times. Of equal importance, the Plague of Cyprian, an unknown disease that began to devastate the Empire from around 249 CE, had by now had a severe impact on the recruitment and existing personnel of the Roman army. It is likely that both the legions and the *auxilia* were very under-strength and ravaged by illness. Nevertheless, although far fewer than the 80,000 men given in the sources, this was still a very large Roman army.

As to the legions, there had been a few changes since the earlier battles. Not least of these was the change ordered by Septimius Severus, who ruled that legionaries should then serve a minimum of twenty-six years before discharge unless illness or disability earned them an early release.

Possibly of more importance, in 212 CE the emperor Caracalla issued the *Constitutio Antoniniana* ('Edict of Caracalla') which gave full Roman citizenship to all free men within the Empire except for groups such as the *dediticii* – tribes settled within the Empire after being defeated in war – and freed slaves. This meant that most men in the Empire were eligible to serve in the legions, with the *dediticii* and others settled in the Empire, along with external tribes, now being the main source of manpower for the *auxilia*. Some of the settled tribes were granted land within the Empire under a *foedus* ('treaty') with specific terms to serve in the army. These were known as *foederati*, a term that would later expand to cover a wider range of troops.

There was also an evolving change in the manner of troop deployment for campaigns. Although theoretically the legions were now settled in permanent barracks along the frontier, these only acted as bases for the legion. A core remained permanently in the barracks, and detachments of these legions were then taken for service in battle or for other duties elsewhere in the Empire. Hypothetically numbering somewhere between 600 and 1,200 men, although the true number was doubtless below this, these troops were known as *vexillationes* after the *vexillum* ('banner') they carried; the legionary standard stayed in the permanent barracks.

The equipment of the army was also undergoing a slow change. Although the legionary *gladius* stayed in use, this was slowly being replaced by longer swords known later as *spathae* (s. *spatha*). Despite the fact that these were longer swords, they were still used mainly for thrusting, a testament to the continuation of Roman training. .

For defence, the armour was also changing. The *lorica segmentata* usually associated with the Roman legionary was being displaced, with the *lorica hamata*, the ring mail that had been common prior to the end of the first century BCE, coming back into general use. However, it was slowly growing longer to protect the upper thighs and the arms. The biggest change was in the helmets. The *Italic* style common in the first and second centuries CE was being phased out for helmets of a heavier, single bowl construction that provided a better defence, but was not as effective when it came to peripheral vision and hearing. Of more importance, although these were probably cheaper to produce, overall they were of poorer quality.

Possibly due to the change in eligibility for the legions reducing the number of specialist troops available to the army, there were troops integral to the legions known as *lanciarii*. Slowly developing during the late second and early third centuries, these troops appear to have been legionaries designated as *lancea subarmales*, implying that they used javelins. If accurate, these *lanciarii* began as legionaries who were capable of acting as skirmishers similar to the earlier *velites*, but it should be noted that the accuracy of this analysis is disputed.

Due to the examination above, it is clear that the Roman army was undergoing a slow evolution, but the nature and speed of this is unknown due to the lack of information in the surviving sources. It is also clear that accepting that Decius commanded 80,000 troops at the battle is open to doubt, with around 50,000 men perhaps being the maximum.

The Opposing Forces: Goths and Allies

The problems associated with establishing the total number of 'Gothic' troops facing Decius, let alone the numbers in each of the divisions, are even worse. The total of 100,000 men given in the sources is obviously far too large. Specialists have estimated that the Roman marching column at the Teutoburger Wald composed of c.20,000 plus attendants was between 9 and 12.5 miles long (c.15 to 20 kilometres). In the case of the Goths, this would mean a single column of at least 27 miles in length. Even when divided, this would mean columns of at least 9 to 10 miles.

As a consequence, it must simply be accepted that the number of men under Cniva is completely unknown, and any attempt to estimate the number is not only fraught with difficulty but is impossible to prove or disprove. Even comparing this number with an estimate of the number of Roman troops is unlikely to help as the size of the Roman army is also unknown. All that can be said is that, when divided into three groups (on which see below), the first two could easily be defeated by Decius but the last group was large enough to finally defeat him.

As to composition and equipment, there is no evidence that during the period between the Battle of Arausio and that of Abritus there was a major change in 'Germanic' warfare, except possibly a slightly greater proportion of cavalry due to an expansion in the aristocracy, caused at least in part by an increase in wealth created by Roman 'subsidies' to both friendly and potentially hostile tribes. Consequently, it is likely that the description of the warriors given for the Battle of Teutoburger Wald remains valid for this battle.

The Course of the Battle

Due to the discrepancies between the accounts, it is necessary to analyze them separately before attempting to form a coherent account of the battle. The one used by most historians to recount the battle itself is that of the pagan Zosimus:

> The Scythians [Goths], taking advantage of the disorder which everywhere prevailed through the negligence of Philip, crossed the Tanais [Danube], and pillaged the countries in the vicinity of Thrace. But Decius, marching against them, was not only victorious in every battle, but recovered the spoils they had taken, and endeavoured to cut off their retreat to their own country, intending to destroy them all, to prevent their ever again making a similar incursion.
>
> For this purpose he posted Gallus on the bank of the Tanais with a competent force, and led in person the remainder of his army against the enemy. This expedition exceeded to his utmost wish; but Gallus, who was disposed to innovation, sent agents to the barbarians, requesting their concurrence in a conspiracy against Decius. To this they gave a willing assent, and Gallus retained his post on the bank of the Tanais, but the barbarians divided themselves into three battalions, the first of which posted itself behind a marsh.
>
> Decius having destroyed a considerable number of the first battalion, the second advanced, which he likewise defeated, and discovered part

of the third, which lay near the marsh. Gallus sent intelligence to him, that he might march against them across the fen. Proceeding therefore incautiously in an unknown place, he and his army became entangled in the mire, and under that disadvantage were so assailed by the missiles of the barbarians that not one of them escaped with life. Thus ended the life of the excellent emperor Decius.

Zosimus, 1.23.1–3.

The second most used source is Jordanes. Although writing much later, he includes quite a lot of detail:

Cniva divided the army into two parts and sent some to waste Moesia, knowing that it was undefended through the neglect of the emperors. He himself with seventy thousand men hastened to Euscia, that is, Novae. When driven from this place by the general Gallus, he approached Nicopolis, a very famous town situated near the Iatrus river. This city Trajan built when he conquered the Sarmatians and named it the City of Victory. When the Emperor Decius drew near, Cniva at last withdrew to the regions of Haemus, which were not far distant. Thence he hastened to Philippopolis, with his forces in good array.

When the Emperor Decius learned of his departure, he was eager to bring relief to his own city and, crossing Mount Haemus, came to Beroea. While he was resting his horses and his weary army in that place, all at once Cniva and his Goths fell upon him like a thunderbolt. He cut the Roman army to pieces and drove the Emperor, with a few who had succeeded in escaping, across the Alps again to Euscia in Moesia, where Gallus was then stationed with a large force of soldiers as guardian of the frontier. Collecting an army from this region as well as from Oescus, he prepared for the conflict of the coming war.

But Cniva took Philippopolis after a long siege and then, laden with spoil, allied himself to Priscus, the commander in the city, to fight against Decius. In the battle that followed they quickly pierced the son of Decius with an arrow and cruelly slew him. The father saw this, and although he is said to have exclaimed, to cheer the hearts of his soldiers: 'Let no one mourn; the death of one soldier is not a great loss to the republic', he was yet unable to endure it, because of his love for his son. So he rode against the foe, demanding either death or vengeance, and when he came to Abrittus [sic], a city of Moesia, he was himself cut off by the Goths and slain, thus making an end of his dominion and of his life. This place is today called the Altar of Decius, because he there offered strange sacrifices to idols before the battle.

Jordanes, Getica, 101–103.

This is the source used by most for the lead up to the battle. Here, Cniva is attested as dividing his army in two, but no mention is made of Ostrogotha. He also gives a figure for the troops led by Cniva alone: 70,000 men. Assuming that Ostrogotha or an unnamed second commander led one-third of the army, this takes the total number to more than 100,000 men. As is usual, this may be too large a number, an exaggeration common among Roman writers.

Interestingly, there is no mention here of the defeat of Decius prior to the sack of Philippopolis. There is, however, the news that Decius was attempting to intercept Cniva as he withdrew and that he had reinforced his army with troops from Novae and Oescus.

The third excerpt is from Dexippus, as recorded later by Syncellus:

Scythians, those called Goths, when they had crossed the Ister River in very great numbers under Decius, began occupying the dominion of Rome. They surrounded the Mysians, who were fleeing toward Nicopolis. Decius, after he had attacked them, as Dexippus records, and had killed thirty thousand, was beaten in battle, with the result that Philippopolis, when it had been taken by them, was sacked and many Thracians were killed. And the same Decius, the fighter against God, when he had attacked Scythians who were returning to their own territory, was killed very piteously in Abrytus [sic], the place called Forum Thembronium, with his son, and the Scythians returned with a great number of captives and much booty. The encamped armies acclaimed sovereign a certain Gallus, who had once been a consul, together with Decius' son Volusianus. And according to Dexippus, they too reigned for eighteen months, having done nothing noteworthy.... And they were slain, after they had been betrayed by their own forces…victims of the same maliciousness as Decius….

Syncellus, pp.459.5–19 = Dexippus, fgrH, 100 f 22.
Trans. Banchich and Lane, 2009, p.100.

In this report, Dexippus claims that Decius had defeated a Gothic army and inflicted 30,000 casualties on them. It is from this source, the contemporary account of Dexippus, that the first section of the battle detailed below is hypothesized.

However, there is the slight problem here that Syncellus/Dexippus implies that Philippopolis was sacked after the defeat at Abritus. It is assumed here that Syncellus has confused events in his interpretation of Dexippus, assuming that Philippopolis could only have been sacked after a major battle and the death of Decius. He does not appear to have realized the he was conflating two separate battles: the first defeat being the Battle of Beroea, dated here to 250, and the second the Battle of Abritus. As a last note, he has made one further mistake: Decius' son was named Herennius Etruscus; Volusianus was Gallus' son.

A further source is Sextus Aurelius Victor:

But most of them report the death of the Decii to be distinguished; for his son, who was more bold in his attack, had fallen in battle; and that his father, when the soldiers were panic-stricken, had much prefaced to console the troops, and said with great vigour that the loss of one soldier seemed to him little. Thus, when the war was renewed, he perished in the same manner as he fought vigorously.

Sextus Aurelius Victor, De Caesaribus, 29.5.

The only detail given here is that, hearing of his son's death in the battle, Decius consoled the troops: 'the loss of one soldier seemed to him little', a phrase expanded by the other sources that mention it.

Finally, there is Zonaras:

Decius, being so disposed toward those revering Christ, before he had completed two whole years in his rule of the Romans, died most shamefully. For when barbarians were plundering the Bosporus, Decius engaged them and killed many. When they were hard pressed and offered to surrender all their loot if they were allowed to withdraw, Decius did not give in, but posted Gallus, one of the men of the senate, on the route of the barbarians, ordering him not to let them pass. But Gallus, betraying Decius, proposed to the barbarians that, since a deep swamp was nearby, they deploy there. When the barbarians so deployed and turned their backs, Decius pursued them. And both he, with his son, and a multitude of Romans fell into the swamp and all perished there, with the result that their bodies, interred in the slime of the swamp, were not found.

Zonaras, 12.20, trans. Banchich and Lane, 2009, p.50.

Along with the other sources, Zonaras has Decius engaging and killing many: 'when barbarians were plundering the Bosporus, Decius engaged them and killed many.' On the other hand, and different to the other sources, Zonaras suggests that Decius had managed to constrict the movements of the Goths so much that they 'offered to surrender all their loot if they were allowed to withdraw'. Obviously, given later events, Zonaras has Decius refusing the offer. Although usually ignored, when combined with the other sources' description it suggests that the Goths were, indeed, hard-pressed during the conflict, although whether they were forced to offer terms is unclear.

Having clarified the sources, it is now necessary to analyze them in more detail before reaching conclusions concerning the nature of the battle.

Analysis

Due to the disparities in the sources, doubtless due to the confusion caused by the differing narratives of the few survivors, it is impossible to be certain as to what actually happened during the battle. What follows is a reconstruction based upon an amalgamation of all the information shown above, but it should be noted that new information (for example, the new fragments of Dexippus mentioned earlier) or new interpretations may make this narrative outdated. It should also be noted that in this description the 'battle' may have taken several days and have taken place in two separate locations rather than being fought in one location at a specific time.

There also remains the problem of Gallus and his alleged betrayal. Two of the sources mention his treachery (Zosimus and Zonaras), but as these are much later they may simply be repeating a traditional fiction aimed at explaining the defeat. As Gallus succeeded Decius, this makes some sense, especially as culturally defeats were either caused by traitors or incompetents. Yet it is not mentioned by Syncellus, quoting Dexippus, and as Dexippus is a contemporary of the event, the fact that he does not mention any betrayal means that the claim is suspicious and may not be accurate.

Obviously the concept that Gallus advised the Goths to deploy behind a swamp is also here discounted. Cniva was clearly a capable and confident military commander, as evidenced by his earlier surprise attack and victory over Decius. As Gallus was not in close proximity to the Goths, the concept that he was able to form a relationship with Cniva strong enough to make Cniva follow his advice rather than rely upon his own skills makes the episode appear to be extremely unlikely, if not impossible.

Consequently it is assumed here that Gallus and a portion of the army was left in Moesia, partly in order to prevent Ostrogotha and his troops from doubling back and ravaging the country, but mainly to intercept any Goths who escaped from Decius and attempted to return across the Danube. It was only after the death of Decius, and possibly much later after Gallus' own death, that the rumour began that Gallus had betrayed the army, causing the death of thousands of his countrymen.

There is one other point on which the sources again disagree. Ostrogouthos/Ostrogotha disappears from Jordanes' account, but in that of Dexippus he takes part in the upcoming battle. Due to Jordanes' temporal distance from events, it is probable that the contemporary Dexippus is more accurate in having Ostrogotha present for the next episode.

With these caveats in mind it is possible to move on to the reconstruction. This is divided into three phases in order to accommodate as much information from the sources as possible.

First Phase

Knowing that Cniva was intent upon returning home and that his most direct route was back through the same region, Decius marched his new army back towards Beroea in order to intercept the Goths. Ostrogotha had also heard of Cniva's success. His earlier attack on Novae had been a failure, so

> ...when Ostrogouthos, the leader of the Scythians, heard that Philippopolis had been taken, and that the Scythians were holding Cniva in the highest regard, and were celebrating him in song, as is their ancestral custom when they have especially good fortune and success in war, whereas they were holding himself [Ostrogotha] in less esteem, accusing him of cowardice and failure in his tactics, he thought it unbearable not to make amends to the Scythian cause by some notable achievement; [so] setting out, he marched quickly with an army of some fifty thousand.
>
> *Dexippus, 194r.*

As Ostrogotha approached Decius, the latter learned of this second army coming near. According to Dexippus, Decius then gave a speech to the troops but, as noted above, before the conclusion of the speech the fragment ends. It is probable that after the speech Dexippus described the battle in detail, but the fact that this is lost means that in the following analysis it has sadly been necessary to resort to speculation, based upon using all the sources and attempting to make a coherent narrative.[5]

Deploying his army, Decius easily defeated the smaller army of Ostrogotha, retaking the many captives Ostrogotha had taken during his march as well as much booty.[6] This may be the 30,000 casualties inflicted on the Goths reported by Dexippus although, as usual, the numbers are doubtless exaggerated.[7] In addition, this is assumed to be one of the three 'battalions' reported by Zosimus.[8]

Second Phase

Having defeated Ostrogotha and with the confidence of the army restored, Decius then sent out scouts to find Cniva. Possibly on the same day but more likely a day or two later, his scouts returned with the report that they had located the Gothic army as it marched towards the Danube.

The description as given in the sources, and usually as taken for granted, is that the Gothic army was advancing in at least two columns. This may give the Gothic force a more 'formal' marching order than was the case. With the booty and captives, it is more likely that the Gothic marching columns were more dispersed than a Roman column would have been. Of more importance, a column of many troops plus baggage, loot and captives would be many miles long. Assessing the sources, it would appear that Cniva had decided that his army would march in two separate columns along the routes north, but with them being near enough that theoretically they would be able to support each other in case of attack. Although some reports have the Goths in several 'groups', it is here suggested that two was the correct number. Not only would these two columns plus Ostrogotha's force be the three battalions reported by Zosimus, but Cniva dividing his own troops into many small groups may not have had the impact necessary for the end result, as will be seen.[9]

Consequently, there may have been one small problem faced by Decius not related in the sources. It seems that his scouts had only located one of Cniva's columns. With only a small portion of the enemy located, Decius led his men towards the Goths as they retired north.

Rather than a piece of tactical brilliance, it is probably better to see the Gothic 'deployment' as the army simply marching along available roads. The fact that there was a marsh nearby and possibly between the two divisions is almost certainly an accident. Also if Zosimus' account is in any way accurate, Decius did not advance to attack the whole of Cniva's army:

> Decius…discovered part of the third, which lay near the marsh.
>
> *Zosimus, 1.23.3.*

The implication is that Decius had located one Gothic column, which was advancing along one edge of a marsh. The other column, this one perhaps led by Cniva himself, was on the other side of the marsh. It may also be that the Goths had their own scouts deployed in case Decius, Gallus or another Roman commander was preparing to block their retreat. One of the possibilities inherent in the sources is that Cniva was informed by his scouts of the Roman advance and was leading his troops through the swamp in the hope of reaching the first column before it could be attacked when heavily outnumbered.

Approaching the Goths, Decius deployed his army and launched an immediate assault. The troops, enthused by their victory over Ostrogotha, smashed through the Gothic force. Unfortunately for Decius but fortunately for Cniva: 'When the barbarians so deployed and turned their backs, Decius pursued them.'[10] The rapid collapse of the Gothic force, plus the earlier defeat of Ostrogotha, resulted in the overconfident Roman army pursuing the Goths deep into the swamp.

It was at this point, with his troops dispersed in the marsh in pursuit of the routing Goths, that Decius 'discovered' the 'third column'. A close reading of the little information available suggests that the Roman army had advanced deep into if not almost through the swamp in their pursuit and that Cniva and his force were at the far side, still on firm ground.

As the Romans floundered in the swamp, the Goths began to bombard them with a hail of missiles:

> He [Decius] and his army became entangled in the mire, and under that disadvantage were so assailed by the missiles of the barbarians, that not one of them escaped with life.
>
> *Zosimus, 1.23.3.*

Only able to come to grips with the Goths in small numbers, the Roman army suffered heavy losses. One of the first was Decius' son:

> The father saw this, and although he is said to have exclaimed, to cheer the hearts of his soldiers: 'Let no one mourn; the death of one soldier is not a great loss to the republic', he was yet unable to endure it, because of his love for his son. So he rode against the foe, demanding either death or vengeance.
>
> *Jordanes, Getica, 103.*

Attempting to come to close quarters with the enemy, Decius shared the same fate as his son:

> The soldiers were panic-stricken, had much preferred to console the troops, and said with great vigour that the loss of one soldier seemed to him little. Thus, when the war was renewed, he perished in the same manner as he fought vigorously.
>
> *Sextus Aurelius Victor, De Caesaribus, 29. 5.*

Both he, with his son, and a multitude of Romans fell into the swamp and all perished there, with the result that their bodies, interred in the slime of the swamp, were not found.

Zonaras, 12.20, trans. Banchich and Lane, 2009, p.50.

[Decius] when he had attacked Scythians who were returning to their own territory, was killed very piteously in Abrytus [*sic*], the place called Forum Thembronium, with his son, and the Scythians returned with a great number of captives and much booty.

Syncellus, pp.459.5–19 = Dexippus, fgrH, 100 f 22.
Trans. Banchich and Lane, 2009, p.100.

The deaths of Decius and Herennius was the first time that any Roman emperor had died in battle at the hands of a barbarian enemy, let alone two of them. The sources portray Decius' death according to their personal bias; after all, Decius had begun a persecution of Christians the year before his death. As a consequence, the pagans tend to portray him in a positive light, whereas the Christians vilify his memory. For example, Zosimus calls him 'the excellent emperor Decius', but the Christian Jordanes states that 'This place is today called the Altar of Decius, because he there offered strange sacrifices to idols before the battle', and Zonaras states that 'Decius, being so disposed toward those revering Christ, before he had completed two whole years in his rule of the Romans, died most shamefully.' Whether he died in shame or bravely at the head of his troops, the defeat was a major turning-point in the history of the Empire.

Aftermath

The battle was one of the worst defeats suffered by Rome: Ammianus Marcellinus goes so far as to class it as being equal to the Battle of the Teutoburger Wald and even Adrianople. The defeat left the region largely unprotected and so open to invasion. In addition, the defeat and death of two emperors convinced others that Roman invincibility was a mirage and so encouraged further invasions and raids. Gallus, the supposed traitor, was forced to agree a treaty with Cniva in which a Roman tribute was paid to avoid further incursions. This may have been in addition to Decius' imperial treasury, which had probably been captured during the battle.

It would only be twenty years later, in 271, that the Emperor Aurelian would restore the reputation of Roman arms in the region by defeating the Goths, killing their leader Cannabaudes (assessed by some as being Cniva due to the similarity of their names), and taking the title *Gothicus Maximus*. However, even with Roman superiority once again established, Aurelian abandoned the trans-Danubian province of Dacia as he believed it to be too difficult and expensive to justify its continued existence. Yet the defeat was soon to be eclipsed by that of another emperor, who was not killed but taken captive.

Select Bibliography

Jordanes: https://people.ucalgary.ca/~vandersp/Courses/texts/jordgeti.html

Publius Herennius Dexippus: https://www.academia.edu/11913736/Further_Dexippus_online

Publius Herennius Dexippus/Syncellus, Banchich, T.M. and Lane, E.N., *The History of Zonaras from the Death of Severus to the Death of Theodosius the Great* (Routledge, 2009), p.100.

Sextus Aurelius Victor: http://www.forumromanum.org/literature/aurelius_victorx.html

Zonaras, Banchich, T.M. and Lane, E.N., *The History of Zonaras from the Death of Severus to the Death of Theodosius the Great* (Routledge, 2009)

Zosimus: https://www.livius.org/sources/content/zosimus

*　*　*

Bursche, A., 'The Battle of Abritus, the Imperial Treasury and Aurei in Barbaricum', *The Numismatic Chronicle* 173 (Offprint, The Royal Numismatic Society, London, 2013), pp.151–170.

Chapter Nine

The Sasanid Threat:
The Battle of Edessa, 260 BCE

The Sources

Unlike most of the battles of the third century, there are many sources that cover, albeit in a frustratingly brief nature, the Battle of Edessa. Sadly the Roman sources tend to contradict each other and this makes it impossible to construct a clear picture of what happened. In addition, they do not give a description of what happened on the battlefield, only describing the battle as a major defeat for the Roman army.

On the other hand, carved into the rock at Shapur I's tomb in Naqš-i Rustam, is the text now known as the **Res Gestae Divi Saporis** (also known as 'The Great Inscription of Shapur I', 'SKZ', or 'ŠKZ'). This is engraved in Greek, Middle Persian and Parthian, and gives the Persian Shah's version of events. Needless to say, this is a very highly biased account and sometimes contradicts the Roman sources, but nevertheless is valuable as an alternative version of events.

Of the Roman sources, several are roughly contemporary. These include the *Life of Plotinus* by **Porphyry**, a philosopher born in Tyre, Syria (c.234–c.305 CE); *De Mortibus Persecutorum* (*On the Deaths of the Persecutors*) by **Lactantius**, a Christian Roman philosopher (c.250–c.325 CE); *Ecclesiastical History* by **Eusebius**, bishop of Caesarea Maritima (c.260/265–339/340 CE); *De Caesaribus* (*On the Caesars*) by **Aurelius Victor**, a Roman historian (c.320–c.390); *Breviarium Historiae Romanae* (*A Brief History of Rome*) by **Eutropius**, a Roman official and historian (c.320–c.390); *Res Gestae* (*Things Done*) by **Ammianus Marcellinus**, a Roman soldier and historian (c.330–c.391/400); *Historiarum Adversum Paganos Libri VII* (*The Seven Books of History Against the Pagans*) by **Orosius**, a Roman priest, theologian and historian (c.375/385–c.420 AD); *Chronographia* (*Chronology*) by **John Malalas**, a Byzantine chronicler (c.491–578); *Historia Nova* (*New History*) by **Zosimus**, a pagan author (fl. first quarter, sixth century CE); and *Epitome Historiarum* (*Epitome of History*) by **John Zonaras**, a Greek historian (fl. c.1120 CE).

All these men wrote works that are used today for assessing events in the third century. However, they all have their problems. For example, Ammianus is classed as one of the greatest Roman historians and wrote a work covering the period from the reign of Nerva (96 CE) to the Battle of Adrianople (378 CE). Sadly those parts covering the period from 96 CE to 353 CE have been lost. Another is that, being Christians, the work of men such as Lactantius, Eusebius and Orosius is heavily biased in tone and omits much in order to keep their work within the remit of their purpose in writing it. In opposition, Zosimus was a pagan and his work is biased against Christians, especially Christian emperors such as Constantine the Great. Finally, writers such as Zonaras – and others already mentioned – were writing long after the events and so were reliant on earlier works, many of which are lost and whose contents are, as a result, of unknown reliability. Consequently where possible more than one autonomous author needs to be cross-referenced in order to reinforce the information contained. Sadly, due to the nature of the works, this is rarely possible for the Battle of Edessa.

In addition to the above there is the *Scriptores Historiae Augustae* (**SHA**), now more commonly known as the *Historia Augusta* (*History of the Emperors*), although the full title on the *Codex Palatinus* manuscript is *Vitae Diversorum Principum et Tyrannorum a Divo Hadriano usque ad Numerianum Diversis compositae* (*The Lives of Various Emperors and Tyrants from the Divine Hadrian to Numerian by Various Authors*). Although the SHA is attributed to 'Various Authors', it is now believed to have been written by a single author in either the late fourth or early fifth century.

The SHA includes thirty *vitae* ('lives'/'biographies') asserted to be of Roman emperors and usurpers of the third century. The difficulty lies in the fact that the author has included fiction in among the facts, distorted events and included possible fictional usurpers, although it should be noted that the coins of usurpers previously believed to be fictional have been found. Despite these problems, due to the lack of other sources for the period it remains an important historical document. Furthermore, included as part of this manuscript is a fragmentary text, the *Life of Valerian*, attributed to **Trebellius Pollio**. Although the reliability of both the SHA and the *Life of Valerian* is obviously uncertain, in recent years it has been subjected to detailed analysis and so, with care, can be used to provide extra details for the third century.

Background

The Gothic threat to the north was not the only external problem faced by Rome. In 224 CE the Parthian Empire was overthrown by the Sasanids under their new Shah Ardashir I (224–240/242 CE). Ardashir immediately promoted an aggressive policy towards Rome, no doubt instigated at least in part by the political need of the new dynasty to focus on external enemies.

The Sasanid claim to the 'Empire of their Ancestors', seen by Western authors as a claim to the Achaemenid Empire (550–330 BCE), meant that, in theory at least, they were claiming a majority of the Eastern half of the Roman Empire. However, it should be noted that they made no attempt to conquer this vast area, instead focusing on control of Armenia and northern Mesopotamia. Rome was left as the 'external enemy' for internal political reasons.

Ardashir himself followed up on his aggressive threats by taking the cities of Nisibis and Carrhae in 238 CE, and his son and successor Shapur I (r.239/240–c.272 CE) continued his aggressive policy. In 240–1 CE he destroyed the kingdom of Hatra (al-Hadr) and asserted control over Osrhoene, until then a Roman client kingdom.

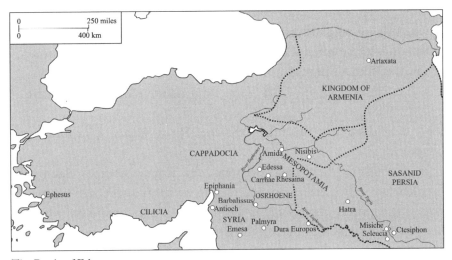

The Battle of Edessa.

The Battle of Rhesaina (243 CE)

This now posed a threat to Syria, and in 242 Rome declared war. The emperor at the time was Gordian III (r.238–244 CE), but as he was only around 17 years of age, it was the praetorian prefect Gaius Furius Sabinus Aquila Timesitheus who took control of events. In either late 242 or more likely early 243 the Roman army won the Battle of Rhesaina. The Sasanids withdrew their armies and Nisibis and Carrhae appear to have been retaken as coins depicting Gordian were minted in the cities.

The Battle of Misiche (244 CE)

Sadly for Rome, soon afterwards Timesitheus, who had been commander of the campaign, died of disease. He was succeeded as praetorian prefect by Marcus Julius Philippus. Despite Timesitheus' death, the Roman army now headed towards the Sasanid capital of Ctesiphon. When they reached Misiche (al-Anbar), they found the Sasanid army waiting for them.

The surviving Roman sources do not mention the battle: the only report comes from the Shapur inscription on the Ka 'ba-i Zardušt at Naqš-i Rustam:

> And as soon as we had become the ruler of the territories, the emperor Gordian conscribed a force taken from the entire Roman Empire, the Gothic and German peoples and marched into Āsūrestān against the Empire of the Aryans and against us; and a great frontal attack took place along the borders of Āsūrestān – in Misok [Misiche]. And the emperor Gordian was killed, and we destroyed the Roman army; and the Romans proclaimed Philip emperor.
>
> *Res Gestae Divi Saporis (Shapur inscription).*

The king allegedly renamed Misiche *Peroz-Shapur* ('Victorious is Shapur').

In contrast to the Persian 'victory', the Roman sources claim that Gordian was killed either on return from a victorious Persian campaign or during a mutiny of the army as they neared Ctesiphon or even while on his way to Persia. It may be that the Roman sources were intent on hiding a major Roman defeat and the death of the young emperor. However,

Zonaras writes that Gordian died after falling from his horse and this clear statement suggests that he was not killed in the battle itself. The result is that Gordian's death has not been accepted as caused during the battle by most Western historians. If Gordian was indeed killed by Shapur, he would have been the first Roman emperor killed by an external enemy and not Decius (see Chapter 8).

Gordian's successor was Philippus Arabicus ('Philip the Arab'), the senior surviving official with the army, who was acclaimed at Zaitha on the Euphrates. As he was from a poor background, his accession was disapproved of by the Senate. As a result, he was blamed for the defeat in the war by many sources, a fact not helped by him having to sign a peace treaty with Shapur in which he ransomed Roman prisoners for 500,000 denarii and which may have resulted in the client kingdom of Armenia passing to Sasanid control.

Affairs in Rome then focused upon internal events, namely a civil war. A man named Decius was proclaimed emperor by his troops and in 249 there was war between Philip and Decius. After Decius' victory, attention turned to the war with the Goths and Decius' death (see Chapter 8). Decius' successor was Gallus, who may have begun a second persecution of Christians. He took his son as co-emperor and began the attempt to restore Roman prestige.

The Battle of Barbalissos (253 CE)

The defeat and death of Decius implied that Rome was weak. Prior to this, in the East Shapur appears to have focused at first upon further expanding and consolidating his empire. With the defeat and death of Decius in 251 CE, Shapur again campaigned along the Roman frontier. In 252 CE his troops occupied Armenia, perhaps cementing his control as agreed in the earlier treaty, but he also made war on Rome again, retaking the city of Nisibis. Meeting with little opposition, in spring 253 he apparently defeated a Roman army at Barbalissos. The battle is claimed as a major victory in Shapur's inscription, but the only possible Roman acceptance of a defeat comes in the *Sibylline Oracle*.[1] Shapur followed the victory by ravaging Syria and perhaps capturing Antioch.

The Battle of Emesa (253 CE)

Shapur's invasion did meet with resistance. Although Shapur took the cities of Larissa, Epiphania and Arethusa, he was defeated in battle at Emesa, although the picture is extremely confused. A usurper named Lucius Julius Aurelius Sulpicius Severus Uranius Antoninus issued coins in Emesa, and a priest of the god Elagabal named either Sampsigeramos or Uranius Antoninus was proclaimed emperor in the city. It was he who allegedly defeated a Persian army near Emesa. However, Uranius Antoninus appears to have seen himself as only a local ruler as his coins do not bear the title 'Augustus'. It is probable that he simply saw himself as a local ruler who intended to protect the region from Sasanid invasions.

The East was not the only problem area. The Goths and the associated tribes launched a sea-borne invasion of Asia Minor and burned the Temple of Artemis at Ephesus. In 253, at the same time as Shapur invaded in the East, they crossed into Moesia Secunda, but this time they were defeated by Aemilian, the governor of Moesia Prima and Pannonia. After his victory Aemilian was proclaimed emperor by his troops.

Gallus ordered troops from Gaul to support him in Italy under the command of a man named Valerian. Gallus was killed in the ensuing chaos. Despite his victory, Aemilian's reign was short-lived: Valerian then arrived with a large army and Aemilian's troops defected. Valerian then became emperor.

Possibly in the following year of 254 CE, deciding that the resistance in the region of Emesa was not worth facing, Shapur appears to have invaded Cappadocia, possibly from Armenia, capturing the city of Satala. Despite the claims of the Sasanid dynasty to rule the regions once owned by the Achaemenids, there does not appear to have been any attempt at conquest: Shapur was content with large-scale raids intent upon capturing plunder and promoting his own prestige.

The Sack of Dura-Europos (256)

The sources are quiet regarding what happened next, but it appears that Valerian, having promoted his son Gallienus to the role of co-emperor, then took steps to protect the East from Shapur while Gallienus took over defence of the West. Despite Valerian's intentions, in 256 Shapur attacked and sacked the frontier fortress of Dura-Europos.

In 257 Valerian seems to have campaigned in the East and regained control of the Roman provinces, protecting them from invasion. However, in 258 the Goths again invaded and ravaged Asia Minor, meaning that Valerian was forced to react and was thus prevented from further campaigns against Shapur. Sadly the campaign against the Goths failed due to another outbreak of plague in the army.

The West

In the meantime, Gallienus had been busy in the West. He drove back the enemies that had penetrated the frontier and fortified some of the cities in Gaul and Germania. As part of his plan, he made an alliance with some of the frontier tribes, aiming to prevent raids and protect the frontier. Despite his work, the Franks invaded Gaul and even penetrated as far as Hispania, and at around the same time the Alamanni actually invaded Italy. Although Gallienus defeated the Alamanni, revolts in Pannonia and Moesia resulted in continuing warfare until 260 CE.

With the northern frontier almost pacified and the revolts diminishing in severity, in 359 CE Valerian ordered troops from Europe to travel to Asia, doubtless with the aim of leading a major campaign against Shapur in 260 CE. However, taking the initiative, in spring 260 Shapur led his armies against the Roman cities of Carrhae and Edessa, placing them under siege. It is likely that Carrhae fell, but Edessa resisted the siege. In response, Valerian led his enlarged army towards the city to face the Sasanids, despite the fact that the army was still being ravaged by the plague. The Battle of Edessa was about to begin.

The Opposing Forces: Rome

Obviously the slow evolution of the Roman army during this period means that it was no different to that fielded by Decius at the Battle of Abritus only nine years earlier. The legions and the *auxilia* were still the basis of the army as described in the previous chapter.

Sadly the Roman sources are confused and have no specific information concerning the army as deployed by Valerian. On the Sasanid side, no written sources cover the battle, but the inscription at Naqš-I Rustam states that:

Valerian Caesar marched against us, and he had with him, from Germān-šahr (Germania), Rešyā-šahr (Rhaetia), Nirkos-šahr (Noricum), Dākyā-šahr (Dacia), Mūsyā-šahr (Moesia), Estriyā-šahr (Istria), Espāniyā-šahr (Hispania), Afrikiyā-šahr (Africa,) Trākyā-šahr (Thracia), Butniyā-šahr (Bithynia), Āsiyā-šahr (Asia), Pamfaliyā-šahr (Pamphylia), Esuriyā-šahr (Isauria), Lūkunyā-šahr (Lycaonia), Galātenyā-šahr (Galatia), Kilikiyā-šahr (Cilicia), Kappadukiyā-šahr (Cappadocia), Frūgiyā-šahr (Phrygia), Sūriyā-šahr (Syria), Funikiyā-šahr (Phoenicia), Jehūdiyā-šahr (Judaea), Arabiyā-šahr (Arabia), Murin-šahr (Mauretania), Germānyā-šahr (Germania), Rodās-šahr (Rhodes), Asenyos-šahr (Osrhoene), and Meyānrōdān-šahr (Mesopotamia) an army of 70,000 men.

Res Gestae Divi Saporis (Shapur inscription).

It is impossible to know whether the list compiled by Shapur is accurate or simply a propaganda tool aimed at further cementing the dynasty in power. Assuming that it is accurate, at least on the whole, there were twenty-seven different provinces attested as providing troops for Valerian's army. Although it is easy to assume that at least some of these regions provided legions, this would be a mistake: by this period whole legions were not redeployed for campaigns. It is far more likely that each region provided one or more *vexillationes* as described in the previous chapter.

Due to the lack of information, it is impossible to gauge whether the claim that Valerian fielded 70,000 men is accurate. All that can be said is that the army was very large, intending to halt the incursions from Sasanid Persia, and included troops from all over the Empire. Consequently it may be that the army numbered at least 40,000 men, with 70,000 men being the extreme upper limit: Shapur is unlikely to have downplayed the number defeated at the battle.

The Opposing Forces: The Sasanids

Like the Roman army, the Sasanid army was to undergo a long evolution over the course of the empire's existence. Obviously Shapur, the *Shahanshah* (King of Kings), was the overall commander of the army and would take personal command of specific campaigns, including the one ending with the Battle of Edessa.

At some point the next rank of leaders was split into four, these being the Shah of Armenia, the Shah of Meshan ('Lower Mesopotamia'), the Shah of Gilan (on the southern coast of the Caspian Sea) and the Shah of Sakastan (on the eastern frontier of the empire). Yet at this early date this system was not yet in place: Armenia had not yet been assimilated into the Sasanid Empire and so this would be impossible. On the other hand, it is likely that Shapur had accepted the shahs of Meshan, Gilan and Sakastan into the hierarchy and that these shahs assumed responsibility for the defence of their regions against invasion.

Cavalry

It is difficult to separate the description of the cavalry units at this early date for the Sasanid Empire from those of later periods. For example, the depiction of the *Shahanshah* Khosrow II Parviz as seen in the reliefs at Taq-e Bostan shows a heavily-armoured cavalryman with the horse wearing armour covering only the front half of the body.

At this earlier period it would appear that the Sasanid army was more a continuation of the Parthian army than was the case later. The absorption of the Parthian elites into the new empire almost certainly resulted in the aristocratic troops continuing to be armed as *cataphracts* as deployed at the earlier Battle of Carrhae (see Chapter 6). These nobles practised warfare extensively and were the main shock elements of the Sasanid army.

Under the direct control of the *Shahanshah* was the guard unit, the *Zhayedan*. Commonly thought to be 10,000 in number to emulate the Immortals of the earlier Achaemenid Empire, this has recently been questioned. The doubt remains valid, since whether the Sasanids copied the earlier empire's methods in any way is open to question. However, the theory that the Sasanids would have been unaware of the earlier Immortals is questionable: to assume that they would not have had access to the Greek writers who described the Immortals or that the 'Persians' did not have their own archives is problematic.

The men forming the *cataphracts* were the *Asavaran/Aswaran/Azadan*, major and minor nobility who formed the core of the Sasanid army. The lower political castes formed the light cavalry, almost exclusively horse archers, again as described in Chapter 6. Alongside these native horse archers were subject cavalry and mercenaries. Although the majority of these were also horse archers, it is possible that some were armed with javelins rather than bows.

The other mounted arm of the Sasanid army was the elephant corps. Although never numerous, elephants provided a platform from which archers in howdahs could shower the enemy with fire from a higher position. Of more importance, elephants were used to create panic and disorder in the enemy – especially those who had little or no experience of fighting against them – and their charge could create large holes in enemy lines that could then be used by the cavalry to create further chaos. To protect the elephants from enemy skirmishers they were supported by archers, slingers and javelinmen, whose task was to keep the elephants safe until they were in position to charge.

Infantry

When it comes to the infantry, the common picture is of peasants armed with long spears and large rectangular shields who were completely useless as an offensive force but could be used defensively, especially as a shield behind which retreating cavalry could reform ready to rejoin the battle.

Although this is in some ways accurate as there were indeed troops of this nature, it is not the whole picture. Alongside the native peasant infantry, the empire could employ allied, mercenary and subject infantry of much higher quality. The most important of these were the Dailami/ Daylami. These were infantry armed with swords, axes and javelins, who at this early date could either skirmish forward of the infantry line, support the cavalry, defend the elephants or take place in the main battle line. Later they would become more heavily armed and be an elite guard formation. There were also other heavy infantry formations, but as these are mainly attested later they may not have existed at this date.

Of greater threat to the Romans, the Sasanids were efficient at siege warfare, employing among other techniques battering rams, siege towers, catapults and mines. As the Romans relied on forts and fortified cities to defend the eastern frontier, this meant that the East was under constant threat. The result was that when Shapur advanced against the cities of Carrhae and Edessa, these were under real threat of destruction.

Although there is some concept of the composition of the Sasanid army, there is absolutely no information regarding the proportion of each troop's type in Shapur's army. Nor is it possible to estimate the numbers involved: at Carrhae in 53 BCE a Roman army of c.39,000 troops was defeated by only 10,000 Parthian cavalry. Consequently, it is possible that Shapur's army facing the alleged 70,000 Romans under Valerian could have numbered anywhere between 20,000 and 80,000 men. However, as Shapur was investing the cities of Carrhae and Edessa, his army was not composed solely of cavalry; therefore it is likely that Shapur's army was nearer in total to that of Valerian rather than being heavily outnumbered.

Location

The exact location of the battle is unknown, but is believed to have been somewhere between the cities of Carrhae and Edessa. Although unknown, what is known is that the region was excellent terrain for a cavalry army to function and it is likely that this was a factor in the upcoming battle.

Deployment

There are no accounts of the deployment employed by either army. All that is known is that Valerian was defeated.

Course of the Battle

When it comes to the battle itself, there is no information in any of the sources concerning the nature and course of the conflict. In fact, the Roman sources tend to downplay the event and even avoid mentioning it at all. For example, Zosimus states that

> In the meantime, Valerian became so effeminate and indolent, that he despaired of ever recovering from the present ill state of affairs and would have concluded the war by a present of money, had not Sapor [Shapur] sent back the ambassadors who were sent to him with that proposal, without their errand, desiring the emperor to come and speak with him in person concerning the affairs he wished to adjust. To which he most imprudently consented, and going without consideration to Sapor with a small retinue, to treat for a peace, was presently laid hold of by the enemy, and so ended his days in the

capacity of a slave among the Persians, to the disgrace of the Roman name in all future times.

Zosimus, 1.36.2.

Zosimus omits any mention of a battle, instead reporting that Valerian was such a coward that he simply wanted to pay the Sasanids to stop the invasions. When Shapur dismissed Valerian's envoys, Valerian agreed to meet in person and so was captured.

Other authors, for example Lactantius, simply state that Valerian was captured, whereas much later sources such as George Syncellus and Zonaras ascribe the capture to Valerian being besieged in Edessa and surrendering to Shapur due to a fear of mutiny among his own troops, this due to Valerian only affecting to lead a campaign against the Persians and the troops recognizing the duplicity. Obviously, in these accounts, the army suffered only minor losses.[2]

Interestingly, Zonaras records an alternative account. In this the cowardly Valerian refused to lead a campaign against the Sasanids, but he then learned that Shapur was besieging Edessa and that the besieged troops were conducting raids from the city and were managing to kill many Sasanids. Encouraged, he decided that he could gain a victory and so marched east. In this account, Valerian was surrounded by a larger Sasanid army. In the course of the battle, large numbers of Roman troops were killed and the army appears to have routed in defeat. It was during the battle that Valerian and many of his courtiers were captured.

This latter account agrees, at least in part, with the description given by Shapur in the reliefs at Naqš-i Rustam. Shapur declares that he won a great battle and that he had captured Valerian with his own hands. Consequently it is the accounts of a great battle as given by Zonaras and Shapur that are accepted here, but the events after the Roman defeat are based upon the Roman accounts.

Faced with mounting pressure on all fronts, Valerian was unsure of which enemy to face and was possibly wary of confronting Shapur. When Shapur advanced and laid siege to Edessa and Carrhae Valerian knew that he had to do something, vacillating between fighting the Sasanids and restoring Roman prestige in the East or of simply paying them off so that he could move to face other threats. However, hearing that the garrison of Edessa was inflicting casualties on the Sasanids, Valerian decided that a victory would not only ease the pressure in the East, but would restore Rome's reputation and so deter attacks on other fronts.

Taking the large army he had gathered east, Valerian deployed opposite the Sasanids besieging Edessa and Carrhae, only to find that he was outnumbered. The site of the battle appears to have been somewhere between the two besieged cities, so it is possible that he drew up his forces to face the enemy at Edessa and was taken by surprise by a second Sasanid army advancing from Carrhae to support the troops at Edessa.

Whatever the case, there followed a great battle, during which the Roman army lost c.10,000 troops (see below). If this is accurate, it is possible that the Sasanid wings routed the opposing cavalry and some of the infantry on the flanks, but that the central core of legions and *auxilia* conducted a fighting retreat into Edessa: if the centre of the army had collapsed, the losses would doubtless have been much higher as the Sasanid cavalry swept in to complete the rout.

The remaining force, c.60,000 men, retreated to Edessa. Here they found that the city was suffering from the effects of the ongoing plague, exacerbated by the Sasanid siege. The Roman sources suggest that, realizing that if he continued to resist then his army could easily rebel and remove him from power, Valerian decided that the only option was a negotiated peace. Accordingly he sent envoys to Shapur, but these were rebuffed and Valerian was told that he would need to seek terms in person. Valerian agreed and left the city to negotiate. At this point Shapur reneged on his promise and Valerian was taken captive.

However, the conclusion of this account includes both of the common Roman *topoi* for dealing with military disasters: incompetent commanders and treacherous barbarians. Consequently it is probably safer to assume that Valerian and his entourage were captured during the battle rather than being trapped by a deceitful Shapur. Writing much later, George Syncellus and Zonaras claim that the remaining Roman army was then besieged in Edessa, where it quickly began to suffer from starvation. This implies that, rather than being 'betrayed' by Valerian, the surviving Roman army – demoralized and besieged in plague-ravaged Edessa – agreed to surrender to escape with their lives. The campaign was over, and the Romans had suffered yet another devastating defeat at the hands of the 'Persians'.

Aftermath

Valerian was to spend the rest of his life in captivity. His fate has invited much speculation. These range from the plausible to the exaggerated and horrific accounts written by Roman historians. Dealing with the Roman accounts first, there are two near-contemporary sources. Eutropius, who wrote shortly after the battle, claims that Valerian 'was overthrown by Shapur king of Persia, and being soon after made prisoner, grew old in ignominious slavery among the Parthians'.[3]

Lactantius, in his heavily biased account, gives a much more lurid account, probably due to both a persecution initiated by Valerian and others instigated by the Sasanid Shahs; in this way he could denigrate both parties simultaneously. Lactantius and Aurelius Victor claim that Valerian was forced to kneel so that Shapur could use him as a stool to aid either his climbing into his carriage or mounting his horse.[4] Furthermore, after his death – or according to some historians while he was still alive – Valerian's skin was flayed from his body, dyed vermilion and kept in a Sasanid temple.[5] The concept that he was flayed is almost certainly inaccurate, and is mainly a theme introduced by Lactantius to highlight the 'barbarity' of the Sasanids. In addition, and despite knowing that the iconographic tradition in both Rome and Persia depicted defeated enemies kneeling in supplication, it is possible that either Lactantius or Aurelius Victor used the visual representations of Valerian kneeling before the mounted Shapur as inspiration for the story of Valerian being used as a footstool.

Despite the suggestion by the Christian writers that Valerian, the instigator of a persecution, died an ignoble death after spending several years being tormented by Shapur, there is another possibility. Near the city of Susa is the *Band-e Kaisar* ('The Dam of the Emperor'). It is feasible that Valerian and at least some of the captured army were sent to this region and, thanks to their building skills, the legionaries – perhaps under the command of Valerian (hence the name of the dam) – built the dam, alongside other Roman-appearing engineering feats in the region. This hypothesis may be reinforced by the claim of the later Persian (Muslim) writer Abu Hanifa Ahmad ibn Dawud ibn Wanand al-Dinawari that Shapur settled the prisoners of war in Gundishapur and released Valerian, as promised, after the construction of the *Band-e Kaisar*.

When Sābūr son of Ardašīr ruled, he raided the land of Rūm and conquered the city of Qālūqīya and the city of Qabadūqīya and massacred the enemy in Rūm. Then he returned to Irāq, and he went to the land of Ahwāz to explore a place in which to build a city in which to settle the prisoners that he had come with from the land of Rūm. He built the city Junday-Sābūr, whose name in Ḥūzīya is Nīlāṭ, and they call its people Nīlāb. Sābūr had taken captive Alyaryānūs, successor to the lord of Rūm. He commanded the building of an aqueduct upon the river Tustar in order to empty it. The king of Rūm sent to it people from the land of Rūm and material, and he built it. When he was finished with it he set him free.

The Book of Lengthy Histories, trans. Michael Bonner.

Although there is no other record of Valerian being released, it is interesting to note that at Naqš-i Rustam Valerian is usually shown holding hands with Shapur I, usually interpreted as a sign of submission rather than of being badly treated.

After his victory, Shapur continued to campaign in Roman territory. He took the city of Caesarea, deporting at least some of its inhabitants to Persia, and then went on to attack Cilicia. At this point the eastern Roman armies had rallied and were able to force him to return home. Sadly for Rome, the commanders of this 'rallied' army – men named Macrianus, Callistus and finally Odenathus of the city of Palmyra – were to take part in the next phase of Roman history.

Effects

The earlier defeats suffered by Rome had caused massive loss of life, but politically they had few consequences. The loss at Edessa was by far the worst defeat inflicted upon Rome by a foreign enemy with regard to both the military and the political repercussions.

Valerian had ordered troops from the Rhine and Danube frontiers. The result was that the tribes across the rivers – for example, the Franks, Alamanni and Quadi – saw an opportunity to raid into the Empire, starting in 260 CE. As already noted, after his victory Shapur continued his advance into the Empire. Pressure increased on every frontier.

Of more importance to the integrity of the Empire, the losses in the East and the invasions in both East and West plus the capture of Valerian resulted in sections of the army losing faith in the remaining emperor, Valerian's son Gallienus. A myriad of usurpers arose, the most important of whom were a man named Postumus who controlled the forces covering the Rhine; Ingenuus, controlling the Danubian forces; and the man named Macrianus who, along with Odenathus, had finally repelled the Sasanids from Roman territory, along with a man named Quietus.

Although Gallienus and those generals who remained loyal were able to slowly recover control over the central region of the Empire, elsewhere things were very different. In the West, Postumus took control of Britain, Gaul and Hispania, establishing a separate entity known as the Gallic Empire. In the East, Odenathus, the ruler of Palmyra, took control of the surviving Roman forces and slowly extended his 'rule'. However, unlike Postumus, he did not assume the title of *Augustus*, instead calling himself *dux Romanorum* (Roman military commander) and *corrector totius Orientis* (chief administrator of the East), but ostensibly still under the (in)direct rule of Gallienus. This is now known as the Palmyrene Empire.

Unlike earlier defeats where after a short period of chaos order had been restored, the Battle of Edessa resulted in the division of the Empire. It would take more than a decade before the unity of the Empire was restored. In 272–3 the emperor Aurelian moved against the Palmyrene Empire, at the time ruled by Odenathus' wife and successor Zenobia, who had taken over the Empire and expanded its frontier further west into Asia Minor as well as taking Egypt. Zenobia was captured and paraded in triumph in Rome.

In 274 Aurelian turned west and launched an assault on the Gallic Empire. In this he was helped by the fact that, prior to the decisive battle, Postumus' successor Tetricus defected to Aurelian, leaving the Gallic army leaderless and easily defeated. Tetricus was rewarded by a senior position in Aurelian's court. Sadly for Rome, Aurelian was assassinated in the following year, but by the time of his death the integrity of the Empire had been restored.

Select Bibliography

Roman

Ammianus Marcellinus, 23.5: https://www.tertullian.org/fathers/index.htm#Ammianus_Marcellinus

Aurelius Victor, *Liber De Caesaribus* (translation by H. Bird): http://www.forumromanum.org/literature/aurelius_victorx.html

Eusebius, *Ecclesiastical History* (Loeb translation by J. Oulton): https://www.ccel.org/ccel/schaff/npnf201.toc.html

Eutropius, *Breviarium* (translation by H. Bird): https://www.livius.org/sources/content/eutropius-short-history

John Malalas, *Chronographia* (translation by Elizabeth Jeffreys, Michael Jeffreys and Roger Scott): https://en.calameo.com/read/000675905f2f4bf509d49

Lactantius, *De Mortibus Persecutorum* (translation by M.F. McDonald): https://www.earlychurch.org.uk/lactantius.php

Orosius, *The Seven Books of History Against the Pagans* (translation by R.J. Deferrari): http://attalus.org/info/orosius.html

Porphyry, *Life of Plotinus* (translation by S. MacKenna): http://ldysinger.stjohnsem.edu/@texts/0260_plotinus/03_life_porph.htm

Scriptores Historiae Augustae (Loeb translation by David Magie), including *The Two Valerians:* https://archive.org/details/scriptoreshistor00magi#:~:text=The%20Scriptores%20Historiae%20Augustae%2C%20or%20Historia%20Augusta%2C%20is,authors%20and%20quotes%20documents%20and%20public%20records%20extensively

https://www.livius.org/sources/content/historia-augusta

https://archive.org/details/scriptoreshistor01camb

Trebellius Pollio, *Life of Valerian* (frags); *Two Gallieni, The Thirty Pretenders* and *The Deified Claudius* included in the *Scriptores Historiae Augustae*: https://www.livius.org/sources/content/historia-augusta

Zonaras, *Epitome Historiarum* (Pinder edition, Bonn, 1841–1897) https://archive.org/details/epitomehistoria00zonagoog/page/n7/mode/2up

Zosimus, *Historia Nova* (translations by J. Buchanan and H. Davis or by R. Ridley): https://www.tertullian.org/fathers/zosimus01_book1.htm

Persian

Res Gestae Divi Saporis (SKZ): http://parthiansources.com/texts/skz/skz-translation

Abu Hanifa Ahmad ibn Dawud ibn Wanand al-Dinawari, *The Book of Lengthy Histories* (trans. Michael Bonner): http://www.mrjb.ca/current-projects/abu-hanifah-ahmad-ibn-dawud-al-dinawari

Chapter Ten

The Sasanid Threat Continues: The Siege of Amida, 359 CE

The Sources

The source for the siege is **Ammianus Marcellinus**. Unlike most events in ancient history, this is not a secondary source: its importance lies in the fact that he was a military staff officer actually present at the siege and is describing things he saw in person rather than relying on others' description of events. Despite this, it should be remembered that although the events he personally saw are, to a great extent, accurate, it is known that two observers of the same event are likely to differ regarding the details. Further, as a staff officer he would have known of the strategies used by the Roman defenders, but any description of Shapur's intentions are almost certainly simply inferred from his actions rather than specific facts. Any areas where Ammianus may be deviating from personal observations will be made clear below.

Background

After the Battle of Edessa in 260 the Roman Empire slowly regained its strength, despite ongoing civil wars for much of the time. The main events between the capture of Valerian and the middle of the fourth century were the division of the Empire into three and its reunification under Aurelian (r.270–75); the reign of Diocletian (284–305), who brought a measure of security to the Empire and established the short-lived 'Tetrarchy'; and the rule of Constantine I 'the Great' (r.306–337), the first Roman emperor to publicly espouse Christianity and hence the consequent conversion of a large proportion of the Empire to the 'new' religion.

During the reign of Diocletian (r.284–305), the Sasanids had defeated the Roman *Caesar* ('Junior Emperor') Galerius at the Battle of Callinicum (Carrhae) in 296/7, but in 299 Galerius had reversed the result at the

Battle of Satala in 298. The resultant peace treaty, signed in 299, expanded Roman territory in the East, changing the border from the Euphrates to the Tigris and so including a region projecting towards the Sasanid capital of Ctesiphon. Fortunately for Rome, the political confusion surrounding the retirement of Diocletian in 305 and the ensuing series of civil wars that ended with Constantine I becoming sole emperor (324) was mirrored to some extent in Sasanid Persia.

Shortly before Constantine died in 337 and rule devolved upon his three sons, the Persian Shah Shapur II began a war attempting to renegotiate the Treaty of 299 more to the satisfaction of the Persians. This would continue until 350, although fighting did not occur in every year. With Constantine dead, it was his son Constantius II who was allotted Greece, Thrace, Egypt and the provinces facing Shapur.

There was to be small-scale warfare throughout Constantius' reign, but there were also three main Sasanid attacks. One was in 338 in which Shapur attempted to take the important fortress city of Nisibis, the headquarters of the Roman commander, the *dux Mesopotamiae*. After a siege lasting two months and with his army ravaged by disease, Shapur finally withdrew.

Six years later in 344, the Battle of Singara was initially a victory for the Romans, but the Romans' need for water meant that they lost cohesion as they captured the Sasanid camp. The reforming Sasanids then counterattacked. Although the Romans remained in possession of

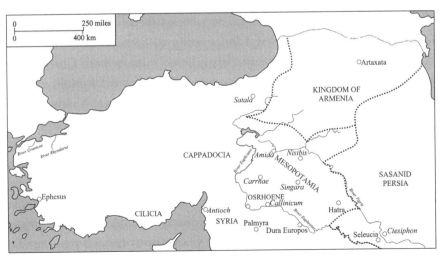

The Siege of Amida.

the camp, allowing them to claim a victory, it would appear that they had suffered the heavier casualties due to the late rally by the Sasanids.

In 346 Shapur again attempted to capture the city of Nisibis, again without success. Undaunted, in 350 Shapur attempted to take the city for a third time. Again the siege lasted for two to three months, but this time Shapur was forced to admit defeat when news came to him of an invasion of Persian territory from the north. Shapur withdrew to face this unexpected attack. For the next few years Shapur was to be distracted by invasion and counterattack along his other frontiers, which was a relief to Constantius as there were problems within the Empire that needed to be dealt with.

While Constantius had been defending the East, his brothers Constantine II and Constans had fought a civil war. In 340 Constantine was killed in an ambush and Constantius was left to rule the West on his own. Constantius and Constans lived in peace, but in 350 the Western troops lost patience with Constans and nominated a usurper named Magnentius. Constans was quickly assassinated.

Appointing his cousin Constantius Gallus as *Caesar* ('Junior Emperor') to maintain the status quo in the East where there was a brief hiatus in hostilities thanks to Shapur being distracted elsewhere, Constantius invaded the West. His campaigns were a success. He defeated Magnentius at the Battles of Mursa Major (351) and Mons Seleucus (353), after which Magnentius committed suicide.

However, the year after his victory Constantius was informed that Constantius Gallus was behaving inappropriately as *Caesar* in the East, displaying a violent nature and being open to corruption. Constantius quickly had him executed. Despite then being sole emperor, Constantius needed a second commander, one to defend the Western frontier against the Germanic tribes and one to defend the East against Shapur. After defeating the Alamanni in 354, in 355 Constantius promoted Gallus' younger half-brother Julian to the rank of *Caesar*. Constantius moved to the East, leaving Julian to command the defence against the northern barbarians.

Once back in the East, Constantius was forced to campaign against tribes who were attempting to use the civil wars as a distraction to invade and pillage across the Danube. In 357 Constantius crossed the Danube and defeated the Quadi and Sarmatians, again demonstrating his military capabilities. Yet the final settlement of his other frontiers and the absence of a strong Roman military commander in the East finally allowed Shapur to focus on Rome once more, this time with the aid of troops supplied by the nations against which he had recently fought.[1]

In 359 Shapur once again invaded Roman territory. Rather than yet another attempt to take Nisibis, Shapur decided that this time he would aim to lead a raid deep into Roman territory. In this he was advised by a Roman named Antoninus, who had been driven to defect to the Sasanids:

> And after long debate to and fro it was decided, on the advice of Antoninus, that since Ursicinus was far away and the new commander was lightly regarded, they should give up the dangerous sieges of cities, pass the barrier of the Euphrates, and push on with the design of outstripping by speed the news of their coming and seizing upon the provinces [i.e. Syria], which in all previous wars (except in the time of Gallienus) had been untouched and had grown rich through long-continued peace.

Antoninus also pointed out to Shapur that a Roman named Sabinianus had been sent to command the Eastern army. Sabinianus is heavily derided by Ammianus, who was a supporter of his predecessor Ursicinus. Accordingly, Shapur led his army past Nisibis and moved towards the city of Amida, wanting to bypass this city in order to attack Antioch, but circumstances would determine otherwise.

The first move was for the army to attack Singara. Shapur may have felt this to be necessary in order to protect his lines of communication and ensure the troops at Singara would not attack the rear of his army as it advanced. The city was captured, as noted by Ammianus (see further below).[2]

The news of both the preparations for the invasion and the invasion itself was reported by spies and deserters, and Ursicinus, only recently removed, was reinstated as the *Magister Equitum per Orient* ('Master of the Horse in the East'). He returned and took steps to ensure that Nisibis was prepared for the expected assault: doubtless at this early stage the Romans expected this to be another attempt to take Nisibis.[3] At the same time he ordered a *comes* ('count') named Aelianus to take reinforcements to Amida. Strategically this was a good move: from Amida the troops could threaten the Sasanid forces either if they besieged Nisibis or if the Sasanid target was Syria. However, at about the same time a message arrived from ambassadors to the Persian court stating that Shapur would 'throw bridges over the Granicus and the Rhyndacus, and invade Asia with a numerous host'.[4] Consequently, it was then ordered that the Roman citizens should retire into the cities and that the crops in the fields were to be burned; 'scorched-earth' tactics as used by defenders throughout history.[5]

However, Shapur marched further north, avoiding Nisibis, both in order to maintain access to supplies and to find an alternative route to Syria. In this way, after defeating advanced forces and scouts of the Romans, the Sasanids reached the fortress of Amida.

Ammianus states that Shapur was not intending to lay siege to the city, but simply bypass it on his way to Syria. Nevertheless, he could not resist the attempt to negotiate the city's surrender:

> The king himself, mounted upon a charger and overtopping the others, rode before the whole army, wearing in place of a diadem a golden image of a ram's head set with precious stones, distinguished too by a great retinue of men of the highest rank and of various nations. But it was clear that he would merely try the effect of a conference on the defenders of the walls, since by the advice of Antoninus he was in haste to go elsewhere.
>
> *Ammianus Marcellinus, 19.1.3.*

Although this description has almost always been accepted at face value, it has recently been noted that Ammianus' description of the king's headgear does not equate with that usually worn by the Sasanid shahs. This was a crenellated crown and the one described, with ram's horns, was associated with the Kidarite ruler Peroz, the ruler of the Chionites, Gelani and Segestani who were present, as displayed on his coins. In addition, Ammianus' attestation of this man being called 'Saansaan' and 'Pirosen' could equally equate to the same 'Šāhanšāh Pērōz', although Šāhanšāh would usually be accorded to Shapur and not one of his allies. This may be more likely than Ammianus' description: it would appear improbable that Shapur would expose himself to enemy fire from the walls of Amida, but instead would send one of his subordinates to attempt the negotiation.

A further question that arises from this passage is how did Ammianus know of Shapur's intentions? Sadly this is nowhere explained, and is probably simply an interpretation used by Ammianus to explain Shapur's direction of attack, although it should be noted that Ammianus may have been accurate in stating that Shapur would not have simply launched a major attack aimed solely at the reduction of Amida.

Whoever arrived to parley, the attempt was rebuffed. Yet some of Shapur's allies felt that a negotiated surrender was still possible. The attempt would backfire:

> And so, at the first dawn of day, Grumbates, king of the Chionitae, wishing to render courageous service to his lord, boldly advanced to the walls with a band of active attendants; but a skilful observer caught sight of him as soon as he chanced to come within range of his weapon, and discharging a ballista, pierced both cuirass and breast of Grumbates' son, a youth just come to manhood, who was riding at his father's side and was conspicuous among his companions for his height and his handsome person.
>
> *Ammianus Marcellinus, 19.1.7.*

His death was lamented among the Sasanid camp before there was a change of plan:

> For the space of seven days all men by communities and companies feasted (lamenting the young prince) with dances and the singing of certain sorrowful dirges. …After the body had been burned and the ashes collected and placed in a silver urn, since the father [Grumbates] had decided that they should be taken to his native land to be consigned to the earth, they debated what it was best to do; and it was resolved to propitiate the spirit of the slain youth by burning and destroying the city; for Grumbates would not allow them to go further while the shade of his only son was unavenged. Accordingly, after two days had been given to rest, a large force was sent to devastate the rich, cultivated fields, which were unprotected as in time of peace; then the city was begirt by a fivefold line of shields, and on the morning of the third day gleaming bands of horsemen filled all places which the eye could reach, and the ranks, advancing at a quiet pace, took the places assigned them by lot.
>
> *Ammianus Marcellinus, 19.1.10–20.2–2.*

The siege of Amida had begun.

The Opposing Forces: Rome

Between the Battle of Edessa in 260 CE and the siege of Amida in 359 CE the Roman Empire had undergone a seismic change. The *Principate*, as founded by the first emperor Augustus and based on the political theory that the emperor was simply first among equals, had been dispensed with and replaced by the *Dominate*, inaugurated by Diocletian after his accession in 284 CE and based on the political theory that the emperor was the 'Lord', above his fellow citizens.

By this date the Roman army was no longer the same as that used during the earlier centuries of the Empire's existence. Major reforms, continued if not initiated by the Emperors Diocletian (r.284–305) and Constantine (r.306–337), supplemented by further changes under succeeding emperors, had resulted in drastic changes to the size, the organization and the equipment in use by the army.

The army was by now composed of three main groups of troops, with the legions remaining the backbone of the force. Although there were now far more legions than in the earlier Empire, they had shrunk in size to a maximum of (probably) between 1,000 and 1,200 men. In addition, they were no longer equipped with the *lorica segmentata*, rectangular *scutum* and *pilum* of the earlier legions. They now wore more traditional ring mail armour (*lorica hamata*), and carried an oval *scutum* and a normal spear. Moreover their main offensive weapon was no longer the short *gladius hispaniensis*, but was now the longer *spatha*, a sword more suited to slashing rather than stabbing. The change was likely due to a combination of a change of emphasis from offensive to defensive warfare, plus a change in fashion from earlier expensive equipment that was difficult to make to a new, cheaper and more cost-effective panoply.

The legions were still supported by *auxilia*, supporting troops equipped similarly to the legions (although it should be noted that the use of armour by the *auxilia* is disputed). Unlike the legions, the number of men in units of *auxilia* remained small, with units probably being on average c.600–800 men in strength.

The cavalry of the imperial army does not seem to have suffered the same level of change as seen in the infantry. The main difference appears to have been the emergence of 'specialist' units, with companies of *equites sagittarii* (horse archers), *catafractarii* and *clibanarii* (heavily-armed cavalry, with even the horses wearing either 'complete' armour or armour covering only the front of the horse), and *equites Illyricani* (skirmishing cavalry with limited armour and carrying javelins) supplementing the traditional *equites*.

However, the main change was in the division of the army into three main categories: the *palatina* ('of the palace'), troops serving directly under the emperor or his *magister militum* ('master of the troops', the most senior officers); the *comitatenses* ('companions', regional 'field armies'); and the *limitanei* ('frontier troops'), units stationed to defend a specific frontier.

According to Ammianus, there were several Roman units within Amida as the Sasanids approached.[6] The garrison of the town was the *Fifth Parthian* legion, with a supporting unit of 'native cavalry'. However, Ursicinus had dispatched reinforcements, the *Magnentiaci*, the *Decentiaci*, the *Tricensimani*, the *Decimani*, the *Fortenses*, the *Superventores* and the *Praeventores* plus the *Comites Sagittarii*.

The *Magnentiaci* and the *Decentiaci* were troops raised by Magnus Magnentius during his short-lived revolt between 350 and 353. They were probably raised as legions, named after Magnentius and his (probable) brother and *Caesar* Decentius. After Magnentius' defeat they were sent east due to them being 'untrustworthy and turbulent'.[7]

The *Tricensimani* ('Thirtieth'), *Decimani* ('Tenth') and the *Fortenses* were probably legions, with the latter sometimes being equated to the *Legio X Fretensis*, although these conclusions are uncertain: the designation of troops was recorded in the *Notitia Dignitatum*, but as this was written much later, these troops are not specifically listed so may have been disbanded or renamed after the defeat at Amida.

The *Superventores* may have been either a legion or a unit of *auxilia*, but both these and the *Praeventores* are sometimes attested as being light cavalry, 'the former…used in surprise attacks and the latter as scouts.'[8] As they had earlier made a sally during a siege of Singara and caused heavy casualties, either of these interpretations remains valid.

Finally, also stationed in the town was the *Comites Sagittarii*, almost certainly a *vexillatio palatina*: the *Comites Sagittarii iuniores* is included in the *Notitia Dignitatum* as a *vexillatio palatinae*, and it appears reasonable to assume that the unit in Amida was the *Comites Sagittarii seniores*, which seems to have disappeared prior to the compilation of the *Notitia*, probably due to its being destroyed at Amida. These are described by

Ammianus as 'squadrons of cavalry…in which all the freeborn barbarians serve, and who are conspicuous among all others for the splendour of their arms and for their prowess.'[9]

So assuming that the traditionally-accepted number of men per unit is in any way accurate, the following would apply:

6 x legions	@	1,200 =	7,200
1 x native cavalry	@	400(?) =	400
2 x light cavalry	@	600 =	1,200
1 x cavalry archers	@	600 =	600
Total			9,400

However, it should be noted that these figures only give these units at full strength. It is highly unlikely that any of these formations were at full complement due to illness, death, detached duties, desertion or some other reason. It is possibly more reasonable to assume an average of two-thirds strength for these units overall, with some being above and some below that number. On the other hand, the *Comites Sagittarii*, being an elite unit, was more likely to have had its numbers supplemented to somewhere close to its nominal strength. Consequently it is assumed here that the Roman troops in Amida amounted to approximately 6,500 men.

This is near to the lowest estimate given for numbers (5,300). Ammianus gives a total of 120,000 defenders of the city, but this includes the citizens who joined the defence and is more likely an estimate of the total population of the city rather than the numbers of the defenders. Yet even here, there is no certainty that Ammianus is accurate in these numbers: the ancients were not above exaggerating for dramatic effect and although, as an active participant in the defence Ammianus could be expected to be accurate, he would not have counted them personally. As a cautionary note, Ammianus later gives the number of Persian dead after the siege as 30,000 men. Yet the passage in question is rarely analyzed:

…when he [Shapur] had invested Amida for seventy-three days with a great force of armed men, he lost 30,000 warriors, as was reckoned a little later by Discenes, a tribune and secretary, the more readily for this difference: that the corpses of our men soon after they are slain fall apart and waste away, to such a degree that the face of no dead man is recognizable after four days, but the bodies of the slain Persians dry up like tree-trunks, without their limbs wasting or becoming moist with corruption – a fact due to their more frugal life and the dry heat of their native country.

Ammianus Marcellinus, 19.2.14.

Ammianus, one of the most respected historians of late antiquity, is willing to accept the number given by Discenes using a questionable method of ascertaining the nationality of corpses. Accepting that Ammianus may not be accurate in his account, at least regarding the numbers involved, it is here accepted that the total number of citizens defending the city was c.30,000, a quarter of the possible population.

The Opposing Forces: The Sasanids

If the numbers of troops defending the city is uncertain, the number of troops in the Sasanid army is completely unknown. Ammianus states that early in the campaign a guarding force of 700 Illyrian (light) cavalry failed in their duty and were 'surprised and put to flight' by 'about 20,000' Sasanid cavalry.[10] During the battle, he claims that Shapur was 'protected by a hundred thousand armed men', but the concept that a force attacking a defended fortification would number less than the defenders appears odd; as noted, Ammianus claims that the defence was 120,000 strong.[11] Whatever the number, the advancing Sasanids then advanced and attacked any troops they met, the majority of the Roman forces retreating to the walls of Amida for protection.

No other numbers are given, so all that is known of the Sasanid army is that it was composed of a large number of troops drawn from different regions. The main strike force of the army was the Asavaran: heavy cavalry, shock troops capable of charging the enemy frontally, but also equipped with bows for long-distance combat. Doubtless a number of horse archers which, as their name suggests, would advance on the enemy and shower them with arrows, in this way disrupting formations, were present. Supplementing these was probably a smaller number of *cataphracts*, the heavily-armed and armoured cavalry whose purpose was to break into enemy formations, allowing the Asavaran and the horse archers to then follow and destroy the enemy. As Shapur was expecting to attack a town, he would have recruited a large number of peasant infantrymen, whose low quality in battle was a possible hindrance, but whose main purpose was to conduct the siege war he expected at some point in the campaign. Finally, the Sasanid army was usually accompanied by a smaller number of specialist troops, equipped and trained to fight as skirmishers or in rough terrain. The most valuable of these was probably the Daylami: tough mountain men who were probably the best infantry available to the Sasanids.

For the Amida campaign the army was accompanied by several allied contingents. These were the Chionitae, recently defeated by Shapur, led by their king Grumbates, described by Ammianus as 'a man of moderate strength, it is true, and with shrivelled limbs, but of a certain greatness of mind and distinguished by the glory of many victories'; the Albani; the Gelani; the Sacae; and the Segestani, described by Ammianus as 'the bravest warriors of all'.[12]

Despite numerous attempts, it is impossible to assert with any confidence how many men there were in Shapur's army. Some have accepted Ammianus' claim of 120,000 defenders at face value, and have obviously been forced to make Shapur's army equal to or greater than this since it is accepted that an army attacking a defended position needs to outnumber the defenders. However, as noted above, this is not necessarily the case. The defence may only have been around 30,000 men, with the vast majority being ordinary citizens. It is probable that Shapur would not have counted these people as being part of the defence as far as serious opposition was concerned, so there is no guarantee that Shapur's army numbered above 30–40,000. Since he may have been more reliant on speed rather than the size of the army, it may have been far smaller than usually assessed. Consequently the attacking army may have numbered as low as 20–25,000 and as high as 40–50,000; there is no way of knowing for certain.

Location

Amida (modern-day Diyarbakir) is situated on the southern flanks of the south-east Taurus Mountains range. Ammianus states that in his day

This city was once very small, but Constantius, when he was still a Caesar, in order that the neighbours might have a secure place of refuge, at the same time that he built another city called Antoninupolis [Antoninopolis], surrounded Amida with strong walls and towers; and by establishing there an armoury of mural artillery, he made it a terror to the enemy and wished it to be called after his own name. Now, on the south side it is washed by the winding course of the Tigris, which rises near-by; where it faces the blasts of Eurus [Greek God of the east wind] it looks down on Mesopotamia's plains; where it is exposed to the north wind it is close to the river Nymphaeus [Batman] and lies under the shadow of the peaks of Taurus, which separate the peoples beyond the Tigris from Armenia; opposite the breath of Zephyrus [God of the west wind] it borders on Gumathena, a region rich alike in fertility and in tillage, in which is the village called Abarne, famed for its warm baths of healing waters. Moreover, in the very heart of Amida, at the foot of the citadel, a bountiful spring gushes forth, drinkable indeed, but sometimes malodorous from hot vapours.

Ammianus Marcellinus, 18.9.1–2.

The city was a major strongpoint in East Rome's defensive system facing the Sasanids. The main city defending the approaches to Syria was Nisibis, in the heart of Roman territory in the region and protecting the main route from Ctesiphon to Antioch. Further south, the routes led through desert territory which, although a shorter route, would need a larger baggage train as supplies of food and water were scarce. Amida guarded the northern route which, although longer, had more access to water and from which an army could gather some supplies to augment those it carried.

It is clear from the sources that Shapur intended to strike at Antioch. Although the northern route was longer, it bypassed Nisibis, the main Roman fortress from which troops could easily attack the rear of a passing Sasanid army. However, this would mean bypassing the (smaller) fortress of Amida, but as Shapur expected Amida to have a much smaller garrison, his army would be less likely to suffer serious casualties from sallies out of the city.

Deployment

As Shapur advanced to the walls, the Roman defenders were doubtless allocated specific areas for guard duty, alerting others should the Sasanids gather in preparation for an assault, but when an attack began many of the available men would head for the area of the assault in order to repel it.

On the Sasanid side, Ammianus gives a detailed description of the troops facing the city:

> The Persians beset the whole circuit of the walls. The part which faced the east fell to the lot of the Chionitae, the place where the youth so fatal to us was slain, whose shade was destined to be appeased by the destruction of the city. The Gelani were assigned to the southern side, the Albani guarded the quarter to the north, and to the western gate were opposed the Segestani, the bravest warriors of all. With them, making a lofty show, slowly marched the lines of elephants, frightful with their wrinkled bodies and loaded with armed men, a hideous spectacle, dreadful beyond every form of horror, as I have often declared.
>
> *Ammianus Marcellinus, 19.2.3.*

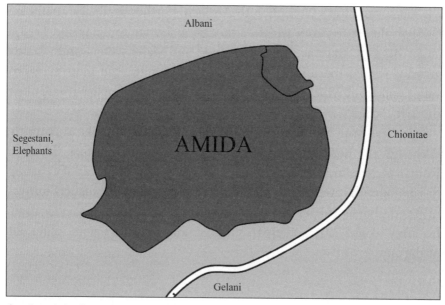

Amida and the Sasanid deployment.

In the east and the south, the River Tigris flowed around the city in a slight bend before continuing east and south to join the Euphrates. These areas were manned by the Chionitae, whose main arm was composed of horse archers, and the Gelani, warriors from the mountainous province of Gilan, both troop types more suitable for defending against an attempt to break out into the region rather than an assault.

The northern side, bordering the Tigris as it flowed south towards Amida, was more open and was guarded by the Albani, troops from the Kingdom of (Caucasian) Albania (the modern-day Azerbaijan region), whose troops came from a topography similar to that around Amida and so may have been presumed a better option by Shapur than the Chionitae and the Gelani in this area.

The western wall was covered by the Segestani, inhabitants of present-day Sistan. Ammianus describes them as 'the bravest warriors of all' and adds that in this area – possibly the most amenable to assault – Shapur also deployed his elephants.

Course of the Battle

The siege would last for seventy-three days, but Ammianus only describes the beginning, the end and some details concerning the rest of the siege. This is understandable as the day-to-day life of the siege would be repetitive and hence be similar to many of the descriptions given.

For the first two days after the funeral celebrations, the Sasanids laid waste to the surrounding region. Finally, with the decision to attack Amida taken, the Sasanid army spent the third day simply forming up outside the city, possibly in the hope that the sight of a formidable army would encourage the Romans to surrender without a fight, but this did not happen.

Consequently on the fourth day the Sasanids launched their first attempt to storm the city. Prior to the attack Grumbates, whose son had been killed, 'hurled a bloodstained spear, following the usage of his country and the custom of our fetial priest…the army with clashing weapons flew to the walls':[13]

Then heads were shattered, as masses of stone, hurled from the scorpions, crushed many of the enemy; others were pierced by arrows, some were struck down by spears and the ground strewn with their bodies, while others that were only wounded retreated in headlong flight to their companions. No less was the grief and no fewer the deaths in the city, whence a thick cloud of arrows in compact mass darkened the air, while the artillery which the Persians had acquired from the plunder of Singara inflicted still more wounds. For the defenders, recovering their strength and returning in relays to the contest they had abandoned, when wounded in their great ardour for defence fell with destructive results; or if only mangled, they overturned in their writhing those who stood next to them, or at any rate, so long as they remained alive kept calling for those who had the skill to pull out the arrows implanted in their bodies. Thus slaughter was piled upon slaughter and prolonged to the very end of the day, nor was it lessened even by the darkness of evening, with such great determination did both sides fight. And so the night watches were passed under the burden of arms, while the hills re-echoed from the shouts rising from both sides, as our men praised the power of Constantius Caesar as lord of the world and the universe, and the Persians called Sapor 'saansaan' and 'pirosen'[14] which being interpreted is 'king of kings' and 'victor in wars'.

Ammianus Marcellinus, 19.2.7–11.

Although Ammianus claims that the battle carried on through the night, he then contradicts this by saying that before dawn of the fifth day the Sasanid army was awakened and as dawn broke the fighting began again as the Sasanids attempted to storm the walls. It is at this point that Ammianus notes that the city was crowded, filled as it was with 'seven legions, a promiscuous throng of strangers and citizens of both sexes, and a few other soldiers, to the number of 120,000 in all'.[15] Many writers have conflated the troops with the citizens and suggested that the city was defended by 120,000 men but, as already noted, this is obviously a mistake.

After a brief description of the wounds and suffering of the besieged, Ammianus then reports that his favourite, Ursicinus, was pleading with the inactive Sabinianus to organize a relief column to support the besieged in Amida. According to Ammianus – although it must be remembered that Ammianus was biased towards Ursicinus – Sabinianus refused, allegedly on secret orders from Constantius.[16] How Ammianus would have known of these 'secret orders' is nowhere explained. Consequently nothing was done, except that Ursicinus sent some messengers into the besieged city.

At this point Ammianus makes a brief digression, in which he first notes the outbreak of a plague in the city due to the inability to bury the dead and then continues onto an outline of the three major 'plagues', i.e. 'endemic', 'epidemic' and 'loemedes' [pestilential].[17] Sadly he does not detail the nature of the plague in Amida, stating simply that 'at last on the night following the tenth day the thick and gross exhalations were dispelled by light showers, and sound health of body was regained.'[18]

The most important aspect of Ammianus' account is his description of the measures and counter-measures employed by the Sasanids and the Romans during the siege:

> But meanwhile the restless Persian was surrounding the city with sheds and mantlets, and mounds began to be raised and towers were constructed; these last were lofty, with ironclad fronts, and on the top of each a ballista was placed, for the purpose of driving the defenders from the ramparts; yet not even for a moment did the skirmishing by the slingers and archers slacken. There were with us two Magnentian legions, recently brought from Gaul (as I have said) and composed of brave, active men, experienced in battle in the open field, but to the sort of warfare to which we were constrained they were not merely unsuited, but actually a great hindrance; for whereas they were of no help with the artillery or in the construction of fortifications, they would sometimes make reckless sallies and after fighting with the greatest confidence return with diminished numbers, accomplishing just as much as would the pouring of a single handful of water (as the saying is) upon a general conflagration. Finally, when the gates were very carefully barred, and their officers forbade them to go forth, they gnashed their teeth like wild beasts. But in the days that followed (as I shall show) their efficiency was conspicuous.
>
> *Ammianus Marcellinus, 19.5.1–3.*

The use of sheds, mantlets, mounds (ramps) and siege-towers is well attested in ancient warfare, but it is interesting to note that, unlike the earlier Roman legions, the 'Magnentian' legions were of little use in siege warfare, being unable to use the artillery pieces and of 'no help...in the construction of fortifications'. The earlier legions were capable builders who constructed much of the infrastructure used by the Empire, but this no longer seems to have been the case, unless these two legions were the exception.

At some point during the siege – after the first few days Ammianus stops using a chronology – one of the inhabitants deserted to the Sasanids. On the south side, overlooking the River Tigris, the walls stood on top of a cliff. At this point there was a large tower above a tunnel that had been carved in order to allow access to the river water. The deserter alerted the Sasanids to this entry point, and seventy archers were guided into the tunnel and so silently took possession of the tower. They then displayed a red cloak, the sign for a general assault.

Once the assault was fully under way the archers began to rain missiles down on the defenders from the tower. At first dismayed, the solution was to redeploy five of the lighter *ballistae* (bolt-shooters) against the tower. These took their toll on the archers, killing most and forcing the remainder to leap from the tower in the hope of saving themselves. Ammianus states that they died in the attempt. With the tower retaken, the *ballistae* were redeployed and eventually the attack was beaten back.[19]

During this part of the siege the Sasanids were slowly building ramps outside the walls with the intention of making the ramps so high that they could look down on the walls and so be able to clear them with missile fire during the next major assault. In response, the Romans began building ramps inside the walls that would overtop those of the Sasanids, allowing them to use their own missiles to suppress the Persian fire.[20]

Possibly on the day after the attack via the tower, the 'Magnentian' legions from Gaul, unhappy with being trapped in the city and seeing the many captives the Sasanids had taken in the surrounding region, demanded to be allowed to sally out against the enemy. They were finally allowed to make an attack. Taking the Sasanids by surprise, they caused a large number of casualties and even thought of advancing into the camp and killing Shapur, but the noise of the attack alerted the Sasanids and slowly the Gauls were pushed back.

The Romans opened the city gates and, without loading them, repeatedly 'fired' the *ballistae* in the hope that the sound of the firing would cause the Sasanids near to the gate to retreat, so allowing the Gauls to retire into the city. The ruse seems to have worked and the sallying legions finally reached the safety of the city, albeit with the loss of 400 trained warriors.[21]

The losses on both sides from this fight were so great that as the next day dawned the Sasanids agreed a three-day truce in order to bury the dead.[22] This was necessary for both sides as they both needed to reorganize their forces and bury the dead to avoid the dangers of disease. Obviously the ceasefire would also allow them to rest and treat the wounded.

It was only then that Shapur abandoned the idea of storming the city, relying instead on siege works, including new towers, to succeed where straightforward assault had failed. Finally, happy with the preparations, Shapur ordered the newly-built 'ironclad towers', higher than the walls and with *ballistae* on top, to be pushed within range of the walls. Alongside these were normal pent-houses, aimed at allowing troops to access the walls and infantry carrying wicker hurdles. Despite the Sasanids' ability to cause large casualties on the walls with their *ballistae* and despite the defences they had constructed to allow them to reach the walls, the defensive fire finally forced the Sasanids to retire towards the end of the day.[23]

In the night the Romans moved the bulk of their catapults to face the enemy towers, and on the following day the towers were destroyed by being struck by large boulders and then set on fire by blazing missiles. In addition, the elephants were also terrified by these missiles, turning tail and causing havoc among the Sasanids. Seeing the damage being caused to his own troops, Ammianus alleges that Shapur himself then took part in the fighting, 'a new thing, never before heard of'.[24]

On the following day, Shapur put his faith in the ramps that had finally been completed, hoping that in this way he would at last gain access to the town. As already noted, the Romans had built their own ramps inside the wall as a counter-measure. It was at this point that disaster struck for the Romans: their own ramp, taller than both the walls and the ramp raised by the Sasanids outside the walls, collapsed forward. It fell over the wall and filled the gap between the Sasanids' ramp and the wall.[25]

At the same time it killed many of the Roman troops defending the wall at that point and caused those nearby to flee from the falling earth. Seeing the collapse, once the ramp had finished its fall Shapur ordered an assault across the fallen ramp while the Romans, rushing to defend the suddenly vulnerable spot, got in each others' way.

Their bravery was hopeless: the vast number of troops now able to pour into the city overwhelmed the defenders and it finally fell to Shapur.[26] Ammianus was one of the few who escaped from the sack, with many of the captured population probably being deported to the Sasanid province of Khuzestan. Although the city had finally fallen, the delay caused by the city's defenders meant that Shapur's plan to attack Syria and possibly Antioch was now impossible due to the weeks spent besieging the city and the heavy losses suffered by the Sasanids, as well as their use of provisions intended for the march to Syria. Shapur withdrew and left the city a wreck.

Aftermath

Thanks to the heavy casualties caused during the siege, Shapur's new allies only served alongside the Sasanids for this campaign season. In the following year, 360, Shapur invaded again, this time taking the fortresses of Bezabde and Singara (again). However, he again suffered heavy casualties and decided that, rather than maintaining an offensive stance, he would restore the captured fortifications as a defence against Constantius II, who had now arrived in the East. In his turn, Constantius II launched a campaign that was to be short-lived: an abortive assault on Bezabde was followed by the news of Julian's revolt in Gaul and Constantius gathered his forces for a campaign to restore his rule in the West. Before the campaign could begin, Constantius died and Julian became sole emperor. Shapur now proposed a peace treaty, but Julian refused and instead began preparations for a major campaign against Sasanid Persia.

Effects

The loss of face caused by the capture of Amida (plus Bezabde and Singara) ensured that Julian, the new emperor, would not be able personally and politically to accede to the Sasanids' success: as a newly-elevated emperor, Julian would want to secure his accession with success in a major campaign. The obvious campaign was against the Sasanids who had only recently humbled Roman power, and this campaign is covered in the next chapter.

Select Bibliography

Ammianus Marcellinus: https://www.tertullian.org/fathers/index.htm#Ammianus_ Marcellinus

Chapter Eleven

The Sasanid Threat Yet Again: Julian's Campaign in Persia, 363 CE

The Sources

There are three main sources for Julian's campaign in Sasanid Persia. The main source, as for the Siege of Amida – and having the same caveats for this campaign as for that siege – is **Ammianus Marcellinus**. For the campaign of Julian, Ammianus is again an eye-witness and here it needs to be remembered that Ammianus was a pagan (with a small 'p'), and although he straddles a fine line between castigating Christians and promoting pagans, his reputation for impartiality is well-deserved. For this section, his high regard for Julian does not restrain him from criticizing Julian when the occasion demanded. Consequently, the detail included by Ammianus is usually accepted at face value.

He accompanied Julian, for whom he expresses enthusiastic admiration, in his campaigns against the Alamanni and the Sasanids. After Julian's death, Ammianus accompanied the retreat of the new emperor, Jovian, as far as Antioch.

The second source is **Zosimus**. A pagan Greek living in Constantinople, Zosimus wrote his *New History* in the late fifth/early sixth century covering the period from 238 to 410, though there are implications that he wanted to go further than this but the work is unfinished. Zosimus is extremely reliant on his sources, particularly Dexippus (for the period 238–270), Eunapius (for 270–404) and Olympiodorus (for 407–410). This reliance goes as far as a change of opinion concerning the people involved when the opinion of his sources changes. In addition, his total adherence to Paganism and rejection of Christianity suffuses the work, meaning that negative events recounted concerning Christians need to be confirmed with other non-related sources if possible.

The third source is **Magnus of Carrhae**, sections of this work being used/paraphrased by the sixth-century chronicler **John Malalas**. The brevity of these entries means that the work is used mainly for supporting evidence in the other sources rather than including additional detail. Where Magnus/Malalas is used separately, a translated quote from the work will be included.

Background

On the death of Constantine I in 337 his three sons (Constantine II, Constans and Constantius II) divided the Empire between them. The emperor of the eastern part, Constantius II, allegedly massacred most of Constantine's relatives who could pose as a threat to the three brothers. The only survivors were two cousins, Constantius Gallus and Julian, and these were banned from having political careers.

In 340 Constantine II invaded the territory of his brother Constans but died. Constans himself was overthrown by the usurper Magnentius ten years later in 350. This left Constantius II in the East as the sole surviving son of Constantine I. Constantius promoted his cousin Gallus to the post of *Caesar* and gave him command of the East while he led a campaign west, overthrowing Magnentius.

Gallus, however, proved incapable of command, terrorizing the East. Constantius ordered his execution, but felt that he needed a second military commander to help defend the Empire. Consequently in 355 he promoted his last surviving relative, Julian, to the post of *Caesar*, married Julian to his (Constantius') sister Helena and gave him command of the Rhine frontier, with Constantius preparing to campaign along the Danube where the barbarians along the frontier had been raiding.

Julian had been studying in Athens, and although he was raised as a Christian, at the age of around 20 he converted to the traditional Roman gods – hence his epithet of 'the Apostate'. He was expected simply to act as a figurehead, behind which Constantius' loyal generals would lead campaigns against the tribes who had begun raiding along the Rhine frontier during the Roman civil war.

Against all expectations, the scholarly Julian proved himself to be a capable general in his own right. In 356 and 357 he led successful campaigns along the Rhine, culminating in the major victory over the Alamanni at the Battle of Argentoratum (Strasbourg). Due to the victory, the troops attempted to acclaim Julian as *Augustus*, an attempt he rejected. In the following year (358) he defeated the Franks and the Chamavi.

At the same time as the Emperor Constantius II was campaigning along the Danube frontier, on the eastern frontier Shapur II invaded and began the siege of Amida (see Chapter 10). Hearing of the incursion and deciding to conduct a major campaign against the Sasanids, Constantius sent orders to Gaul demanding that a large proportion of Julian's army be transferred east for the upcoming campaign. The Gallic troops, unhappy about being sent away from their homes, again acclaimed Julian as their new *Augustus*. This time he acceded to their wish, and a new round of civil wars was about to begin.

Embroiled in the East, Constantius sent an embassy to Julian asking that he resign and revert to *Caesar*. In the meantime, he attempted to retake some of the fortresses lost to the Sasanids, with casualties incurred on both sides. Although these attempts failed, the losses suffered by the Sasanids, coupled with those they had lost in the Amida campaign, meant that Shapur was not in a position where he could mount a further campaign of his own. Consequently, when Constantius realized that he had no option but to confront Julian, Shapur did not attack along the eastern frontier.

Constantius left Antioch and began the march west. As he reached Mopsuestia, in Cilicia it became clear that he was extremely ill. He died on 3 November 361, allegedly nominating Julian as his successor. Julian duly inherited the Empire from Constantius; he also inherited a war with Sasanid Persia.

Despite the pressure in the East, Julian did not continue the war. Instead he began to implement reforms of the bureaucracy. His studies had led him to see earlier emperors, for example Hadrian, as the epitome of Roman rule. Consequently he acted in a way not seen for many years, essentially attempting to revert the government to the *Principate*, where the ruler was seen as *primus inter pares* ('first among equals') rather than the *Dominate* (from *dominus*, 'lord'), where the ruler was set above the people. Alongside these reforms he drastically cut the number of bureaucrats, alienating the educated people who would later condemn his rule. However, his main claim to fame is that he attempted to restore the traditional gods to the forefront of the Empire, putting in place a religious structure similar to that employed by Christianity.

Having enforced his reforms, in 362 Julian finally moved to Antioch in preparation for a war with Sasanid Persia. Politically this was a necessity: he had been acclaimed by the Western army, but the Eastern army had been prepared to oppose this in battle. He needed a military victory to cement his position. However, once in the city, tensions arose between Julian and the Christian citizens who were opposed to his pagan sympathies, and his attempts to act as an earlier emperor in the *Principate* tradition simply reinforced their contempt.

Julian's reforms were dedicated to his aim and specific in their function, suggesting that he was a very intelligent individual who could plan for change and who had the ability to organize. This is reinforced by his plans for the Persian campaign. Not only did he gather the troops ready for the invasion, but he also concerned himself with the logistics for the campaign:

> He was followed by his troops carrying provisions along with them, who likewise embarked according to the orders they received. The navy was by this time come up. It consisted of a great number of vessels; six hundred were made of wood, and five hundred of skins, besides which were fifty ships of war, and others that followed them for the construction of bridges [pontoons], if requisite, that the army should pass the rivers on foot.
>
> A great number of other vessels likewise followed, some of them carrying provisions for the army, others timber for the construction of engines, and some battering engines for a siege which were ready made.
>
> *Zosimus, 3.13.2–3.*

As further evidence of the seriousness of the invasion, one of his senior commanders was Hormizd, one of Shapur II's brothers. Feeling that he was under threat, Hormizd had fled from the Sasanid Empire during the reign of Constantine I. There is a theory that Julian was planning to replace Shapur with his brother, but as Hormizd had been at the Roman court for forty years, it is unlikely that the Sasanid court would accept him as ruler. Yet this should not be dismissed out of hand: Julian may have felt that the threat of a second Roman invasion would allow Hormizd to rule, despite any objections from the Sasanid aristocracy.

With or without the threat of a replacement for his throne, for Shapur the prospect of a major campaign was undesirable. Consequently he sent envoys to Julian in the hope of agreeing a peace treaty, but these were simply dismissed.[1] On 5 March 363, Julian led his troops from Antioch and advanced against the Sasanids.[2]

The Opposing Forces: Rome

With only four years separating the siege of Amida and Julian's campaign it is obvious that there was little chance for major changes to have been made to the army between the two affairs. Yet it should be noted that it is impossible to say this with utmost certainty due to the speed of Julian's other reforms, plus the possibility that any reforms he made to the army would have been to the army he was commanding personally. It is here assumed that any changes implemented by Julian were minor and unlikely to have been carried through elsewhere.

The composition of the army is nowhere described, so it is again assumed that it was a standard Roman army with a core formed by the legions supported by *auxilia* but also with specialist troops supplied either by subservient tribes or allies. However, as the proportion is not attested, it is uncertain if Julian had made any specific deployments to suit the terrain and opponent. Ironically, some of the troops who had led his usurpation in Gaul due to the threat of being sent to the east now accompanied him on his Persian campaign.

When it comes to the numbers of troops, we have two numbers given by Zosimus:

> He [Julian] therefore thought it prudent to leave in that country eighteen thousand men under the command of Sebastianus and Procopius, while he himself crossed the Euphrates with the main body of his forces in two divisions. He thus rendered them fully prepared to oppose the enemy wherever they should meet with them, and prevent the devastations which they committed wherever they came.
>
> *Zosimus, 3.12.5.*

In the following section he states that:

Having made these arrangements at Harran [Carrhae], a town that separates the Roman from the Assyrian dominions, he had an inclination to view the army from some eminence, the infantry and cavalry of which in the whole amounted to sixty-five thousand men.

Zosimus, 3.13.1.

Although historians have struggled to equate the figures given here with those given by Ammianus, there is a problem that has sometimes been overlooked: Ammianus actually contradicts Zosimus:

Startled by this cruel disaster, Julian (as he had previously planned) instantly put 30,000 picked men under the command of the aforesaid Procopius, and joined to him with equal powers Sebastianus, formerly a military commander in Egypt, and now a count, with orders to keep for the present on this side of the Tigris and to watch carefully everywhere and see that nothing unexpected should happen on the unprotected side, such as he had heard often occurred.

Ammianus, 23.3.5.

As Ammianus was an eye-witness and is therefore to be preferred, it is here assumed that Sebastianus and Procopius were given 30,000 men, not the 18,000 claimed by Zosimus. Consequently the question of numbers does not include the 18,000 men in Zosimus. The result is that, when Julian then reviewed the army as narrated by Zosimus, only two figures are possible: if the review was after the division, Julian had amassed 95,000 troops for the campaign and personally led 65,000 men in the invasion; if the review was before the division, Julian had amassed 65,000 men, then detached 30,000 and so led 35,000 in person.

Yet obviously, if the number of 18,000 men is considered doubtful, this throws doubt on the number of 65,000, also given by Zosimus. Sadly there is no other information in the sources, so the latter figure of 65,000 men is here accepted, although with reservations. It is also assumed, based on logistic factors and the information given by Ammianus, that the 65,000 was the total force and that, after the division of the army, Julian led 35,000 men on his invasion. The reasons for this will become clear below.

Allies

During the course of the invasion Julian was approached by a number of 'Saracens':

> At night he rested in a tent, where some princes of the Saracenic tribes came as suppliants, bringing him a golden crown, and adoring him as the master of the world and of their own nations: he received them graciously, as people well adapted for surprises in war.
>
> *Ammianus Marcellinus, 23.3.8.*

These 'Saracens', Arabic tribes from Rome's desert border, supplied Julian with a number of troops, but the number and composition of these forces is completely unreported.[3] It is possible that they supplied a variety of troops, but as they are later reported as capturing Sasanid skirmishers it is clear that at least some of them were used as skirmishers in front of the Roman army.[4]

The Opposing Forces: The Sasanids

As this campaign was only four years after the siege of Amida, the equipment and nature of the Sasanid forces would have been the same as those found in the previous chapter.

If there are difficulties concerning the number and nature of the Roman army at this point – even when it is covered by Roman sources and where one is an actual eye-witness – there is no evidence for the numbers employed by the Sasanids and we are rarely given an indication as to the proportions of troops available. In part this is due to the nature of the campaign, in which Julian faced different Sasanid armies at different places. Consequently, and where possible, these factors will be discussed at the relevant place within the narrative.

Julian's Persian Campaign

In the winter prior to the campaign, Julian ordered the army he had gathered for the invasion to disperse to winter quarters throughout the region. In addition he sent envoys to Arsaces, king of Armenia, ordering him to make his own preparations for a war with Persia.[5]

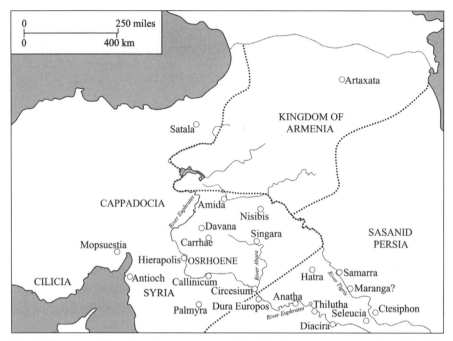

Julian's Campaign. Note that the exact course of the frontiers is uncertain and not all of the place names' locations given in the text are known.

These preparations did not go unnoticed: both Shapur in Persia and the neighbouring Saracen/Arabic tribes knew that an attack was imminent. Shapur sent envoys seeking peace, but these were rebuffed and 'many nations' sent embassies with offers of help. These were also rebuffed by Julian.[6]

On 5 March 363 Julian left Antioch, ordering his troops to leave their winter quarters and amass for the attack.[7] On 10 March he arrived at Hierapolis (Manbij), and waited there for three days while his troops and the ships assembled. Then he gave command of the ships to a man named Hierius and led the combined army east.[8] He first travelled to Batnae (Suruç), crossing the Euphrates on a pontoon bridge when the fleet with the equipment caught up.[9]

Leaving Batnae, Julian led the army to Carrhae (Harran). From Carrhae there were two roads he could use for the invasion: the northern route past Nisibis and down the River Tigris, or the southern route via Circesium and the River Euphrates. Zosimus claims that Julian was unsure of the route he would take, but as the large fleet he had assembled could not take the northern route this is doubtful; he almost certainly planned to take the southern route all along.[10] Therefore it is probably better to follow Ammianus, who claims that the march to Carrhae was with the hope that this would convince Shapur that he was taking the route past Nisibis and so aiming to march down the Tigris, a route for which supply dumps had also been ordered beforehand and that would allow him to join forces with the Armenian King Arsaces.[11]

At Carrhae he delayed for a short period, during which time it is claimed by Ammianus that he nominated Procopius as his successor in a secret meeting.[12] After this he was informed of Persian raiding and finally made the decision to move.[13] However, according to both Ammianus and Zosimus he didn't want to leave without protecting the region from further raids, and it was now that he detached either 30,000 (Ammianus) or 18,000 (Zosimus) men under Sebastianus and Procopius. These had a further set of orders that is sometimes overlooked: Ammianus notes that, once the frontier was secure, if possible they were to join Arsaces of Armenia and invade:

> Corduene and Moxoëne, lay waste in passing by Chiliocomum, a fruitful region of Media, and other places, and meet him [Julian] while he was still in Assyria, so as to aid him in cases of necessity.
>
> *Ammianus, 23.3.5.*

Before setting off Julian reviewed the army, given by Zosimus as being 65,000 men.[14] As this was at Carrhae and the division of troops was also at Carrhae, as already noted it is highly likely that the review also included the troops being detached under Sebastianus and Procopius (see above). It may be at this point that Julian's strategy becomes clear.

The Possible Invasion Strategy

The division of the army, with some left to defend the frontiers, is sometimes seen as the whole of Julian's strategy for the invasion, but this appears to be mistaken. As noted above, he had made contact with Arsaces of Armenia with the intent of having an army invade from the north. In this context, his advance to Carrhae and apparent movement to the north tied in with the proposed campaign from Armenia.

Consequently Julian may have hoped that Shapur would commit his forces to the expected attack from the north, leaving Julian to attack Ctesiphon and then swing north to take Shapur in the rear. This may have been his plan all along, but neither Ammianus nor the sources available to Zosimus were in a senior position where they would be admitted to the military councils and so be able to report them accurately.

The Army Divides

If these suppositions are accurate and the hope was that at some point the detached force under Sebastianus and Procopius would travel to Armenia and take part in an invasion from the north, Julian would have wanted to maintain morale across the whole force. Consequently, when he reviewed the army at Carrhae, it is likely that the 65,000 men attested by Zosimus as under review included the 30,000 being sent north.[15] Not to have addressed these men may have damaged their morale, possibly being seen as of less import than the body travelling with Julian.

Following the review, the army divided. Sebastianus and Procopius may have waited for a short period in case of further Persian incursions before heading along the northern route towards Nisibis. In the meantime, Julian effectively reversed direction and headed south, first reaching Davana at the source of the River Belias and then going on to Callinicum, where he was met by both the fleet and the 'Princes of Saracen nations'.[16] The fleet at this point comprised 1,000 cargo ships, with supplies and siege engines, 50 warships and 'bridge-making equipment', either the timber needed for construction and/or boats to be used for pontoons.[17] Finally the army reached Circesium, where a pontoon bridge was built to cross the River Abora before then being dismantled for further use.[18]

At this point another fleet carrying supplies arrived, proving the efficiency of the Roman logistical arm when well-led.[19] At this point Julian addressed the troops before giving each man 130 pieces of silver.

It was only then that the army crossed the frontier into Persia. Both Ammianus and Zosimus give a description of the order of march:

And being a general trained by experience and study of the art of war, and fearing lest, being unacquainted with the terrain, he might be entrapped by hidden ambuscades, he began his march with his army in order of battle. He also arranged to have 1,500 mounted scouts riding a little ahead of the army, who advancing with caution on both flanks, as well as in front, kept watch that no sudden attack be made. He himself in the centre led the infantry, which formed the main strength of his entire force, and ordered Nevitta on the right with several legions to skirt the banks of the Euphrates. The left wing with the cavalry he put in charge of Arintheus and Ormisda, to be led in close order through the level fields and meadows. Dagalaifus and Victor brought up the rear, and last of all was Secundinus, military leader in Osdruena.

Ammianus Marcellinus, 24.1.2.

Zosimus states that command of the cavalry was given to Hormisdas, a member of the Sasanid dynasty who had fled to safety under threat from his brother during the reign of Constantine I, and a man named Arintheus. The infantry was placed under a man named Victor and a man named Lucilianus was put in command of the 1,500 scouts sent ahead of the army:[20]

The emperor, on entering Persia, placed the cavalry on the right, and proceeded along the bank of the river, the rear guard marching at the distance of seventy stadia. Between these and the main body were placed the beasts of burden, which carried the heavy armour and provisions, the attendants, that they might be secure, being enclosed on every side by the army. Having thus arranged the order of his march, he thought proper to send before him fifteen hundred men, in order to reconnoitre and observe whether any enemy approached either openly or in ambuscade. Of these he made Lucilianus captain.

Zosimus, 3.14.1.

Interestingly, Ammianus records that Julian ordered the troops into extended order in the belief that this would make the Persians think he had more troops than he really had. Ammianus adds that the column then stretched for 10 miles, suggesting that the high numbers sometimes given by the sources and historians are in error.[21]

Having prepared his men, Julian finally crossed the frontier. The army passed Zaitha/Lautha and then Dura-Europos, which had been taken and destroyed by the Sasanids in 256–7, with the journey taking two days.[22] Then, after a march of four or seven days, the army arrived at Anatha/Phathusae, a fortified island in the Euphrates.[23]

Fortified islands along the Euphrates were one of the defence-in-depth methods used on the Eastern frontier. Covering the routes along the river, these could either slow down attacks if the invader decided to assault them or threaten the rear of an invader should they be left undefeated. This fortress would only be the first of a series passed by the invading army.

At this early stage Julian appears to have decided to attempt to take these fortresses as his army advanced. Consequently, Julian ordered Lucilianus and 1,000 of the advanced scouts to go aboard some of the ships in the hope of a speedy attack taking the fortress by surprise. The surprise attack failed but, fortunately for Julian, Hormisdas managed to convince the defenders to surrender. They were sent back to Chalcis under guard.[24]

At this point there was a hurricane that destroyed some of the ships but, undeterred, Julian continued the advance.[25] Reaching another island fortress named Thilutha, he attacked but was repulsed. However, the defenders agreed not to attack his forces if they were left alone and a similar arrangement was made with the next island fortress of Achaiachala, but the following fortress was abandoned and so the Romans simply set fire to it.[26]

Two days later the Roman army reached Baraxmalcha, averaging around 21 miles per day on the march. On the next day they reached Dacira/ Diacira. The town was abandoned, but among the booty left behind was a large quantity of corn.[27] The town was then fired and the march resumed, reaching the likewise abandoned town of Ozogardana.[28]

According to Zosimus, after Dacira the army passed the towns of Sitha, Megia and Zaragardia, the latter of which was burned.[29] It is probable that Ammianus' Ozogardana and Zosimus' Zaragardia were the same town, as after burning the town the army is attested by both authors as resting for two days.[30]

At this point Julian became wary, since they had not yet faced any opposition from the Sasanid army. As Ammianus and Zosimus are more concerned with Julian's actions the specifics concerning Shapur's response are unclear, but it would seem that Julian's diversionary strategy had worked: Shapur may have taken the main Sasanid army north to face an expected attack from the direction of Armenia.

Hoping to discover any enemy force, Julian dispatched Hormisdas at the head of a scouting party to reconnoitre the region. The descriptions given by Ammianus and Zosimus differ, but combining them gives a coherent account of what happened: the Surena attempted to ambush Hormisdas. Ammianus states:

> But their [Sasanid] attempt failed, because the river at that point is narrow and very deep, and hence could not be forded. At daybreak the enemy were already in sight, and we then saw them for the first time in their gleaming helmets and bristling with stiff coats of mail; but our soldiers rushed to battle at quick step, and fell upon them most valiantly. And although the bows were bent with strong hand and the flashing gleam of steel added to the fear of the Romans, yet anger whetted their valour, and covered with a close array of shields they pressed the enemy so hard that they could not use their bows.
>
> *Ammianus Marcellinus, 24.2.4–5.*

> In this expedition Hormisdas and his soldiers were all near perishing, had they not been unexpectedly preserved by a fortunate accident. A person called Surena, which is a title of distinction among the Persians, had planted an ambuscade in a particular place, expecting Hormisdas and his troop to pass that way, and intending to surprise them as they passed. This hope would have been successful, had not the Euphrates burst its banks, and running between the enemy and Hormisdas, obstructed the march of his men. Being compelled by this cause to defer the journey, the following day they discovered the ambuscade of Surena and his troops, with whom they engaged. Having killed many, and put to flight others, they admitted the remainder of them into their own army.
>
> *Zosimus, 3.15.5–6.*

It would appear that the ambush was placed, but the burst banks altered the direction of Hormisdas' march. By approaching from an unexpected direction, the Sasanids' ambush was detected. Hormisdas then proved himself a capable commander, ordering his troops to close quickly and engage the enemy hand-to-hand, so minimizing losses from missile fire and causing the Sasanids to break and run.

The enemy force appears to have comprised *cataphracts* and horse archers – unless Ammianus is resorting to a *topos* (a traditional description) in his portrayal – and these would be vulnerable if quickly attacked at close quarters. However, the claim by Zosimus that after the skirmish some of the Sasanid troops joined the attacking army can only mean that a few men decided to join with Hormisdas rather than being taken prisoner.

The Roman army then advanced as far as the village of Macepracta, where the river appears to have branched and from where many canals had been cut to irrigate 'Babylon', meaning that a large part of the area was 'marshy'.[31]

The infantry crossed on bridges, but the cavalry and baggage animals attempted to wade through some shallows. However, here they were attacked by enemy archers and slingers; many were killed and others swept away.[32] Lucilianus and the lightly-armed scouts had gone ahead and, according to Zosimus, Victor was sent with a further detachment to find Lucilianus and, with their combined force, cross the river and attack the Sasanid defenders from behind, at which point the Sasanid force was defeated and fled.[33]

Crossing the river, the Romans then reached Pirisabora/Bersabora, a heavily defended city with two walls and a main citadel.[34] The city was too large to be left to the army's rear, so Julian was forced to begin a major siege operation:

> The emperor, after riding up and inspecting the walls and the situation, began the siege with all caution, as if he wished by mere terror to take from the townsmen the desire for defence. But after they had been tried by many conferences, and not one could be moved either by promises or by threats, the siege was begun.... Then the defenders, who were strong and full of courage, spread over the ramparts everywhere loose strips of haircloth to check the force of the missiles, and themselves protected by shields firmly woven of osier and covered with thick layers of rawhide, resisted most resolutely... in the first stillness of night many kinds of siege-engines were brought to bear and the deep trenches began to be filled up. When the defenders, who were watching intently, made this out by the still uncertain light, and besides, that a mighty blow of the ram had breached a corner tower, they abandoned the double walls of the city

and took possession of the citadel connected with them, which stood on a precipitous plateau at the top of a rough mountain.… And now the soldiers with greater confidence rushed through the city, seeing it deserted, and fought fiercely with the inhabitants, who from the citadel showered upon them missiles of many kinds. For although those same defenders were hard pressed by our catapults and ballistae, they in turn set up on the height strongly stretched bows, whose wide curves extending on both sides were bent so pliably that when the strings were let go by the fingers, the iron-tipped arrows which they sent forth in violent thrusts crashed into the bodies exposed to them and transfixed them with deadly effect…on the following day, they continued the battle most fiercely, many fell on both sides, and their equal strength held the victory in balance.… Julian gave orders that the engine called Helepolis should quickly be built.… To this huge mass, which would rise above the battlements of the lofty towers, the defenders turned an attentive eye, and at the same time considering the resolution of the besiegers, they suddenly fell to their prayers, and standing on the towers and battlements, and with outstretched hands imploring the protection of the Romans, they craved pardon and life.… Mamersides, commander of the garrison, was let down on a rope and taken to the emperor, he obtained (as he besought) a sure promise of life and impunity for himself and his followers.… Then the gates were thrown open and they came out, shouting that a potent protecting angel had appeared to them in the person of a Caesar great and merciful. The prisoners numbered only 2,500; for the rest of the population, in anticipation of a siege, had crossed the river in small boats and made off. In this citadel there was found a great abundance of arms and provisions; of these the victors took what they needed and burned the rest along with the place itself.

Ammianus Marcellinus, 24.2.9–22.

Following the fall of the city, Ammianus describes another clash with the Surena, although it should be noted that Zosimus claims that the skirmish took place during the siege.[35] Whichever is true – and as noted earlier, Ammianus is preferred here – the Surena had obviously been observing events from a distance, presumably because he did not have the troops available for a definitive battle. The Persian force had ambushed a Roman scouting party of three units, routing them and capturing a standard. Julian counterattacked, defeating the Persians and retaking the standard. Julian also punished the troops who had retreated, deserting their standard to the enemy.[36]

Following his victory in taking both the city and defeating the Surena, Julian led the army on, bypassing Phissenia and reaching an area flooded by the Sasanids.[37] Here the engineers constructed bridges and filled the deeper areas with earth, allowing the army through to reach the town of Bithra.[38]

Here palm trees were common and due to the abundance of food the army was well-fed.[39] Leaving the area, Ammianus notes that there was an attack by enemy archers, certainly horse archers, that was beaten back, after which the army paused to set fire to another deserted town before reaching the city/castle of Maiozamalcha, perhaps named by Zosimus simply as a castle near to 'a populous city called Besuchis'.[40] Making a careful camp, Julian set off to scout the city. Here a party of ten men came out of the city and attempted to kill Julian while he was practically undefended. Fortunately for Julian, the attack was defeated and he escaped unscathed.[41]

Having scouted the city, Julian moved his camp to a safer position in preparation for a siege.[42] The baggage animals were placed in a nearby palm grove, no doubt with the hope of them grazing in the area and so needing less fodder. Seeing this, the Surena launched an attack, aiming to kill the baggage animals and so hinder the invasion. Julian, however, seems to have placed an adequate guard in place as the attackers were driven off.[43]

Julian then began the siege in earnest, with the infantry conducting the siege and a mixed force of cavalry and infantry under Victor scouting and foraging in the nearby region.[44] The siege in many respects followed the progress of the earlier one so will not be recounted here, except to note that a mine was dug and a ramp raised under the command of Nevitta and Dagalaifus, while Victor was sent to scout the road to Ctesiphon, returning with no sign of the enemy.[45] After a siege of two days, the walls were stormed and the city taken. In addition, Julian was informed of an enemy force lurking in caves near the city and ready to take the Romans by surprise: these were smoked out and destroyed.[46]

Ammianus now narrates a march over several bridges to 'two fortresses built with special care', but Zosimus continues his narrative with an advance past several cities until the army arrived at one named Mainas Sabatha that was stormed by a section of the army.[47]

Marching on, Zosimus names the next city-fortress as Arintheus, and it is here that he has the Roman army first encountering serious opposition from the Sasanids.[48] Although Ammianus does not name the place, their accounts are similar in that a son of Shapur and some other nobles attempted to halt the Roman advance at a river crossing, but when he saw the size of the main body of the Roman army when it came into view, he retreated.[49]

Shortly after, the Romans reached a fertile region used by the Sasanid shahs for hunting and butchered the captive animals.[50] Moving on, they entered the region of Seleucia, erecting a camp and resting for two days.[51]

After breaking camp, the army had only advanced a short distance when

> While three *cohorts* of light-armed skirmishers were fighting with a band of Persians which had burst forth from the suddenly opened gates of a town, others who had sallied forth from the opposite side of the river cut off and butchered the pack-animals that followed us, along with a few foragers who were carelessly roaming about.[52]
>
> *Ammianus Marcellinus, 24.5.5.*

Angered by the defeat but at last coming near Ctesiphon, the army neared another fortress and Julian again went ahead to observe the nature of the defences. As before, he came under missile fire and, enraged, he ordered the siege and destruction of the fortress.[53] Yet this time there was a major difference: the defenders believed that Shapur was approaching with the main Sasanid army and Julian feared this to be true.[54]

Before the siege engines were ready, at night the defenders repeated their previous attack, with a sally from the gates practically destroying a Roman unit, while others crossed the river and attacked the Romans from the rear.[55] Wary that the attack across the river was made by reinforcements arriving from the main Persian body, Julian redoubled the attack before Shapur could intervene. Finally the defenders were overcome and the fortress taken, after which the army was allowed a short rest.[56]

Marching on, the army arrived at the Naarmalcha ('King's Canal'), the canal allegedly dug by Trajan to join the Euphrates and Tigris but which had been blocked by the Persians. In order to allow his fleet to cross rivers, Julian caused the dams and debris to be cleared, with the force of the water entering the newly-cleared canal finishing the task.[57] The fleet was then transferred from the Euphrates to the Tigris, while the army built bridges to cross the rivers and reach the same place, given by Ammianus as Coche.[58] After the effort of dam-clearing and bridge-building, Julian again allowed the army to rest for a time.[59]

Resuming the advance, the army came to the banks of a river – possibly the Tigris but Zosimus claims that the crossing of the Tigris was later – only to find the opposing banks, which here were steep and difficult to climb, manned by Sasanid troops determined to repel the crossing. The accounts given by Ammianus and Zosimus are so close that only one needs to be given:[60]

[Julian] unloaded the stronger ships of those which carried provisions and artillery, and manned them each with eight hundred armed soldiers; then keeping by him the stronger part of the fleet, which he had formed into three divisions, in the first quiet of night he sent one part under Count Victor with orders speedily to cross the river and take possession of the enemy's side of the stream. His generals in great alarm with unanimous entreaties tried to prevent him from taking this step, but could not shake the emperor's determination. The flag was raised according to his orders, and five ships immediately vanished from sight. But no sooner had they reached the opposite bank than they were assailed so persistently with firebrands and every kind of inflammable material, that ships and soldiers would have been consumed, had not the emperor, carried away by the keen vigour of his spirit, cried out that our soldiers had, as directed, raised the signal that they were already in possession of the shore, and ordered the entire fleet to hasten to the spot with all the speed of their oars. The result was that the ships were saved uninjured, and the surviving soldiers, although assailed from above with stones and every kind of missiles, after a fierce struggle scaled the high, precipitous banks and held their positions unyieldingly.

Ammianus Marcellinus, 24.6.4–7.

With the bridgehead secure the rest of the army was able to cross the river, only to find themselves facing a large Persian army. Julian was to fight a battle in front of the walls of Ctesiphon.

The Battle of Ctesiphon

Although the crossing had been forced, the Roman army then found itself facing a Sasanid force determined to protect Ctesiphon from attack. Again, the accounts of Ammianus and Zosimus are close, but only Ammianus gives specific detail:[61]

> The Persians opposed to us serried bands of mail-clad horsemen in such close order that the gleam of moving bodies covered with densely fitting plates of iron dazzled the eyes of those who looked upon them, while the whole throng of horse was protected by coverings of leather. The cavalry was backed up by companies of infantry, who, protected by oblong, curved shields covered with wickerwork and raw hides, advanced in very close order. Behind these were elephants, looking like walking hills, and, by the movements of their enormous bodies, they threatened destruction to all who came near them, dreaded as they were from past experience.
>
> Hereupon the emperor, following Homeric tactics, filled the space between the lines with the weakest of the infantry, fearing that if they formed part of the van and shamefully gave way, they might carry off all the rest with them; or if they were posted in the rear behind all the centuries, they might run off at will with no one to check them. He himself with the light-armed auxiliaries hastened now to the front, and now to the rear.
>
> So, when both sides were near enough to look each other in the face, the Romans, gleaming in their crested helmets and swinging their shields as if to the rhythm of the anapaestic foot, advanced slowly; and the light-armed skirmishers opened the battle by hurling their javelins, while the earth everywhere was turned to dust by both sides and swept away in a swift whirlwind. And when the battle-cry was raised in the usual manner by both sides and the trumpets' blare increased the ardour of the men, here and there they fought hand-to-hand with spears and drawn swords; and the soldiers were

freer from the danger of the arrows the more quickly they forced their way into the enemy's ranks. Meanwhile Julian was busily engaged in giving support to those who gave way and in spurring on the laggards, playing the part both of a valiant fellow-soldier and of a commander. Finally, the first battle-line of the Persians began to waver, and at first slowly, then at quick step, turned back and made for the neighbouring city with their armour well heated up. Our soldiers pursued them, wearied though they also were after fighting on the scorching plains from sunrise to the end of the day, and following close at their heels and hacking at their legs and backs, drove the whole force with Pigranes, the Surena, and Narseus, their most distinguished generals, in headlong flight to the very walls of Ctesiphon. And they would have pressed in through the gates of the city, mingled with the throng of fugitives, had not the general called Victor, who had himself received a flesh-wound in the shoulder from an arrow, raising his hand and shouting, restrained them; for he feared that the excited soldiers, if they rashly entered the circuit of the walls and could find no way out, might be overcome by weight of numbers.

Ammianus Marcellinus, 24.6.8–13.

Sadly for modern readers, the battle as described by Ammianus lacks clarity in some of the detail. It seems clear that the main troops facing the Romans were the *cataphracts*, the 'levy' infantry, and the elephants, but this would appear to be Ammianus depicting the battle for his contemporaries rather than for posterity. Doubtless there were skirmishers, both mounted and on foot, plus auxiliary forces recruited to defend Ctesiphon in the absence of the main Sasanid army. These are nowhere depicted and so their actions remain lost in obscurity.

The aim of the Sasanid commander appears to have been to use the *cataphracts* to break through the Roman lines, causing confusion and an ensuing rout. Doubtless these were supported by horse archers, aiming to cause casualties at the point of impact before the *cataphracts* contacted the Romans. The levy and elephants appear to have formed a second and third line respectively. In theory, the levy would give the *cataphracts* and horse archers cover behind which to reform should they be repulsed, and the elephants could be used either as a third wave to complete the victory or as a reserve should they be needed.

As for the Romans, the claim that Julian 'filled the space between the lines with the weakest of the infantry' is vague. It could mean that they were deployed alternatively with the 'stronger' units in the lines or that they formed the second of three lines (the *triplex acies*). Given that Julian had deployed his army in three lines in the victory over the Alamanni at the Battle of Argentoratum (Strasbourg, 357 CE) six years earlier, it is likely that this was again his deployment and merely reflected his standard strategy rather than a failing in part of the army.

The course of the battle appears to have been determined by Julian. During the battle he moved from one area to another, encouraging the attackers and deploying the reserves where needed, but his actions may not have been wholly necessary: the Roman line advanced quickly in order to avoid heavy casualties from the horse archers and other skirmishers ('the soldiers were freer from the danger of the arrows the more quickly they forced their way into the enemy's ranks'), and contacted the *cataphracts* before they could deliver a devastating charge. Stationary cavalry caught by infantry were always vulnerable due to being outnumbered in a small area and having a lack of manoeuvrability when not charging, and these appear to have slowly given way before routing towards Ctesiphon 'with their armour well heated up'.

The Romans pursued the *cataphracts* (and possibly the horse archers and other skirmishers), resulting in the levy infantry and elephants also fleeing as the *cataphracts* attempted to pass them. The pursuers actually reached the walls of Ctesiphon, but here Victor halted them for fear that, entering the city and being vastly outnumbered, they would be slaughtered. So ended the battle.

Analysis

The Battle of Ctesiphon was a major victory for the Roman army, although sometimes it is not counted as such since the end of the campaign was to be a disaster. It is clear from the description that the Sasanid army was composed of cavalry (described as *cataphracts*, but doubtless including many horse archers and other skirmishers), infantry (described as 'protected by oblong, curved shields covered with wickerwork and raw hides...in very close order', so the troops usually seen as a 'levy' (poor quality infantry)) and the (almost) obligatory elephants.

Yet there is no mention of Shapur being present, so this was a regional force tasked with defending Ctesiphon while Shapur was absent. Consequently, although the Romans inflicted heavy casualties for very few themselves – Ammianus claims 2,500 enemy for only 70 Roman casualties, Zosimus 2,500 for 75[62] – the fact that this was not the main Sasanid imperial army implies that it was a force of secondary status with little chance of defeating Julian's experienced army.

Julian Changes Strategy

Zosimus now notes that the army crossed the Tigris to a more fertile region, arriving at Abuzatha and halting for five days.[63] Such a long rest would be advisable given the strain of the days before.

It was at this point that a fateful decision was made. As this determined the ensuing events, it is printed here:

Having held council with his most distinguished generals about the siege of Ctesiphon, the opinion of some was adopted, who felt sure that the undertaking was rash and untimely, since the city, impregnable by its situation alone, was well defended; and, besides, it was believed that the king would soon appear with a formidable force. So the better opinion prevailed, and the most careful of emperors, recognizing its advantage, sent Arintheus with a band of light-armed infantry, to lay waste the surrounding country, which was rich in herds and crops; Arintheus was also bidden, with equal energy to pursue the enemy, who had been lately scattered and concealed by impenetrable by-paths and their familiar hiding-places. But Julian, ever driven on by his eager ambitions, made light of words of warning, and upbraiding his generals for urging him through cowardice and love of ease to loose his hold on the Persian kingdom, which he had already all but won; with the river on his left and with ill-omened guides leading the way, resolved to march rapidly into the interior. And it seemed as if Bellona herself lighted the fire with fatal torch, when he gave orders that all the ships should be burned, with the exception of twelve of the smaller ones, which he decided to transport on wagons as helpful for making bridges. And he thought that this plan had the advantage that the fleet, if abandoned, could not be used by the enemy, or at any rate, that nearly 20,000 soldiers would not be employed in transporting and guiding the ships, as had been the case since the beginning of the campaign.

Ammianus Marcellinus, 24.7.1–4.

Although Julian quickly repented of his decision and attempted to save the ships, he was too late: all but the twelve smaller ships were lost.[64] Realizing that advancing further into Persia was futile, after deliberation Julian decided to march northwards towards Corduene.

The Sasanid commanders were quickly apprised of the burning, and in recognition of Julian's obvious intention to turn away from the river, set fire to the fields across which the Roman army needed to advance, pinning them in their camp until the fires had burned out. In addition, once the Roman army began to move they were harassed by the horse archers, but sometimes with close-order troops – particularly *cataphracts* – to give the impression that Shapur had finally arrived.[65]

Ammianus gives no details, but Zosimus states that the Romans advanced to a place called Noorda where they defeated a Sasanid attack, before carrying on to the River Durus and crossing it after building a bridge.[66]

On 16 June 363 the army again broke camp and headed north.[67] Before it could go far a large cloud of dust appeared on the horizon. Unsure whether this was Shapur or the Armenian King Arsaces and the detachment sent under Sebastianus and Procopius, the army was gathered and camped in a valley near a stream.[68] On the following morning it became clear that this was a Sasanid army. The troops wanted to fight, but although Julian refused to give permission, a small-scale battle did happen as the Roman light troops fought their Sasanid counterparts in the area between the two armies.[69] Finally the Sasanid troops were routed and the Roman army was able to move on.

Reaching the town of Barroptha,[70] some Persian scouts retreated before the Roman army, but then gathered together and attacked the Roman baggage. Julian himself took command of the troops and led them against the attack, driving off the Sasanid forces and allowing the army to continue to the town of Hucumbra/Symbra.[71] Here the advanced scouts drove off some Persian forces, and the main army took the town. Finding abundant supplies there, the Romans rested for two days to regain their strength.[72]

Resuming the march, at a place between the towns of Danabe and Synca the Sasanids attacked the rearguard and inflicted heavy casualties, but received more themselves and were driven off: at this point Daces/Adaces, a Persian satrap, fell.[73]

The Battle of Maranga

From here the Romans marched for 70 *stadia* (c.13 km/8 miles), via the town of Acceta,[74] to Maranga/Maronsa.[75] According to Zosimus, the Persians then attacked the rearguard, but Ammianus gives details of a set-piece battle.[76] As Ammianus is an eye-witness, his account is preferred here:

Near daybreak a huge force of Persians appeared with Merena, general of their cavalry, two sons of the king, and many other magnates. Moreover, all the companies were clad in iron, and all parts of their bodies were covered with thick plates, so fitted that the stiff joints conformed with those of their limbs; and the forms of human faces were so skilfully fitted to their heads, that, since their entire bodies were plated with metal, arrows that fell upon them could lodge only where they could see a little through tiny openings fitted to the circle of the eye, or where through the tips of their noses they were able to get a little breath. Of these some, who were armed with pikes, stood so motionless that you would think them held fast by clamps of bronze. Hard by, the archers (for that nation has especially trusted in this art from the very cradle) were bending their flexible bows with such wide-stretched arms that the strings touched their right breasts, while the arrow-points were close to their left hands; and by a highly skilful stroke of the fingers the arrows flew hissing forth and brought with them deadly wounds. Behind them the gleaming elephants, with their awful figures and savage, gaping mouths could scarcely be endured by the faint-hearted; and their trumpeting, their odour, and their strange aspect alarmed the horses still more…. Although these sights caused no little fear, the emperor, guarded by troops of armed men and with his trustworthy generals, full of confidence, as the great and dangerous power of the enemy demanded, drew up his soldiers in the form of a crescent with curving wings to meet the enemy. And in order that the onset of the bowmen might not throw our ranks into confusion, he advanced at a swift pace, and so ruined the effectiveness of the arrows. Then the usual signal for battle was given, and the Roman infantry in close order with mighty effort drove the serried ranks of the enemy before them. And in the heat of the combat that followed, the clash of shields, the shouts of the men, and the doleful sound of the whirring arrows continued without intermission. The plains were covered with blood and dead bodies, but the Persian losses were greater; for they often lacked endurance in battle and could with difficulty maintain a close contest man to man, since they were accustomed to fight bravely at long range, but if they perceived that their forces were giving way, as they retreated they would shoot their arrows back like a shower of rain and keep the enemy from a bold pursuit. So by the weight of great strength the Parthians were driven back, and when the signal for retreat was given in the usual manner, our soldiers, long wearied by the fiery course of the sun, returned to their tents, encouraged to dare greater deeds of valour in the future. In this battle (as was said) the loss of the Persians was clearly the greater, while that of our men was very slight. But noteworthy among the various calamities of the combats was the death of Vetranio, a valiant fighter, who commanded the legion of the Zianni.

Ammianus Marcellinus, 25.1.11–19.

After this victory, the Sasanids agreed to a three-day truce. Although in part they needed time to regain their strength as much as the Romans, they had onc major advantage: they were being supplied, whereas the Romans continued to use their meagre store of food and were continually hungry.[77]

Breaking camp once again, the Romans continued the retreat, past Tummara (where Zosimus claims that they burned the last of their ships) and fought another skirmish with the Sasanid army.[78]

The Battle of Samarra

At around noon of the following day, the Sasanids again gathered their forces and attacked the Roman rearguard. Julian at this point was in the van, 4 miles ahead of the rearguard,[79] and his actions when the news arrived were to be the defining moment of his reign:[80]

And while the flanks were strongly protected and the army, as the nature of the ground made necessary, advanced in square formation, but with the battalions in open order, it was reported to the emperor, who even then unarmed had gone forward to reconnoitre, that the rear guard had suddenly been attacked from behind. Excited by the misfortune, he forgot his coat-of-mail, and merely caught up a shield in the confusion; but as he was hastening to bring aid to those in the rear, he was recalled by another danger – the news that the van, which he had just left, was just as badly off. While he was hastening to restore order there without regard to his own peril, a Parthian band of mailed cavalry on another side attacked the centre companies, and quickly overflowed the left wing, which gave way, since our men could hardly endure the smell and trumpeting of the elephants, they were trying to end the battle with pikes and volleys of arrows. But while the emperor rushed hither and thither amid the foremost ranks of the combatants, and as the Persians turned in flight, they hacked at their legs and backs, and those of the elephants. Julian, careless of his own safety, shouting and raising his hands tried to make it clear to his men that the enemy had fled in disorder, and, to rouse them to a still more furious pursuit, rushed boldly into the fight. His guards, who had scattered in their alarm, were crying to him from all sides to get clear of the mass of fugitives, as dangerous as the fall of a badly built roof, when suddenly – no one knows whence – a cavalryman's spear grazed the skin of his arm, pierced his ribs, and lodged in the lower lobe of his liver. While he was trying to pluck this out with his right hand, he felt that the sinews of his fingers were cut through on both sides by the sharp steel. Then he fell from his horse, all present hastened to the spot, he was taken to camp and given medical treatment.

Ammianus Marcellinus, 25.3.2–7.

Although the death of Julian is usually represented as being in a 'minor skirmish', or an 'insignificant skirmish', the account given by Ammianus suggests that it was in fact a major coordinated assault by the Sasanid forces on the front, rear and left flank of the Roman marching columns.

The fighting was only halted by nightfall. Opinion differs as to who 'won' the battle, with Ammianus simply stating that losses were heavy on both sides, whereas Zosimus implies a Roman victory.[81] Although the information given can be used to some extent to support both arguments, it is probably safer to say that neither side was defeated tactically, but that the Sasanids gained a strategic victory: the battle resulted in a delay in the retreat as the officers decided upon a new emperor while the army continued to use their dwindling supplies of food. The new emperor would not have the strength of will and determination possessed by Julian.

Aftermath

On the day after Julian's death (27 June) the army commanders attempted to choose a new emperor, but the troops elected a man named Jovian.[82] When the appointment was announced to the troops, the standard-bearer of the Joviani – a personal enemy of Jovian – deserted to the Sasanids and told Shapur what had happened. Shapur quickly resumed the assaults upon the marching Romans.

On 1 July the Roman army, continuing the attempt to march out of Sasanid territory, arrived at Dura, after which they were attacked by 'Saracens' (Arab tribesmen) annoyed that Julian had refused to pay them subsidies. Shortly after, the Romans were pinned in place for four days by the Sasanid army. Reaching the Tigris, the troops demanded to be allowed to cross the river and reach Corduene and safety. At first permission was refused as the river was in flood, but finally detachments of Gauls and Germans made the attempt. They succeeded and defeated the Sasanids positioned on the far bank, but the floods stopped the rest of the army from following. Pinned against the river for two days and with starvation setting in, the Romans were surprised when Shapur then sent envoys. The ensuing discussions lasted for four days, during which time, Ammianus laments, they were only 100 miles from Corduene and safety, and could have reached there with regular marches.

The terms demanded by Shapur were harsh, intending to at least restore the territory lost to Rome in the treaty signed in 299 CE during the reign of Diocletian (see Chapter 10). Shapur demanded Arzanene, Moxoëne, Zabdicene, Rehimene (unknown) and Corduene, plus Singara, Castra Maurorum and Nisibis.[83] Jovian had little option but to agree as he needed the army to confirm his elevation. However, he managed to insert a condition that the populations of Nisibis and Singara, plus the troops in the Roman fortresses, should be allowed to remove to Roman territory. Of equal importance, Jovian had to agree not to support Arsaces of Armenia if attacked by Sasanid Persia. Possibly during Julian's invasion, Arsaces had devastated Chiliocomum and Shapur wanted revenge.

Although the treaty was agreed, many men still died during the march out of Persian territory. Once safe, Jovian had to take steps to minimize the damage caused by the treaty, which delayed his travel to Constantinople for his confirmation. That event was never to happen as Jovian died en route at Dadastana after a reign of only eight months. He was succeeded by a man named Valentinian, who appointed his brother Valens as co-*Augustus* with command over the East.

Effects

It is difficult to underestimate the importance of Julian's failed invasion. Internally Julian was the last pagan emperor and had attempted to reverse the growth of Christianity by subsidizing and reorganizing the pagan hierarchy. It is unlikely that his attempts, and those of a possible pagan successor had Julian survived and been able to nominate such an individual, would have been enough to reverse the eclipse of paganism, but a long-term attempt, plus a completely different sequence of Roman emperors, would have completely changed the course of later events.

Externally the defeat and the ensuing humiliating treaty resulted in the emperor Valens, who succeeded to the (Eastern) throne in 364, being focused on reversing the treaty and regaining Roman prestige. In part due to his desire for new sources of troops, he allowed the Tervingi to cross into the Empire in 376. The net result was the revolt of the Tervingi and the defeat and death of Valens at the Battle of Adrianople in 378. Although the impact of that battle was minor for the East, after a complicated series of events the descendants of some of the Tervingi went on to sack Rome in 410 and create a kingdom following their settlement in Gaul in 418–19.

Possibly more than any other defeat in Roman history to this point, the defeat and death of Julian had a complicated, long-lasting and devastating effect on the future history of Rome. As a consequence, this analysis is the longest and most complicated in this series of battles.

Select Bibliography

Ammianus Marcellinus: https://www.tertullian.org/fathers/index.htm#Ammianus_
    Marcellinus
Zosimus, 3.12.1–2: https://www.tertullian.org/fathers/zosimus03_book3.htm

Chapter Twelve

Civil Wars: The Battle of the (River) Frigidus, 5–6 September 394

Sources

There are six major sources for the Battle of the River Frigidus. The variety of the sources means that they need to be cross-referenced whenever possible to assure the greatest accuracy. Below is a list of these authors, starting with the earliest.

Paulus Orosius (c.375–c.420 CE) wrote the *Historiarum Adversum Paganos Libri VII* (*Seven Books of History Against the Pagans*) at the request of (Saint) Augustine of Hippo. The book's aim is to compare the pagan past with the Christian present, in effect claiming that, despite the sack of Rome in 410, the condition of humanity had improved thanks to the Empire's conversion to Christianity. His work is usually praised for its attempt to be unbiased and to present the past in a factual manner. However, as it had a specific aim, it is undoubtedly biased and this should be remembered at all times.

Philostorgius (368–c.439 CE) wrote the *Historia Ecclesiastica* (*Church History*), a history of the Arian controversy between 425 and 433. The work survives only as an epitome written in the ninth century, but excerpts also appear in the works of other writers. Due to the nature of the surviving work, its accuracy must remain questionable so the work needs to be used with caution.

Socrates Scholasticus (c.380–after 439 CE) wrote the *Historia Ecclesiastica* (*Church History*), a work covering the years 305 to 439, during the lifetime of Emperor Theodosius II, grandson of Theodosius I. The aim of the book was to continue the work of Eusebius of Caesarea. Socrates is one of the better historians covering the period, as although a Christian he writes calmly and clearly of the events between the rise of Constantine I and his own lifetime/time of writing.

Sozomen (c.400–c.450 CE) wrote a history of the Church in two volumes, but sadly the first volume has been lost. The second volume, dedicated to Emperor Theodosius II, is based largely on the scheme laid out by Socrates Scholasticus, but including information from other sources not found in Socrates' work. His work is accepted as being generally accurate as far as events are concerned, but as usual it is biased due to its being written from a Christian viewpoint.

Zosimus (fl. late fifth to early sixth century CE) was an Eastern Roman writing in Constantinople, who composed the *Historia Nova* (*New History*). Unlike the other writers, Zosimus was a pagan who blames Christianity for the decline of Rome. In theory his work can be used as a counter-balance to the Christian authors, but sadly his writing is strewn with inaccuracies and so must be used with extreme caution.

Jordanes (fl. sixth century CE) was an Eastern Roman, probably of Gothic descent, who wrote two important works. One was *De summa temporum vel origine actibusque gentis Romanorum* (*The High Point of Time, or the Origin and Deeds of the Roman People*), usually shortened to *Romana* (*On Rome*), an epitome of events from creation to the victory of the general Narses over King Teia of the Goths (552 CE). The second was *De Origine Actibusque Getarum* (*On the Origins and Deeds of the Goths*, usually abbreviated to *Getica*). Both were written in the mid-sixth century. Although the latter is an important work, its accuracy is debatable with many events and descriptions almost certainly being apocryphal. Due to this, it must always be used with extreme caution.

Background

Following the disastrous Battle of Adrianople in 378 in which the Eastern Empire had lost a large number of men, the Western Emperor Gratian had appointed a man named Theodosius as the new Emperor of the East. However, in 383 a man named Magnus Maximus rebelled in Britain. The Emperor Gratian was deserted by his troops, captured and executed (23 August 383). The Western half of the Empire was then divided, with Maximus securing control of Britain, Spain and Gaul while the child Emperor Valentinian II, the legitimate successor to Gratian, ruled the remainder of the West.

Although in 382 Theodosius had brought the Gothic War (378–382) to an end, in the East tensions remained high with Sasanid Persia. Taking advantage of Theodosius' poor political position, Maximus sent envoys to Theodosius demanding either 'peace and alliance or civil war'.[1] Despite his problems in the East, in 384 Theodosius led a minor expedition to the West to demonstrate his support for Valentinian, a move that appears to have intimidated Maximus, who backed down and made no move against Valentinian.

Finally, in 387, Theodosius concluded a decisive peace with Persia, freeing troops stationed on the Eastern front for service elsewhere. Aware that Theodosius might then act against him, Maximus decided on a pre-emptive attack and later in 387 he invaded Italy. Valentinian fled to Thessalonica in the East and asked Theodosius for help.

Unable to respond in 387 as by the time Valentinian reached Thessalonica the campaign season was over, when the campaign season of 388 opened

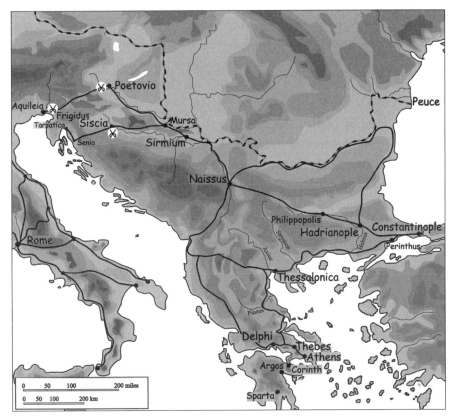

The Civil Wars in the Balkans.

Theodosius acted with surprising speed. He used Thessalonica as his base and launched a two-pronged attack, with a naval invasion of Italy being sent at the same time as he led the majority of his troops in person by land into Italy. A large percentage of his forces appear to have been composed of Gothic *foederati*: Gothic troops serving Rome under their own leaders in accordance with the peace treaty of 382. Alongside them were Huns and Alans, as well as a large force of regular Roman troops, including units from both the East and some that had followed Valentinian from the West.[2]

Theodosius defeated Maximus' advance forces at the Battle of Siscia ('the Save'), and then met Maximus' main force at Poetovio. After a hard-fought battle the Western armies were defeated. Maximus retired to Aquileia, but when Theodosius' advance guard arrived at the city Maximus was handed over to them and on 28 August 388 he was beheaded.

Theodosius acted with clemency to the defeated West. Only a few individuals were executed and Maximus' immediate family – with the exception of his son Victor who Maximus had promoted to *Augustus* – were allowed to live. However, Theodosius was left with a problem. Valentinian was clearly not yet ready to assume the full responsibility of being an *Augustus*. Previously Valentinian had been well served by the Frankish general Bauto, but Bauto had recently died and so Arbogast, another Frankish general trusted by Theodosius, was made *magister militum* ('Master of the Troops') and appointed to serve Valentinian.

The appointment of Arbogast proved to be a problem as Valentinian was soon complaining about his subordination to the Frank.[3] Losing patience, Valentinian formally dismissed Arbogast but Arbogast refused to retire, stating flatly that Valentinian had not appointed him and so could not dismiss him.[4] On 15 May 392 Valentinian was found hanged in his residence, either a suicide or murdered by Arbogast.[5] Soon afterwards Arbogast nominated a new emperor: on 22 August 392, only three months after the death of Valentinian, he promoted a man named Eugenius, a former *magister scrinorum*, to the post of *Augustus*.

Theodosius refused to acknowledge the new emperor. Instead he recruited foreign mercenaries and once again called on the Goths to fulfil their treaty obligations by supplying a large number of troops; they allegedly sent 20,000 men for the upcoming campaign.[6] With his preparations complete, Theodosius marched with his army from Constantinople towards Italy.

In response, and learning from the mistakes of Magnus, Arbogast decided that defending the passes was secondary to keeping his army as a large single force under his personal control. As a consequence, Theodosius crossed the Alps unopposed and descended towards the city of Aquileia, so entering the valley of the River Frigidus. Here they encountered the army of Arbogast encamped near the river.

Location

Although the precise location of the battle has not yet been discovered, taking into account the local topography it is most likely that the battle was fought in the valley of the River Frigidus (Vipava) where the road approaches the modern town of Ajdovščina. Here the road across the Alps winds its way out of the mountains and into a valley with hills on either side, a vital factor if the account of the battle in the sources is accepted as accurate.

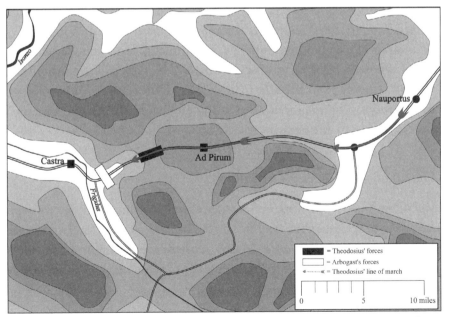

Theodosius' route and possible location of Arbogast. Arbogast's position shows the relative ease with which he could command the lines of advance over the Alps.

The Opposing Forces: East Rome*

Although almost half a century had passed between the Siege of Amida and the Battle of the Frigidus, any changes made to the organization of the army are unrecorded and, since they were usually implemented due to the whim of an individual emperor, it is probably safe to assume that any changes made were only small-scale and did not affect the overall composition and configuration of the army so are not analyzed here.

Despite modern attempts, it is impossible to calculate the origin and number of the troops led by Theodosius, with the possible exception of the 20,000 troops allegedly being supplied by the Goths. Modern authors have attempted to use the list of troops in the *Notitia Dignitatum* to reach an acceptable figure, but this is unsatisfactory for at least two reasons. The first is that it is unclear whether Theodosius took all the troops available in the Balkans or whether he left some behind as a garrison covering the Danube frontier. As there were nominally three armies in the region – two *Praesental* armies (armies 'in the presence' of the emperor and nominally under his direct control) and the Army of Thrace – this means that the invasion force could have numbered from the low thousands to many tens of thousands. The second is that no ancient source has stated whether the Goths were the only *foederati* ('barbarian' troops serving the Roman Empire as allies) who accompanied Theodosius. With such a large variation in potential numbers, it is impossible to know how many troops were under Theodosius' command. However, Theodosius had recently spent time in the West and so had doubtless gained knowledge of the West's military potential, so it is likely that his forces outnumbered those available to Arbogast.[7]

The Opposing Forces: West Rome

Much like Theodosius' forces, Arbogast's Roman army had gone through the series of reforms initiated by Diocletian and Constantine. However, there were some differences. Many of these were minor: Diocletian's reforms had mainly impacted upon the East, which had been under his

---

* The changes outlined here are a very simplified version of the reforms with many local and national variations being employed.

direct control. When Constantine had come to power he had implemented further reforms, but these appear to have been mainly implemented in the West; he appears to have retained many of the reforms of the eastern army implemented by Diocletian without change.

There may be two further major differences between the armies. The division of the Empire into East and West had had a financial impact: the richer East was a more financially viable entity than the poorer West, so the Eastern army *may* have had access to modern replacements for equipment, whereas the Western troops may have had to rely on inherited arms and armour.

The second factor was recruitment. In the Gothic War (376–382), fought between the Goths (rebelling due to their maltreatment) and the Eastern Empire, the Eastern Emperor Valens had been killed at the Battle of Adrianople (378). The Western Emperor Gratian had then appointed a new emperor, Theodosius, and given him control of the whole of the Balkans. This included the Western province of Illyricum as this was also being ravaged by the Goths and its allocation to Theodosius ensured that there would be no division of command during the war. However, once the Gothic war ended, Illyricum was not returned to the West. The result was that the Eastern Empire had gained control of the Illyrian recruiting grounds that had furnished the best recruits for the Western Empire. Consequently the West lost access to the best recruits and the East gained access to them.

Furthermore, despite the presence of Sasanid Persia on the Eastern frontier, in many respects the East was easier to defend as the Sasanids were politically more advanced than the 'barbarian' tribes facing the West and so it was easier to secure a stable frontier by signing a peace treaty with a political entity that stuck to the terms. The fragmented and more volatile tribes pressing on the Rhine and the Danube frontiers were far more difficult to deal with.

Yet despite these difficulties and differences, the armies that were to fight at the Frigidus were remarkably similar: both comprised a mixture of Roman and non-Roman troops. The army of Theodosius was supplemented by a large number of Goths and other 'barbarians'. Alongside the regular Roman troops that he had concentrated from Gaul and Italy, Arbogast's army included both Franks and Alamanni that he had recruited while campaigning on the Rhine.[8] Nevertheless, there appears to have been one major difference: despite augmenting his troops with federates from Gaul and across the Rhine, Arbogast's forces were not as strong as those of the Eastern Emperor.

The Battle

Outnumbered, Arbogast adopted a defensive strategy and drew up his forces in front of the exit to the pass he expected Theodosius to use. Furthermore, he stationed troops on all the strategic high points surrounding the exit so that when Theodosius emerged from the pass he would find himself partially surrounded. It would appear from later events that Arbogast was relying on his troops to hold their position and, once Theodosius' assault had failed, Arbogast could then send troops to the rear of the pass in order to block Theodosius' exits. With a failed assault and then being surrounded, Theodosius could be expected to surrender. By accurately calculating Theodosius' movements and by taking efficient steps to counter them, Arbogast had proved himself to be strategically superior to Theodosius.

Theodosius acted in exactly the manner predicted by Arbogast. When Theodosius descended from the pass, he saw that Arbogast had deployed his forces so as to block the exit towards the river and had simultaneously limited the space in which Theodosius himself could deploy. He also became aware of troops stationed on strategic heights blocking possible alternative routes down from the pass. These troops posed an additional threat to his flanks.

Realizing that he was in danger of being surrounded and unable to deploy his whole army, Theodosius had no option but to order the troops in the army's vanguard to attack. Accordingly he gave the command for the Gothic *foederati* and other *auxilia* at the head of the marching columns to make a headlong assault on the enemy.[9] He was probably hoping that, even if they did not break through the enemy's lines, they could at least force Arbogast's forces to recoil, giving Theodosius' forces more room in which to deploy.[10] After a ferocious assault – during which there was allegedly an eclipse of the sun[11] – both the *foederati* and the other units were repulsed with heavy losses: according to Orosius, 10,000 Goths lost their lives in the battle.[12] As night fell the troops of the West celebrated a victory and Arbogast sent detachments of troops around the flanks of the Eastern army to secure the passes to their rear.

Although many ancient and modern writers have assumed that the decision by Theodosius to send the Goths in first was political and made in order to weaken the Goths as a political force, this would appear unlikely: the local topography ensured that he did not have the luxury of choosing which of his troops attacked first and there was definitely no guarantee of a victory. Although the end result would in reality weaken the Goths, it was not intentionally so.

As night fell and with the Gothic assault repulsed, the opposing armies settled down for an uneasy night. At this point Arbogast and the Western army doubtless believed that the battle was won: the enemy was unable to deploy properly, the first massive assault had been held, and in addition Arbogast was confident enough to detach forces from his main battle line and send them to occupy strategic points in the pass to trap Theodosius where he was. In contrast, the Eastern army's morale would have been low due to the defeat and their poor circumstances. The failure of the initial assault led Theodosius to spend the night desperately praying to God for help.[13]

Overnight the situation changed. The troops Arbogast had sent to cut Theodosius off instead deserted to the Eastern emperor, allegedly swayed by the emperor's persuasive personal arguments.[14] Seeing their defection as a good omen and a sign that God was with him, Theodosius renewed the battle on the following day. He attacked early in the morning, taking Arbogast by surprise since he believed Theodosius to be surrounded and without hope.[15] Theodosius' confidence was to be further reinforced. After the fighting had begun, a local wind, the *Bora*, began to blow from behind the Eastern forces towards the Western army (though it should be noted that this may have been simply a local storm rather than the *Bora*). As the Eastern army advanced, large amounts of dust were disturbed and this was blown into the defenders' faces. Legend has it that the wind was so strong that it blew the defenders' missiles back at them, which may be possible as the *Bora* has been measured at around 60 mph. Confused and unable to see properly, the Western army wavered and broke. Punching through the centre, Theodosius' men reached the enemy camp where Eugenius was captured and later executed. Seeing that he had lost, Arbogast fled. Realizing that his position was hopeless, Arbogast finally committed suicide rather than allowing himself to be captured by Theodosius.[16]

Aftermath

The battle was over. It had spanned two days of intensive fighting. Both sides had taken heavy losses. For the East the losses were not as devastating as they had a larger pool of manpower and were far richer, thus having the ability to replace lost men and equipment. In addition, the worst losses had been on the first day and had been suffered by the Gothic *foederati* who had led the assault. Consequently the losses for the army of the East had been small, but for the West the defeat was a disaster. It is likely that the losses suffered during the three battles of Siscia, Poetovio and Frigidus were far greater than those suffered by the Eastern Empire at Adrianople. The need to rebuild the army in the following years would prove to be too great a strain for the Western Empire to bear. However, immediately after the battle such a conclusion would have been unthinkable. Theodosius had reunited the Empire under one ruler, who had now proved himself capable in war and a strong leader. Theoretically the West could now be supported by the greater resources of the East.

Effects

The fact that the battle was part of a civil war has resulted in the importance of the battle (and of the two preceding it) being ignored or overlooked by many writers, largely due to their focus being upon the reign of Theodosius 'The Great' and his reuniting of the two halves of the Empire. Furthermore, due to the circumstances surrounding the battle, there were detrimental outcomes, especially for the West, concerning both the victorious and the defeated antagonists.

Dealing with the triumphant Eastern army first, after the battle Theodosius was acknowledged as the sole emperor of the Empire. Theoretically, the stronger Eastern Empire could now support the weaker West, but the fact that Theodosius planned to elevate his son to the post of Western Emperor emphasizes that any perceived unity was not one of equals; in effect, the West was still going to be left to deal with its own problems.

Of more immediate concern for both East and West, however, was the reaction of a large section of the Gothic warriors that had served in the victorious army. These Gothic federates had been employed as shock troops on the first day of battle, sustaining very heavy losses (10,000 according to Orosius) in a fruitless attack on the Western lines. As noted above, the acceptance by many ancient and modern authors that Theodosius' decision to send the Goths to attack was a political one aimed at weakening the Goths is mistaken. However, it would appear that an immediate claim to this effect by Roman sources acted to reinforce a similar belief among the Goths: they had been used as 'cannon-fodder' by a cynical Roman emperor. Less than a year after the battle a violent Gothic revolt began, led by a man named Alaric who was later to lead his men in the first Sack of Rome since the Gauls 800 years earlier. However, this revolt was not to be focused upon the East whose emperor had committed the Goths to their disastrous attacks; the East was far too strong to be overcome. Instead it was eventually to be directed against the West.

Although the battle is sometimes relegated to the footnotes in modern histories, in reality it was of more profound importance than even the earlier Battle of Adrianople. After Adrianople, the Eastern army was forced to resort to a strategy of delay and control, restricting the movement of the victorious Goths and blockading them in the mountains until hunger and fatigue had forced them to negotiate with Theodosius. This gave Theodosius time to recover the army's strength and train new recruits from its large pool of manpower.

In direct contrast, the Western army had been heavily defeated by Theodosius at the earlier battles of the Siscia ('the Save') and Poetovio in 388 against Magnus Maximus. Before having had enough time to fully recover, the rebellion of Arbogast and Eugenius embroiled the West in yet another civil war. It would prove impossible for the West to recover from the extremely heavy losses suffered by the Western army at the Battle of the Frigidus, largely because the West did not have access to the large reserves of manpower available to the East. In this context, the later desire of Stilicho to risk going to war with the East to recover the Illyrian recruiting grounds makes sense: without them he was struggling to maintain the integrity of the West. In the fifth century the West's inability to recover from these devastating losses was one of the factors enabling a diversity of 'barbarian' tribes to invade Western territory, which in turn was the cause of a number of internal rebellions that further weakened the West. It is difficult to over-emphasize the importance of the Battle of the Frigidus in the history of the (Western) Roman Empire.

Select Bibliography

Jordanes, *Getica:* https://archive.org/details/gothichistoryofj00jorduoft
Orosius: https://sites.google.com/site/demontortoise2000
Philostorgius: https://www.tertullian.org/fathers/philostorgius.htm
Socrates Scholasticus: https://ccel.org/ccel/schaff/npnf202/npnf202.i.html
Sozomen: https://ccel.org/ccel/schaff/npnf202/npnf202.i.html
Zosimus: https://www.tertullian.org/fathers/zosimus04_book4.htm

Secondary Source
Williams, S. and Friell, G., *The Empire at Bay* (Yale, 1995).

Chapter Thirteen

The Vandal Disaster:
The Battle of Cape Bon, 468

The Sources

The most detailed description we have of what happened comes from **Procopius** (c.500–after 565 CE). His description of events is contained in the *De Bello Vandalico* (*War Against the Vandals*) which, although mainly concerned with the conquest of Vandal Africa by the Byzantine general Belisarius, also includes a brief history of the manner in which the Vandals had conquered and maintained control of Africa.[1] His account is taken from **Priscus** (410s–after 472 CE), possibly one of the better writers in Late Antiquity, who wrote an eight-volume historical work entitled the *History of Byzantium*, which covered the period from 433 until 474 AD. Sadly his works have been lost and only exist in extracts, including this one in Procopius.

Priscus is considered a reliable and sober historian, and as he was alive during the war with the Vandals his work is therefore extremely valuable. Despite the plaudits for Priscus, the usual care needs to be taken: although the information derives from Priscus, Procopius may have edited events described in the originals to fit his own narrative. However, as it is the most detailed narrative it is used here for the basis of the account.

Zosimus (fl. late fifth-early sixth century CE) was an Eastern Roman writing in Constantinople who composed the *Historia Nova* (*New History*). Unlike the other writers, Zosimus was a pagan blaming Christianity for the decline of Rome. In theory his work can be used as a counterbalance to the Christian authors; however, his writing is strewn with inaccuracies so must be used with extreme caution.

---

* A version of this battle can be found in Hughes, I., *Patricians and Emperors: The Last Rulers of the Western Roman Empire* (Barnsley, 2015).

As noted in the previous chapter, **Jordanes** (fl. sixth century CE) was an Eastern Roman, probably of Gothic descent, who wrote *De summa temporum vel origine actibusque gentis Romanorum* (*The High Point of Time, or the Origin and Deeds of the Roman People*, usually shortened to *Romana* (*On Rome*)), an epitome of events from creation to the victory of the general Narses over King Teia of the Goths (552 CE), and *De Origine Actibusque Getarum* (*On the Origins and Deeds of the Goths*, usually abbreviated to *Getica*) with both being written in the mid-sixth century. It is the *Romana* that covers the Battle of Cape Bon, but as this is a chronicle the entry is brief. This gives an example of the type of entry common to the chronicle tradition:

> [Valde Leo erravit] Basiliscum cognatum suum – id est fratrem Augustæ Verinæ – Africam dirigens cum exercitu, qui navali proelio Carthaginem sæpe aggrediens, ante eam, victus cupiditate, pecuniis vendidit regi Wandalorum, quam in Romanorum potestatem redegerat.

> [Leo erred greatly] Sending his brother-in-law [Flavius] Basiliscus – that is, the brother of his Augusta, [Ælia] Verina – to Africa with an army, a man who, often attacking Carthage in naval battles, being conquered by avarice, sold it to the king of the Vandals for money rather than subjecting it to Roman power.
>
> *Jordanes, Romana, 337.*

The brevity of the entry and the lack of any supporting details mean that Jordanes is omitted from the analysis except to add veracity to other sources. The same is true of Georgius Cedrenus, Marcellinus *Comes* and other chronicles, unless where otherwise stated.

Background

In December 406 CE a large force of Vandals, Alans and Sueves had crossed the Rhine into Gaul. After plundering Gaul they crossed the Pyrenees and settled in Hispania in 409. The Siling Vandals, the Asding Vandals, the Alans and the Sueves settled in different regions. However, after a long period of warfare the Goths who sacked Rome in 410 were also forced over the Pyrenees and induced by the Romans to launch a devastating attack on the Siling Vandals and the Alans in return for land to settle in Gaul. The Silings and Alans were so badly defeated that the remnants fled to live with the Asding Vandals in Gallaecia.

The next few years saw the Asdings come under increasing pressure, and their king Gunderic led them south to Baetica before his death in 428, then in 429 their new king Gaiseric led them across the Straits of Gibraltar and into Africa. Once across the Straits, they slowly moved east until coming up against the African army stationed in the province of Africa. After twice defeating the army, in 435 they were allowed to settle on lands in Africa.

This was only a brief interlude as in 439 Gaiseric took advantage of Roman troubles to invade and capture Carthage, the capital of Roman Africa. Despite Roman pressure, Gaiseric managed to maintain his grip on the region and signed a new treaty in 442 acknowledging his control of the provinces of Africa, Byzacena and part of Numidia in return for continuing the supply of grain and other goods to Italy and especially Rome. The West could not resist Gaiseric as they were facing other problems in mainland Europe and so did not have the resources to retake Africa. However, Gaiseric's victory was a major disaster for the West as in one blow he had deprived Rome of its most productive and taxable region. Consequently the rulers in Rome (and Constantinople) were constantly planning to retake Africa.

In 455 the Roman Emperor Valentinian III was assassinated on the orders of a man named Petronius Maximus, who then took the throne. Taking advantage, Gaiseric annexed Sardinia, Corsica, the Balearic Islands and Malta. More famously, on 31 May the Vandals landed in Italy and sacked Rome; a far more methodical sack than that of the Goths in 410. Alongside the traditional plunder, Gaiseric captured Eudoxia, the widow of Valentinian III, and her daughters Eudocia and Placidia. Eudocia was later to marry Gaiseric's son Huneric, creating further political problems for Rome.

Despite internal problems, Western Rome did make a major attempt to reconquer Africa. In 460 the Emperor Majorian conducted major campaigns in the West in an attempt to restore Rome's fortunes. First he subdued the Goths in Gaul and then the Sueves in Hispania, both of whom had been attempting to expand their powers. He then moved the army south, aiming to cross the Straits of Gibraltar, following in the wake of the original Vandal invasion. The attempt was a failure: Gaiseric launched a naval attack on the ships Majorian had had built – after taxing the aristocracy in Rome – and destroyed or captured the Roman fleet at the Battle of Elche. Majorian was assassinated as the price of his failure.

In 468 there was to be one more attempt to reconquer Vandal Africa, this time a major campaign using the resources of both the Eastern and Western Roman Empires.

The Opposing Forces: Rome

For the campaign the eastern Emperor Leo emptied the Eastern treasury, possibly spending four years' worth of revenues in order to gather a formidable army:

> And the Emperor Leo…was gathering an army against them [the Vandals]; and they say that this army amounted to about one hundred thousand men. And he collected a fleet of ships from the whole of the eastern Mediterranean…[and]…they say, thirteen hundred *centenaria* were expended by him.
>
> *Procopius, 3.6.1–2.*

> Whereupon the emperor, aroused to anger, collected from all the eastern sea 1,100 ships, filled them with soldiers and arms and sent them against Gaiseric. They say that he spent 1,300 *centenaria* of gold on this expedition.
>
> *Priscus, fr. 42, trans. Gordon, 120–1.*

According to the original text the number given by Priscus was 100,000 ships. This has been emended by the translator to 1,100 as the original number is obviously far too large and the latter corresponds to the 1,113 vessels claimed by Cedrenus.[2]

> Joannes Lydas [Lydus, John the Lydian]…says that 65,000 pounds of gold and 700,000 pounds of silver were collected. [And]…those that administered these things reveal 47,000 pounds of gold were raised through the prefects, 17,000 pounds of gold through the count of the treasury, and 700,000 pounds of silver, apart from adequate

amounts raised from the public funds and from the [Western] Emperor Anthemius.

Candidus, fr. 2, trans. Gordon, 121.

In addition, Theodorus Lector gives a figure of 7,000 sailors/marines to man the fleet.[3] Although possibly a realistic number, there is then the problem that if the Latin word *nauta* is translated as the usual 'sailor', this gives an average of only six sailors per vessel: in that case, the fleet was probably not as large as the sources claim. Assuming that it would, for example, take only 20 sailors to man a vessel, this would give a fleet of 350 ships. This may be more likely than the 1,000 vessels assumed by Cedrenus, but if the latter is to be accepted then the 7,000 men attested by Theodorus needs correction. This has led to at least one modern historian translating *nauta* as 'marines', so bypassing the need to lower the number of ships. Obviously certainty is impossible, but the lower number of ships is more realistic given the number of men involved. This would account for the speed and decisiveness of later events.

Sadly there is no other information concerning the origins or numbers of the troops so the details are unknown. As a result, any attempt to estimate them is merely guesswork: all that can be said with certainty is that from the context this was the largest military force assembled to campaign in the West in the last days of the Western Empire.

In addition to these difficulties, Leo had planned a three-fold attack. Unfortunately it is not made clear whether the troops used by Marcellinus and Heraclius were included in the total given by Procopius. If so, as seems likely, then obviously the invasion fleet aimed at Africa would have been far smaller than that given for the whole campaign. Marcellinus would need a large fleet to carry his troops and ensure that they could land safely in Sardinia, and it is clear from later evidence that Heraclius was accompanied by a fleet as he traversed the North African coast.[4] Furthermore, despite modern estimates, no numbers are given for the men assigned to either Marcellinus or Heraclius and all the numbers suggested are based on figures proposed for other armies, which are themselves often conjecture. As a result, and despite temptation, no numbers will be given for any of the armies used by Marcellinus, Heraclius and Basiliscus. Yet one thing is certain: the diversion of ships and men away from the main projected invasion of Africa means that Basiliscus probably would not have the overwhelming superiority in men and ships usually accorded in the sources and accepted by some more modern accounts.

The Opposing Forces: Gaiseric

There is no figure given in any of the Roman sources for either the men or the ships available to the Vandals. This is understandable as attention was focused more upon the Roman commanders than upon the strategic and tactical skill of Gaiseric.

If the number of c.350 ships given above for the Roman invasion force is accepted, then the Vandal navy may have been of approximately equal strength, but it is likely that Roman intelligence would know of the number of Vandal ships and so ensured that they had a superiority. Consequently it is assumed here that the Vandals had a fleet of c.200–250 ships, enough to facilitate the conquest of the Western Mediterranean but less than the fleet used by Rome.

Location: The Roman Campaign

The Roman campaign was to be a major operation, orchestrated by the Eastern Emperor Leo. It was a three-pronged assault, with two aimed at drawing off Vandal resources before the third launched a major blow aimed at Carthage itself. One force would attack the Vandals' possessions in the western Mediterranean. A second force was to muster in Egypt before travelling across the northern coast of Africa, seizing Tripolitania before moving on to Carthage itself. The third and main attack would be a direct assault on the Vandals' African territories, carried out by a large fleet and supporting army.

The first task force was under Marcellinus, *magister militum per Dalmatiae* ('Master of the Troops in Dalmatia'). With a mixed army of Eastern and Western troops, Marcellinus landed in Sardinia, where 'he drove out the Vandals and gained possession of it with no great difficulty.'[5] Doubtless the intention was to either distract the Vandal garrison or destroy it, or at least ensure that it could not be removed to protect Africa until after it had been heavily defeated and demoralized.

The second attack was led by a man named Heraclius, who had probably previously been a *comes rei militaris* ('Count of the Military') alongside an

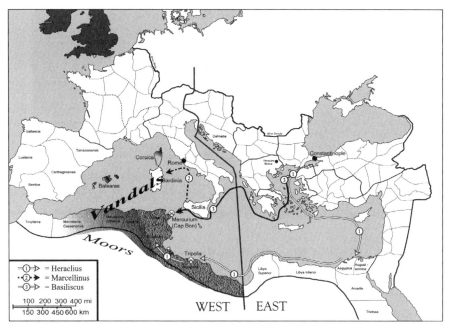

The African Campaign of 468.

Isaurian named Marsus.[6] Heraclius travelled first to Egypt to collect 'an army drawn from Egypt, the Thebaid and the desert'.[7] The inclusion of 'the desert' suggests that Heraclius may have had a contingent of 'Saracen' (Arab) allies. Travelling west, they caught the Vandals by surprise.[8] However, unlike Marcellinus, Heraclius had to defeat the enemy in a pitched battle:

> And Heraclius was sent from Byzantium to Tripolis in Libya, and after conquering the Vandals of that district in battle, he easily captured the cities, and leaving his ships there, led his army on foot toward Carthage. Such, then, was the sequence of events which formed the prelude of the war.
>
> *Procopius, 3.6.9.*

It would appear that Heraclius had been transported by a fleet from Egypt to Tripolis, where he had landed and fought the Vandals. After this, wary of the threat of the Vandal fleet nearer to Carthage, he had left the ships in Tripolis. As already noted, when combined with the campaign against Sardinia, the strategy of attacking on three fronts weakened the main invasion fleet which was commanded by Basiliscus, the brother of Leo's wife Verina, who was almost certainly given the post of *magister militum praesentalis*.[9] Priscus describes him as 'a successful soldier but slow-witted and easily taken in by deceivers'.[10]

Africa

Not waiting for the whole fleet to be amassed, Basiliscus apparently used part of his newly-acquired navy to attack Vandal shipping: 'When no small force from the East had been collected, he engaged frequently in sea fights with Gaiseric and sent 'a large number of ships to the bottom'.[11]

After the success of Marcellinus in Sardinia and Heraclius in Tripolis, Basiliscus finally set sail for Africa, doubtless using Sicily as a staging point for the landings. Unlike Majorian, Leo had eschewed the subtle approach – a landing via Spain – for a direct frontal assault on Carthage with his main force.

> But Basiliscus with his whole fleet put in at a town distant from Carthage no less than two hundred and eighty *stades* [a *stadion* was 185 metres in length, therefore the landing was around 52 kilometres or c.32 miles from Carthage]…[at a place] named Mercurium [Cape Bon].
>
> *Procopius, 3.6.10.*

The fact that Basiliscus landed so far from Carthage was obviously seen by Procopius as a mistake, reinforcing his depiction of Basiliscus as a weak commander.[12] On the other hand, it should be noted that coordinating the movement of a large fleet of ships over a large distance without the close communication equipment now available was fraught with danger: the least that could be expected was that the ships would become dispersed as they travelled. If this was to happen, the fleet would be vulnerable to an attack by Gaiseric's large fleet manned by experienced crews.

Finally, Basiliscus had landed in Africa with the troops.[13] Procopius sees this as the defining moment of the campaign:

If he [Basiliscus] had not purposely played the coward and hesitated, but had undertaken to go straight for Carthage, he would have captured it at the first onset, and he would have reduced the Vandals to subjection without their even thinking of resistance; so overcome was Gaiseric with awe of Leo as an invincible emperor, when the report was brought to him that Sardinia and Tripolis had been captured, and he saw the fleet of Basiliscus to be such as the Romans were said never to have had before. But, as it was, the general's hesitation, whether caused by cowardice or treachery, prevented this success.

Procopius, 3.6.11–12.

As is usual with ancient historians, the fate of a whole campaign rests solely on the negative interpretation of a commander's actions. Although it is possible that Basiliscus acted too cautiously in not advancing directly on Carthage, the majority of military experience tells against such an interpretation. By the time Basiliscus landed he would have known that news of the victories in Sardinia and Tripolis would have reached Gaiseric. On the other hand, having been in Sicily and at sea for quite a time, Basiliscus would not have known Gaiseric's reaction. The most likely response to being attacked would surely have been for Gaiseric to recall as many of his troops as possible and gather them at the capital in preparation for a counter-strike. If that was the case, Basiliscus would have erred on the side of recklessness to order his men to land and then move against Carthage: an attack on Basiliscus' ill-prepared forces as they marched towards Carthage would have been devastating. Basiliscus did the correct thing in landing, making a beachhead secure and sending out scouts for information on Gaiseric's activity.

According to Procopius, Gaiseric took advantage of the lull in Roman activity:

And Gaiseric, profiting by the negligence of Basiliscus, did as follows. Arming all his subjects in the best way he could, he filled his ships, but not all, for some he kept in readiness empty, and they were the ships which sailed most swiftly. And sending envoys to Basiliscus, he begged him to defer the war for the space of five days, in order that in meantime he might take counsel and do those things which were especially desired by the emperor. They say, too, that he sent also a great amount of gold without the knowledge of the army of Basiliscus and thus purchased this armistice.

Procopius, 3.6.12f.

By the early sixth century the story that Basiliscus had been 'bribed' by Gaiseric was common, since this is also included in the history of Theodorus Lector.[14] Procopius' claim concerning the 'perfidious' nature of Gaiseric's negotiations, stating that he only asked for an armistice in order to amass his forces, also has a precedent in Roman historiography: Ammianus states that the Gothic leader Fritigern had fraudulently opened negotiations with Valens prior to the Battle of Adrianople in 378.[15] Interestingly, in both cases the end result was a catastrophic defeat and it is simply a common Roman excuse that they could only be defeated by either the treacherous nature of their barbarian enemies or the incompetence of the Roman commander.

Basiliscus' reaction to the Vandals' envoys is understandable. He was at the head of (probably) the largest army assembled by the Empire for many years and, in conjunction with his overwhelming fleet, it was only natural for him to believe that Gaiseric would want to come to terms with the Empire before his 'kingdom' was annihilated. What Basiliscus did not take into account is that Gaiseric was one of the greatest commanders the barbarian kingdoms would ever produce. A study of Gaiseric's history clearly shows that he was a superb military and political leader. He had taken control of Africa in two campaigns, one ending in 435 when he made a treaty with Rome and the other in 442 when his conquest of Carthage was accepted by both East and West. Furthermore, he had easily defeated Majorian's attempt at reconquest and had then been able to politically isolate the West from the East. Sadly Basiliscus appears to have underestimated his opponent.

Unfortunately for Basiliscus, Gaiseric had quickly recognized that without the support of the fleet the Roman army would struggle to feed itself in a hostile environment, and Gaiseric had enough troops to ensure that Africa remained hostile to the Romans. What Gaiseric needed was to destroy the 'mobile supply base' that was the Roman fleet. He used the negotiations as a way of both buying the time necessary to make his own preparations and for the weather to come to his assistance.

The Battle of Cape Bon

> And [Gaiseric arranged for the truce], thinking, as actually did happen, that a favouring wind would rise for him during this time…. The Vandals, as soon as the wind had arisen for them which they had been expecting…raised their sails and, taking in tow the boats which, as has been stated above, they had made ready with no men in them, they sailed against the enemy. And when they came near, they set fire to the boats which they were towing, when their sails were bellied by the wind, and let them go against the Roman fleet. And since there were a great number of ships there, these boats easily spread fire wherever they struck, and were themselves readily destroyed together with those with which they came in contact. And as the fire advanced in this way the Roman fleet was filled with tumult, as was natural, and with a great din that rivalled the noise caused by the wind and the roaring of the flames, as the soldiers together with the sailors shouted orders to one another and pushed off with their poles the fire-boats and their own ships as well, which were being destroyed by one another in complete disorder.
>
> *Procopius, 3.6.17–21*[16]

Although as already noted the whole disaster is usually laid at the feet of Basiliscus, it is clear that Gaiseric deserves a great deal of the credit for the victory. By agreeing to an armistice he had bought time for himself to organize his defences in case the opportunity to strike presented itself. When the time came he acted with speed and determination, and his ability is highlighted by the decisiveness of the attack. However, the Vandals were not willing to simply let the fireships go in and await the outcome. Even as the fires were spreading among the Roman fleet:

> Already the Vandals too were at hand ramming and sinking the ships, and making booty of such of the soldiers as attempted to escape, and of their arms as well. But there were also some of the Romans who proved themselves brave men in this struggle, and most of all John, who was a general under Basiliscus and who had no share whatever in his treason. For a great throng having surrounded his ship, he stood on the deck, and turning from side to side kept killing very

great numbers of the enemy from there, and when he perceived that the ship was being captured, he leaped with his whole equipment of arms from the deck into the sea. And though Genzon, the son of Gaiseric, entreated him earnestly not to do this, offering pledges and holding out promises of safety, he nevertheless threw himself into the sea, uttering this one word, that John would never come under the hands of dogs.

Procopius, 3.6.22–24

In 1588 the use of fireships by the English navy scattered the Spanish armada, but it was the ensuing storm that finally destroyed the Spanish fleet. In 468 there was no storm: the Roman fleet was disordered and many ships were burned by the fireships, but the decisive action was the follow-up by the Vandal fleet, ensuring that the Romans were so heavily defeated that their fleet ceased to exist as an effective force.

Basiliscus was then cut off from supplies except for what he could forage in Africa, which was probably not enough to feed his large army on enemy soil, especially when the Vandals could harass any Roman troops gathering food. Further, without a fleet he had no way of effectively laying siege to the city of Carthage: the Vandal fleet could not only keep the city supplied with food but could transport reinforcements into the city. In addition, the fleet could take troops out of the city and land them to the rear of the Roman siege lines, possibly with devastating results. There was now little chance of the campaign successfully taking Carthage. Using the remaining ships, Basiliscus embarked the army and sailed to Sicily, where he was joined by Marcellinus.

Aftermath

Ancient historians almost universally believed that individuals were responsible for victories and defeats. An energetic and capable commander won and an ineffective and incapable commander lost. However, where the Romans had (apparently) overwhelming superiority then the ancient sources rarely accept that either incompetence or the ability of enemy commanders could account for a defeat. The traditional method of assigning blame for such defeats, especially in the Later Empire, was 'treachery'. Where exactly the blame was to lie depended on the popularity of the military commander. In 460 the failure of Majorian's campaign against the Vandals was given as 'treachery' on behalf of unknown individuals; Majorian was popular and the failure could not be ascribed to him.[17] Basiliscus was not popular. The fact that he had lost a campaign that seemingly could not be lost meant that he was the scapegoat for some contemporary historians. As a result, the majority of the sources castigate Basiliscus.

Over time Basiliscus' failure was transformed. Procopius claimed that 'Basiliscus, either as doing a favour to Aspar (an Eastern military commander) in accordance with what he had promised, or selling the moment of opportunity for money, or perhaps thinking it the better course' waited blindly for Gaiseric to strike, and so a large part of the fleet was either destroyed or captured.[18] Later the tale took a more sinister twist. For example, according to Malalas, Basiliscus 'accepted bribes from Gaiseric and betrayed the ships and all the men in them. Basiliscus was in the only ship to escape, all the rest being sunk.'[19]

Possibly the only deviation from the theme is that of Theophanes, who claims that Leo was willing to accept the defeat as he was more concerned about the primacy of Aspar, needing Basiliscus, Heraclius and Marsus to defend himself against Aspar.[20] In this narrative, although Basiliscus is still at fault, the defeat was in some ways a blessing for Leo as he could from then on focus on internal affairs and the removal of Aspar from his seat of power.

Whether caused by incompetence, treachery or simply due to the underestimation of an opponent, Basiliscus knew that his failure had been catastrophic. On his return to Constantinople and fearing for his life, he immediately sought sanctuary in the Church of St. Sophia. Fortunately for Basiliscus, his sister Verina interceded with her husband in order to save his life.[21] Possibly of more importance, Leo still needed supporters in his escalating conflict with Aspar, his *magister militum*. In this context, Basiliscus' survival is less surprising. However, for a period after the defeat it would be inappropriate to restore Basiliscus to his previous status and he was exiled to Heraclea Sintica in Thrace.

Despite the reprieve, Basiliscus' reputation among later generations was to be secured by events in the mid-470s. In January 475 Basiliscus was officially proclaimed emperor, evicting Zeno, Leo's successor. Unfortunately his rule was so inept that after only twenty months, in August 476 Zeno was allowed to return to Constantinople. Basiliscus died shortly afterwards in captivity. The nature of his rule assured that later historians would ridicule his memory, leaving us with the image of a misguided, inept commander who was easily duped by Gaiseric, when in reality he was probably a competent, if cautious, commander who failed to take into account Gaiseric's outstanding military ability and readiness to take a risk.

When Heraclius received news of Basiliscus' defeat, he was still on the way towards Carthage. Realizing the futility of continuing the advance, Heraclius withdrew – probably to Tripolitania – before taking ship to Constantinople.

Marcellinus' fate was different. After the reconquest of Sardinia it seems that he returned to Sicily, possibly to prepare to join the campaign in Africa. He was never to leave the island.[22] Shortly after Basiliscus' return, in August 468 he was 'destroyed treacherously by one of his fellow officers'.[23] Although Marcellinus *comes* claims that he was in Africa at this point, this would seem to be in error.[24]

Effects

The devastating loss at Cape Bon ensured that the East and West would never combine again in an attempt to defeat the Vandals. Instead, Gaiseric was able to extend his dominions and, thanks in part due to his longevity – he reigned from 428 to 477, a period of forty-nine years during which a long line of Roman emperors came and went – he secured the kingdom for his son Huneric, married to Eudocia, daughter of Valentinian III.

For the West, the permanent loss of Africa was eventually to prove fatal. At the mercy of Gaiseric due to the need for African grain to feed the city of Rome and without the revenues of the West's richest province, Rome could no longer maintain an army of sufficient strength to defeat its enemies. Without the ability to secure a military reputation, short-lived emperors were crowned and overthrown, the ensuing confusion being one of the two major factors in the fall of the West.

If the campaign had been successful, it is possible that the Western Roman Empire would have lasted longer, but it remained too weak to regain its former status and so would have fallen eventually. Defeated, it was clear to all that the Empire was now in its final throes and the vultures – in the form of the Germanic tribes massed along its northern border, in Gaul and in Hispania – were quick to take advantage. The loss at Cape Bon ensured that the West would be lost.

Select Bibliography

Ammianus Marcellinus: https://www.tertullian.org/fathers/index.htm#Ammianus_ Marcellinus

Cassiodorus, *Chronicle* https://r.search.yahoo.com/_ylt=AwrC3L4QMYZiUmg AngMnnIlQ;_ylu=Y29sbwNiZjEEcG9zAzEEdnRpZAMEc2VjA3Ny/ RV=2/RE=1652990353/RO=10/RU=https%3a%2f%2fwww.roger-pearse.com%2fweblog%2fwp-content%2fuploads%2f2014%2f12%2fC assiodorus_Chronicle_Procee_2014.pdf/RK=2/RS=e6bXR3RJ48GWt.vLkmdb3ULYDTc-

Cedrenus: http://www.documentacatholicaomnia.eu/30_20_1100-1200-_Georgius_ Cedrenus.html (Greek and Latin)

Fasti Vindibonenses Priori (in the *MGH*): https://archive.org/search. php?query=monumenta%20germaniae%20historica (Latin)

Hydatius, 195 [200], s.a. 460: http://thelatinlibrary.com/hydatiuschronicon.html (Latin) See also Burgess, R.W., ed. and trans., *The Chronicle of Hydatius and the Consularia Constantinopolitana* (Oxford, Clarendon Press, 1993) and/or Mommsen, T. (ed.), *Chronica minora saec. IV.V.VI.VII., volumen II* (*Monumenta Germaniae Historica, Auctores Antiquissimi*, vol. 11, Berlin, Weidmann, 1894)

John Malalas: https://topostext.org/work/793

Jordanes, *Romana*: http://www.harbornet.com/folks/theedrich/Goths/Romana. htm#top

Marcellinus *comes*, *Chronicon*: http://www.documentacatholicaomnia.eu/04z/z_ 0474-0534__Marcellinus_Comes__Chronicum__MLT.pdf.html (Latin)

Paschchale Camp, s.a. 468 (in the *MGH*) https://archive.org/search. php?query=monumenta%20germaniae%20historica (Latin)

Photius, *Bibliotecha*, 79: https://www.tertullian.org/fathers/photius_01toc.htm

Priscus, fragments, Blockley, R.C. (2009, see below)

Procopius, *History of the Wars*: https://archive.org/details/b24750281_0002/ page/n9/mode/2up

Theodorus Lector, 1.25: https://books.google.co.uk/books?id=QF02EF4y4_4C& pg=RA1-PA395&lpg=RA37-PA394&dq=%22patrol.+gr.+LXXX&redir_ esc=y#v=onepage&q&f=false (Greek)

Theophanes, Mango, C. and Scott, R. (trans.), *The Chronicle of Theophanes Confessor: Byzantine and Near Eastern History AD 284–813* (Oxford, 1997)

Vita Daniel Stylites: https://sourcebooks.fordham.edu/basis/dan-stylite.asp

Zachariah of Mitylene/Zacharias Rhetor: https://www.tertullian.org/fathers/ zachariah00.htm

Zonaras: https://archive.org/details/epitomehistoria00zonagoog/page/n7/mode/ 2up (Greek)

Secondary Sources

Blockley, R.C., *The Fragmentary Classicising Historians of the Later Roman Empire*, Vol. II (Cambridge, United Kingdom, 2009)

Conclusions

Hopefully the preceding chapters have clearly demonstrated that, despite popular myth, the Roman army was anything but invincible. Rather it was largely victorious thanks to factors still appreciated in military circles today: a series of competent Roman commanders opposed by some incompetent opposition; an increasingly professional army wearing standardized armour facing armies of amateurs, often without armour, intent mainly on raid and plunder; and a logistical system far more efficient than those of the majority of their opponents.

If anything, what has been highlighted is that in many cases the battles were probably far greater defeats than the Roman sources have stated. The majority of casualties caused in ancient warfare were when one side routed and the other pursued the fleeing men, striking down individuals who were not attempting to protect themselves. In many cases, it was Roman professionalism, organization and discipline that allowed them to prevail, simply outlasting the enemy and then inflicting heavy losses as the enemy ran. However, what has been shown is that there were times when this failed and it was the Romans that endured the ignominy of defeat, suffering large casualties as they either routed or were pinned in place and unable to fight effectively.

Although in the main the defeats have been glossed over by many (especially Roman) historians, it is hoped that the foregoing has shown that, despite the impressions given in the sources, the Roman army was not infallible and was often defeated, thanks to either incompetence or over-confidence. In addition, in many cases, rather than victories determining the reaction of the Romans and the direction of their policies, it was the defeats that had the greatest impact upon Roman mentality, diplomacy and strategy; two obvious examples being the *metus Gallicus* after the Battle of the Allia (resulting in Rome's attitude to the Gauls being one of fear and trepidation until after Julius Caesar had conquered Gaul), and the Teutoburger Wald (after which no further attempts were made to expand the border of the Empire beyond the Rhine).

It is obvious that during the long existence of the Roman Empire, from the earliest Republican period until the deposition of the last emperor, the Roman army won the vast majority of the battles it fought, especially following the change to a professional force facing amateur opposition. Yet although these victories determined the rate of expansion and final size of the Empire, in some cases it was the catastrophic defeats suffered that had the greatest impact on the Roman psyche and helped to determine the future of the Empire.

Notes

Chapter One
1. https://www.livius.org/sources/content/diodorus
2. Plutarch, *Camillus*, 15.3–4.
3. Livy, 5.35.
4. Diodorus Siculus, 14.113.4.
5. Plutarch, *Camillus*, 17.2–5.
6. Livy, 5. 36.
7. Diodorus, 14.113.4–5.
8. Dionysius, 12.1.
9. Livy, 5.36; Dionysius, 12.2.
10. Livy, 5.36.
11. Livy, 5.37.
12. For more details on this style of warfare and an analysis of the transformation, see e.g. Armstrong, 2016, 85ff. cf. Chapter 2.
13. Diodorus, 14.114.3.
14. Dionysius, 12.12.
15. Plutarch, *Camillus*, 18.4.
16. cf. Livy, 9.30.
17. Livy, 5.36; dates, Armstrong, 2016, 75.
18. On Consular Tribunes, see Armstrong, 2016, esp. 74ff.
19. Livy, 8.8.
20. Livy, 5.37.
21. For more detail on this hypothesis, see Cornell, 2006, 316f.
22. Strabo, *Geography*, 5.2.3.
23. Diodorus, 14.117.7.
24. Caesar, *Gallic Wars*, 4.24f.
25. Livy, 5.37.
26. Plutarch, *Camillus*, 18.6.
27. Livy, 5.38.
28. E.g. Diodorus, 12.2.
29. Offending the gods and illness, e.g. Plutarch, *Camillus*, 28; 'Incredibly dubious', Armstrong, 2016, 88.
30. Strabo, *Geography*, 5.2.3.
31. *Brewer's Classical Dictionary*: https://www.infoplease.com/dictionary/brewers/alliensis
32. Diodorus, 13.7.

Chapter Two
1. Livy, 8.8.
2. Livy, 8.9.14; 8.10.2–4.

3. This section is based on Erdkamp, 2011, p.56.
4. Livy, 8.8.8.
5. Livy, 8.9.14; 8.10.204.
6. Cato in Varro, LL 7.58.
7. *Leves*, Livy, 8.8.5; *Rorarii*, Paulus, *Epit. Fest.*, 13, 323.
8. Erdkamp, 2011, p.56.
9. The *hasta* was still being used against Pyrrhos; Dionysius of Halicarnassus, 20.11.2.
10. *Pilum* probably copied from the Samnites; Sallust, *Bellum Catilinae*, 51.38.
11. Forsythe, 2005, 304.
12. 40,000, Dionysius of Halicarnassus, 16.1.3; 50,000, Constantine Porphyrogenitus, *The Embassies*, 6; cf. App. Sam. 1.pos=28.
13. Salmon, 2010, 224–5.
14. Salmon, 2010, 225; Wiley, *Ancient Battles*, Part IV, Chapter 18, p.7.
15. Salmon, 2010, 223; cf. Livy, 8.37.4–5, 12. 9–10; Auct, de Vir ill. 32.
16. Livy, 9.1.
17. Livy, 9.2.
18. Livy, 9.2.
19. Livy 9.4; cf. Ox. pop. ad an. 320/319; Cicero, *Cato Maior*, 12.41; Cic. de off. 3.30.109; App. Samn., 4.2; Dio, frg. 36.9–14; Zonaras, 7.26.
20. Livy, 9.3–4; Constantine Porphyrogenitus, *The Embassies*, 7, 9–10.
21. These were performed by the Fetial College; c.f e.g. Tenney, Frank, 'The Import of the Fetial Institution', *Classical Philology*, Vol. 7, No. 3 (July 1912), pp.335–342.
22. Forsythe, 2005, 298; cf. Livy, 9.5.2–4.
23. Forsythe, 2005, 7.
24. Livy, 9.4.
25. Livy, 9.7.
26. Salmon, 2010, 229.
27. cf. Livy, 9.21.2.
28. Frontinus, 5.16.

Chapter Three
1. Diod. Sic., 20.104.
2. Livy, 10.2.
3. Cass. Dio., 39
4. Plutarch, *Pyrrhus*, 7–12.
5. Pol., 6.20–35.
6. Pol., 6.21–39.
7. Pol., 6.23–46.
8. Pol., 6.23–46.
9. Pol., 18.30.
10. Pol., 6.19–26.
11. Plutarch, *Pyrrhus*, 15.
12. Dionysius, *Fr. Didot.*, xx. 2; Plutarch, *Pyrrhus*, 16; Florus I. 18. § 7.
13. Dion. Hal., 19.13f.
14. Livy, 12.
15. Front., Strat., 2.21.
16. Dion., 20.5.
17. Dion., 20.1–20.

18. Dion., 20.5.
19. Pol., 18.28.
20. Frontinus, Strat., 2.21.
21. Cic. De Fin., 2.19.
22. Plutarch, Pyrrhus, 21.9.

Chapter Four
1. Polybius, 6.20–35.
2. Strabo, Geography, 3.4.18.
3. Livy, 21–30 (26).
4. Livy, 21.57.5.
5. Fighting style, Polybius, 3.65.6.
6. Polybius, 2.28.
7. Polybius, 3.114.
8. Propertius, Elegies, 4.10.46–7.
9. Polybius, 3.83.
10. Polybius, 3.83.

Chapter Five
1. Livy, Periochae, 67.1.
2. Sallust, Bellum Jugurthinum (The War with Jugurtha), 86.2.
3. cf. Sallust, Bellum Jugurthinum, esp. 51.2.
4. E.g. Velleius Paterculus (2.12.2) sees them as German, whereas Plutarch (Marius 11.1) admits that this is conjecture. Much later, Orosius (15.16.1) adds the Tigurini and the Ambrones to the coalition and states that this was 'a conspiracy to destroy the Roman Empire'. For comprehension, the Tigurini and the Ambrones are ignored in this description.
5. Sallust, Bellum Jugurthinum, 114.2.
6. Plutarch, Marius, 11.2.
7. Orosius, 5.16.1.
8. Granius Licinianus, 33L 11.25.
9. Cassius Dio, 27, 91.1–2.
10. A similar thing may have happened to some degree at the later Battle of Adrianople in 378.
11. Orosius, 5, 16.3–4.

Chapter Six
1. Sources: Plutarch, Crassus, 17–33L; Cassius Dio, 40.20.
2. Defeat of Silaces, Dio, 40.12.2; Greek/Macedonian cities, Dio, 40.13.1; Plutarch, Crassus, 17.2–3.
3. Dio, 40.13.1–2; Plutarch, Crassus, 17.3.
4. Plutarch, Crassus, 17.4.
5. Dio, 40.13.3.
6. Plutarch, Crassus, 19.1.
7. Dio, 40.20.3.
8. Plutarch, Crassus, 18 1.
9. Plutarch, Crassus, 18.2–4.
10. Omens and Crassus' response, Plutarch, Cassius, 18.5; officer intervention, Plutarch, Cassius, 18.4.

11. Plutarch, *Crassus*, 22.2.
12. Ibid, 22.3.
13. Ibid, 20.1–2.
14. Ibid, 21.1f.
15. Ibid, 22.2–3.
16. Dio, 40.20.4.
17. Plutarch, *Crassus*, 23.3.
18. Ibid, 23.3–4.
19. Ibid, 20.1.
20. Ibid, 18, 24.
21. Spear, Plutarch, *Crassus* 27, Antony, 45; Dio, *Cassius* 40.22; Herodian, 4.30; Two men, Plutarch, *Crassus*, 27.
22. Plutarch, *Crassus*, 21.
23. Ibid, 23.5–6.
24. Plutarch, *Crassus*, 23.6; cf. Dio, 40.21 2–3.
25. Plutarch, *Crassus*, 23.7–24.3.
26. Ibid, 25.1.
27. Ibid, 23.7–24.4.
28. Ibid, 23.7–24.5.
29. Plutarch, *Crassus*, 25.2–5; but cf. Dio, 40.21 2–3.
30. Plutarch, *Crassus*, 25.6–11.
31. Ibid, 26.1–4.
32. Ibid, 26.5–27.1.
33. Plutarch, *Crassus*, 27.1–2; Dio, 40.22 1–5.
34. Dio, 40.23 1.
35. Ibid, 40.23 1.
36. Plutarch, *Crassus*, 27.5–6; Dio, 40.25 1.
37. Plutarch, *Crassus*, 27.7.
38. Ibid, 27.8.
39. Ibid, 28.1–2.
40. Ibid, 28.4–5.
41. Dio, 40.25.3.
42. Plutarch, *Crassus*, 28.4; Dio, 40.25.4.
43. Plutarch, *Crassus*, 28.5.
44. Ibid, 28.6.
45. Ibid, 28.7.
46. Plutarch, *Crassus*, 31.1–5; Dio, 40.27.1.
47. Plutarch, *Crassus*, 33.1.
48. Dio, 40.28.1.
49. Ibid, 40, 28.2–3.
50. Florus, *Epitome of Roman History*, 2.13.14.

Chapter Seven
1. The standard size of a *turma* during the Republican period and in the *cohors equitata* was thirty men. However, Arrian (*Ars Tactica*, 17.3) states that an *ala* had 512 men, so each *turma* should be 32 men. No definitive answer to the dilemma has yet been found, other than to say that numbers varied slightly from region to region.
2. Vell. Pat., 2.117.1.
3. Tacitus, *Annals*, 1.61.62.

4. Cass. Dio, 56.21.3–5.
5. Ibid, 56.22.2.
6. Ibid, 56.22.2.
7. Suetonius, *Augustus*, 23.4.

Chapter Eight

1. *cum pauculis, qui fugere quiuerant*, Jord., *Get.*, 102.
2. Dexippus, 194v 2–3; 194v 9.
3. Ibid, 194v.
4. Bursche, 161.
5. Dexippus, 194r.
6. Zosimus, 1.23.1–3; 'Decius, marching against them, was not only victorious in every battle, but recovered the spoils they had taken.'
7. Syncellus, pp.459.5–19 = Dexippus, fgrH 100 f 22. Trans. Banchich and Lane, 2009, p.100.
8. Zosimus, 1.23.2.
9. Ibid, 1.23.2.
10. Zonaras, 12.20, trans. Banchich and Lane, 2009, p.50.

Chapter Nine

1. 13.108–112.
2. George Syncellus, 466.9–13; Zonaras, 12.23–24.
3. Eutropius, 9.7.
4. Aur. Vict., 32.6.
5. Lactantius, *de Mortibus*, 5.

Chapter Ten

1. Ammianus Marcellinus, 18.4.
2. Ibid, 19.2.9.
3. Ibid, 18.6.8.
4. Ibid, 18.6.17–18.
5. Ibid, 18.7.4.
6. Ibid, 18.9.3–4.
7. Ibid, 18.9.3.
8. Ammianus Marcellinus I, trans. J.C. Rolfe, Loeb, 1982, p.464, n.4.
9. Ibid, 18.9.4.
10. Ibid, 18.8.1.1–3.
11. Ibid, 19.6.11.
12. Ibid, 18.6.22.
13. Ibid, 19.2.2.
14. See the assessment of 'Saansaan' and 'pirosen' earlier in the text.
15. Ammianus Marcellinus, 19.2.12–13.
16. Ibid, 19.3.1.
17. Ibid, 19.4.7.
18. Ibid, 19.4.8.
19. Ibid, 19.5.4–7.
20. Ibid, 19.6.6.
21. Ibid, 19.6.6–10.

22. Ibid, 19.6.13.
23. Ibid, 19.7.2–5.
24. Ibid, 19.7.6–8.
25. Ibid, 19.8.2.
26. Ibid, 19.8.4–5.

Chapter Eleven
1. Libanius, *Oration*, 12, 76–77.
2. Ammianus Marcellinus, 23.2.6.
3. cf. Ammianus Marcellinus, 23.5.1.
4. Ibid, 24.1.10.
5. Ibid, 23.2.1.
6. Ibid, 23.2.1.
7. Date, Ammianus Marcellinus, 23.2.6.
8. Zosimus, 3.12.1–2.
9. Bridge, Ammianus Marcellinus, 23.2.7; 23.3.1.
10. Zosimus, 3.12.3.
11. Ammianus Marcellinus, 23.3.6.
12. Ibid, 23.3.2.
13. Ammianus Marcellinus, 23.3.4; Zosimus, 3.12.3.
14. Zosimus, 3.13.1.
15. Ibid, 3.13.1.
16. Ibid, 23.3.7; Zosimus, 3.13.1.
17. Ammianus Marcellinus, 23.3.9.
18. Ibid, 23.5.9; cf. Zosimus, 3.13.1.
19. Ibid, 23.5.6; Zosimus, 3.13.2.
20. Zosimus, 3.13.3–3.14.1.
21. Ammianus Marcellinus, 24.1.3.
22. *Zaitha*, Ammianus Marcellinus, 23.5.7–8; two days, Ammianus Marcellinus, 24.1.5; also two days, Zosimus, 3.14.2, where *Zaitha* is called *Lautha*.
23. Four days, Anatha, Ammianus Marcellinus, 24.1.6; Seven days, Phathusae, Zosimus, 3.14.2. It is possible that the local settlement was called Phathusae and that the island fortress was called Anatha.
24. Ammianus Marcellinus, 24.1.7–9; Zosimus, 3.14.3–4.
25. Ammianus Marcellinus, 24.1.11.
26. Thilutha, Achaiachala and abandoned fortress, Ammianus Marcellinus, 24.2.1–3; Attacks repulsed and defenders agreeing not to interfere, Zosimus, 3.15.1–2 where no names are given.
27. Diacira, Ammianus Marcellinus, 24.2.3; Dacira, Zosimus, 3.15.2.
28. Ammianus Marcellinus, 24.2.4; Zosimus, 3.15.4.
29. Zosimus, 3.15.3.
30. Ammianus Marcellinus, 24.2.4; Zosimus, 3.15.4.
31. Ammianus Marcellinus, 24.2.6–7; cf. Zosimus, 3.16.1.
32. cf. Zosimus, 3.16.1, where they became entangled in mud.
33. Zosimus, 3.16.2–3.17; Ammianus Marcellinus, 24.2.8 simply states that the Sasanid force was defeated.
34. Pirisabora, Ammianus Marcellinus, 24.2.9; Bersabora and description, Zosimus, 3.17.4–18.6.

35. Ammianus Marcellinus, 24.3.1; Zosimus, 3.19.1–2.
36. Ammianus Marcellinus, 24.3.1; cf. Zosimus, 3.19.1–2.
37. Zosimus, 3.19.3. Zosimus claims that the 'King's river' was here, but this is unclear.
38. Bithra, Zosimus, 3.19.4.
39. Ammianus Marcellinus, 24.3.10–11; Zosimus, 3.20.1.
40. Zosimus, 3.20.1–5. From this point the account of Ammianus is preferred to that of Zosimus, who appears to have struggled with interpreting his sources.
41. Ammianus Marcellinus, 24.4.3–4; cf. Zosimus, 3.20.2–3.
42. Ammianus Marcellinus, 24.4.6.
43. Ibid, 24.4.7; Zosimus, 3.20.4.
44. Ibid, 24.4.9; cf. Zosimus, 3.20.6, 3.21.5.
45. Ibid, 24.4.13; Zosimus, 3.21.4.
46. Ammianus Marcellinus, 24.4.29–30.
47. Zosimus, 3.23.3–4.
48. Ibid, 3.24.31.
49. Ammianus Marcellinus, 24.4.31.
50. Ibid, 24.5.1–3.
51. Ibid, 24.5.3.
52. cf. Zosimus, 3.24.1.
53. Ammianus Marcellinus, 24.5.6–7.
54. Ibid, 24.5.8.
55. Ibid, 24.5.8–9.
56. Ibid, 24.5.11–12.
57. Ibid, 24.6.1–2; cf. Zosimus, 3.24.2.
58. Ammianus Marcellinus, 24.6.2.
59. Ibid, 24.6.3.
60. cf. Zosimus, 3.25.1–4.
61. Ibid, 3.25.6–7.
62. Ammianus Marcellinus, 24.6.15; Zosimus, 3.25.7.
63. Zosimus, 3.21.1.
64. Ammianus Marcellinus, 24.7.5; cf. Zosimus, 3.26.2. Zosimus claims eighteen Roman and four Persian vessels were saved, 3.26.3.
65. Ammianus Marcellinus, 24.7.7.
66. Noorda, Zosimus, 3.26.3; Durus, Zosimus, 3.26.4.
67. Ammianus Marcellinus, 24, 8,1–5.
68. Ibid, 24, 8.8.
69. Ibid, 25.1.1–3; advanced light troops, Zosimus, 3.26.5.
70. Zosimus, 3.27.1.
71. Hucumbra, Ammianus Marcellinus, 25.1.4; Symbra, Zosimus, 3.27.2. The events recounted here imply that the two named towns are actually the same.
72. Town taken, Zosimus, 3.27.3; rest, Ammianus Marcellinus, 25.1.4.
73. Adaces, Ammianus Marcellinus, 25.1.6; Daces, Zosimus, 3.27.4.
74. Zosimus, 3.28.1.
75. Maranga, Ammianus Marcellinus, 25.1.10–11; Maronsa, Zosimus, 3.28.1–2.
76. Zosimus, 3.28.2.
77. Ammianus Marcellinus, 25.2.1.
78. Zosimus, 3.28.3.
79. Four miles, Ammianus Marcellinus, 25.5.6.

80. cf. Zosimus, 3.28.4–29.1.
81. Ammianus Marcellinus, 25.3.13–14; Zosimus, 3.29.2.
82. Ammianus Marcellinus, 25.7.1.
83. Ibid, 25.7.9.

Chapter Twelve

1. On the proposals, Zosimus, 4.37.
2. Philos. HE, 10.8.
3. Zosimus, 4.53.4.
4. Ibid, 4.53.3–4.
5. Examples of sources that claim he was murdered: Zosimus, 4.54.3; Soc. 5.25; and Orosius 7.35. Uncertain about events: Sozimus, 7.22.
6. 20,000 men, Jordanes, *Getica*, 28.145: 'a large number', Soc. 5.25.
7. Orosius, 7.
8. Williams and Friell, 1995, 132.
9. Sozimus' claim (7.24) that it was Theodosius' vanguard that attacked the opposition supports the theory that Theodosius was compelled to use the troops at the front of the column without regard to strategical or tactical niceties.
10. Zosimus, 4.58.2; Sozimus, 7.24.
11. Zosimus, 4.58.3.
12. Orosius, 7.35.
13. Sozimus, 7.24, 'he fell prone upon the earth, and prayed with tears'; Soc. 5.25, 'he cast himself in great agony upon the ground, and invoked the help of God in this emergency.'
14. Orosius, 7.35.16; Sozimus, HE, 7.24.5.
15. Zosimus, 4.58.
16. Zosimus, 4.58; *Fasti Vindobonenses priores* no. 522.

Chapter Thirteen

1. Proc., 3.6.8f.
2. Cedrenus, p.613 (however, this appears to be '1115' in the *Migne Patrologia Graeca*; p.667).
3. Theod. Lect., 1.25.
4. See below.
5. Proc., 3.6.8.
6. Proc., 3.6.9; Marsus, Theoph., Ammianus Marcellinus, 5963.
7. Theoph., Ammianus Marcellinus, 5963.
8. Ibid.
9. PLRE 2, *Basiliscus 2*, 213. Brother of Verina, Prisc. fr. 53.1; Vit. Dan. Styl. 69; Marc. *com.* s.a. 475; Jord. Rom. 337; Zach. HE, 5.1; Proc., 3.6.2 etc. On his competence, see below.
10. Prisc., fr. 43.
11. Prisc., fr. 53.1. There is a *lacuna* in the text that is sometimes amended to a specific number.
12. Although in 533 Belisarius landed nearer to Carthage, it should be noted that he landed at Sicily first and had the good fortune to find out that the Vandals were not expecting his attack: Hughes, 2009, 79f.
13. Proc., 3.6.10.

14. Theod. Lect., 1.25.
15. Ammianus Marcellus, 31.12.13f.
16. cf. Theoph., Ammianus Marcellinus, 5961.
17. Traitors, Hyd. 195 [200], s.a. 460.
18. Proc., 3.6.16.
19. Joh. Mal., 14.44, cf. Prisc. fr. 53; Phot. Bibl., 79; Theod. Lect. Epit. 399; Zon., 14.1.24–6.
20. Theoph., Ammianus Marcellinus, 5963.
21. Proc., 3.6.26; Nic. Call. HE, 15.27.
22. cf. Marc. *com.* s.a. 468, who clearly expected Marcellinus to be in Africa.
23. Date, Fast. Vind. Prior., s.a. 468; Quote, Proc., 3.6.25: cf. Pasch. Camp., s.a. 468; Cass. Chron., s.a. 468; Marc. *com.* s.a. 468; Cons. Ital., s.a. 468.
24. Marc., *com.* s.a. 468.

Index

Abarne, 175
Abgar, 98, 101–2, 105, 107
Abora, River, 192, 196
Abritus, 128–46, 153
Abuzatha, 204
Acarnanians, 51, 53
Accensi, 24–5
Acceta, 206
Achaemenid, 149, 152, 155
Achaiachala, 194
Adaces, 206
Adrianople, Battle of, 145, 148, 210, 212, 217, 220–1, 232
Adriatic, 3, 29
Aelianus, 167
Aemilian, 152
Aemilianus, S., 59, 62
Aetolians, 51, 53
Africa, 44, 61–3, 69, 71, 73–4, 79, 154, 223–30, 232, 234, 236
Agema, 43, 54
Aginnum, Battle of, 78
Ahenobarbus, 114
Ajdovščina, 215
ala Milliaria, 117
ala Quingenaria, 117
Alae, 'wings', 42, 52
Alae, Cavalry, 118
Alamanni, 158, 161, 166, 183–4, 203, 217
al-Anbar, 150
Alans, 214, 224–5
Alaric, 221
Alaudae, Legio V, 112–13
Albani, 174, 176–7
Albania, 177
Albinus, 24, 29
Albis, River, see Elbe, River
al-Dinawari, 160, 163
Alexander Severus, 129
Alexander the Great, 37, 43–4, 58, 96, 98–9, 101
Alexander, King of Epirus, 23, 36
Aliso, 125
Aller, River, 112
Allia, Battle of the River, 1–21, 23, 24, 32, 83, 92, 238

Allia, River, 12–16, 18
Allobroges, 61
Alps, 3, 20, 61–2, 77–8, 87, 92, 137, 215
Ambracians, 53
Amida, 164–83, 185, 187, 189, 216
Amisia, River, see Ems, River
Amisos, 131
Anagni, 49
Anatha, 194
Andromachus, 108
Anti-elephant wagons, 50, 53–4
Antigonus, 37
Antoninopolis, 175
Antoninus, Lucius Julius Aurelius Sulpicius Severus Uranius Antoninus, 152
Antoninus, Roman deserter, 167–8
Apennines, 22, 40, 49, 63–4
Apulians, 31, 55
Aquae Sextiae, Battle of, 92, 95
Aquileia, 214–15
Arausio, Battle of, 75–93, 94, 102, 112
Arbogast, 214–19, 221
Archidamus III, 36
Ardashir, 149
Arethusa, 152
Argentoratum, Battle of, 184, 203
Argos, 58
Argyrippa, 54
Ariminum, 63
Arintheus, 193, 199, 204
Armada, Spanish, 234
Armenia, 97–104, 109, 149, 151–2, 155, 175, 189, 191–2, 194, 205, 210
Arminius, 114–15, 118, 124–7
Arno, River, 64
Arretium, 63
Arsaces, 189, 191, 205, 210
Artavasdes, 97–101, 103–4, 109
Artemis, Temple of, 152
Arzanene, 209
Asaak, 99
Asavaran, 155, 173
Asculum, Battle of, 34–58, esp. 50 ff
Aspar, 235
Aspis, 25
Asprenas, Lucius Nonius, 125

Assisi, 73
Assyrian, 188
Āsūrestān, 150
Aswaran, 99
Athamanians, 51, 53
Athenian, 101
Athens, 41, 184
Athesis, Battle of, 92
Attic helmets, 25, 27, 39
Augusta Traiana, 131
Augustus, 74, 92, 109–10, 113, 116, 125
Aurelian, 146, 162, 164
Aurelius Victor, 129, 139, 144, 147, 160
Aurunci, 23
Azadan, 99

Babylon, 196
Baetica, 225
Balearic Islands, 44, 68, 225
Balearic slingers, 70
Balissus, River, 101–2, 105
Ballistae, 180–1, 197
Band-e Kaisar, 160
Baraxmalcha, 194
Barbalissos, Battle of, 151
Barroptha, 205
Basiliscus, 224, 227, 230–6
Bastarnae, 131
Batman, River, 175
Batnae, 190
Bauto, 214
Beli Lom, River, 133
Belias, River, 192
Belisarius, 223
Beneventum, Battle of, 58
Beroea, 11, 133, 137, 139, 141
Bersabora, see Pirisabora
Besuchis, 198
Bezabde, 182
Bithra, 198
Boiorix, 84
Bora, 219
Boudicca, 115
Bovianum, 32
Brennus, 4, 11, 13, 15–16, 18
Bructeri, 113, 118, 136
Bruttii, 51, 53
Bulgaria, 133
Byzacena, 225

Caepio, Quintus Servilius, 78, 84–91
Caere, 10–11, 18–19
Caesar, Gaius Julius, 17, 20, 91–2, 95–6, 100, 110, 112, 238
Caesarea, 147, 161, 211
Caetra/Caetrati, 67

Caius Cassius Longinus, see Cassius
Calabria, 44
Calatia, 24, 29
Cales, 23, 31
Callistus, 161
Calvinus, Titus Veturius, 24, 29
Camillus, 2, 19, 24
Campania, 23, 51
Campanian League, 23
Candidus, 227
Cannabaudes, 146
Cannae, 32, 59, 68–9, 74
Canusium, 29
Cap Bon, Battle of, 223–37
Capite Censi, 79
Cappadocia, 152, 154
Capua, 23, 49
Caracalla, 134
Carbo, Gnaeus Papirius, 77–8
Carnuntum, 133
Carpi, 131–2
Carrhae, 94–110, 150, 153, 158–9, 188, 190–2
Carrhae, Battle of, 94–110, 155
Carrhae, Battle of (296–7), 164
Carthage, 1, 25, 60–1, 74, 224–5, 228–32, 234, 236
Carthaginians, 57, 60, 62–3, 65–6, 69, 71, 73
Cassius, 101–2, 108–9
Cassius Dio, 54–5, 75, 85–6, 95, 97, 111, 114–16, 120–3
Castra Maurorum, 209
Casus Belli, 96
Cataphracts, 104–7, 155, 173, 196, 202–3, 205
Cato, 25
Catulus, 92
Caudine Forks, Battle of, 21–34, 38–9, 78
Caudini, 29
Caudium, 29
Cedrenus, Georgius, 224, 226–7
Celtiberians, 67
Centennius, Gaius, 73
Centurion, 39, 81
Chaionians, 53
Chalcidian, 39
Chalcis, 194
Chamavi, 185
Chariots, 11–12, 16–17, 55, 68
Chatti, 113, 118
Chauci, 113, 118
Cherusci, 113–16, 118
Chiliocomum, 191, 210
Chionites, 168
Cicero, 21, 34
Cilicia, 154, 161, 185

Cimbri, 77–8, 82–8, 90–2, 95, 112
Cineas, 43, 49
Circesium, 190, 192
Cisalpine Gaul, 20, 84, 87
Cleonymus, 36
Clibanarii, 170
Clusians, 4–5
Clusium, 4–5, 10–11
Cniva, 131–3, 135, 137–8, 141–6
Cohort, 18, 45, 79–81, 102, 106, 108, 117, 199
Colline Gate, Battle of, 95
Comitatenses, 171
Comites Sagittarii, 171–2
Companions, 43, 48, 115, 171
Constans, 166, 184
Constantine I, the Great, 148, 164, 170, 184, 186, 193, 211, 216–17
Constantine II, 166, 184
Constantius Gallus, 166, 184
Constantius II, 165–6, 178–9, 182, 184–5
Constitutio Antoniniana, 134
Coponius, 108
Corcyra, 37
Corduene, 191, 205, 209
Corsica, 225
Cortona, 65
Coruncanius, Tiberius, 49
Crassus, Marcus Licinius, 95–6, 99–103, 105–10
Crassus, Publius, 96, 100, 102, 106–7
Crete, 44
Croton, 37
Crustuminian Mountains, 12
Ctesiphon, 97, 99, 102, 150, 165, 175, 192, 198–9, 201–4
Ctesiphon, Battle of, 201–4

Daces, *see* Adaces
Dacia, 131, 146, 154
Dacira, *see* Diacira
Dadastana, 210
Dagalaifus, 198
Dailami/Daylami, 156, 174
Danabe, 206
Danube, River, 114, 131–3, 136, 141–2, 161, 166, 184–5, 216–17
Dauni/Daunian, 51, 54
Davana, 192
Decentiaci, 171
Decentius, 171
Decian Persecutions, 129
Decimani, 171
Decius, emperor, 55–7, 129–33, 135–45, 151, 153
Decius, Trajan, 129
see also Trajan

Decius Vibelius, 49
see also Vibelius
Dediticii, 134
Devotio, 57
Dexippus, Publius Herennius, 129–32, 138–42, 145–6, 183
Diacira, 194
Diadochi, 37
Dies Alliensis, 19
Dies Nefastus, 19
Dio, Cassius, 54–6, 76, 85–6, 94, 97, 99, 102, 107–8, 111, 114–16, 120–3
Diocletian, 117, 128, 164–5, 170, 209, 216–17
Diodorus Siculus, 1, 4–5, 9, 11, 13, 15
Dionysius of Halicarnassus, 9, 19, 34, 48, 50, 52–6
Discenes, 172–3
Dobrudja, 131
Dominate, 170, 185
Drusus, Nero Claudius, 113–14
Ducarius, 72
Dura, 209
Dura Europos, 152, 193
Durus, River, 205

Ebro, River, 60–1
Ecbatana, 99
Edessa, 153, 156–9, 161
Edessa, Battle of, 98, 105, 147–64
Eggius, 125
Egypt, 37, 96, 162, 165, 188, 228–9
Elagabal, 152
Elbe, River, 112–14, 126
Elche, Battle of, 226
Elephants, 43–4, 48, 50–7, 61–2, 156, 176–7, 181, 201–3, 206, 208
Emesa, Battle of, 152
Endemic, 179
Ephesus, 152
Epidemic, 179
Epiphania, 152
Epirote League, 37, 48, 53–5
Epirus, 23, 34, 36–7
Equitata/e Milliaria, 117
Equitata/e Quingenaria, 117
Equites Illyricani, 171
Equites Sagittarii, 170
Etruria, 49, 63, 73
Etruscans, 3, 40, 72
Etrusco-Corinthian Helmet, 25, 27
Etruscus, 129, 139
see also Herennius
Eudocia, 225, 236
Eudoxia, 225
Eugenius, 214, 219, 221

Euphrates, 96–7, 101, 109, 151, 165, 167, 177, 187, 190, 193–5, 200
Eurus, 175
Euscia, 137
Eusebius, 147–8, 211
Eutropius, 147, 160

Fabians/Fabii, 4–6, 73
Fabius, Gnaeus Mallius, 78
Fabius, Quintus Ambustus, 4–5
Fabius, Quintus Maximus, 73
Fabricus, 49
Falerna, 31
Fireships, 233–4
Flamen, 18
Flaminius, 63, 65–6, 69–70, 72–3
Florus, 111–12
Foederati, 134, 214, 216, 218, 220
Foedus, 30, 134
Fortenses, 171
Forum Thembronium, 138, 145
Framea, 118
Franks, 153, 161, 185, 217
Fregellae, 23, 31
Frentani, 51
Frentanian, 48
Fretensis, 171
Frigidus, Battle of, 211–22
Frisii, 113
Fritigern, 232
Frontinus, 50, 52, 53

Gabinius, Aulus, 96
Gaiseric, 225–6, 228, 230–6
Galerius, 164
Gallaecia, 225
Gallic Empire, 162
Gallienus, 152–3, 162, 167
Gallus, 131–2, 136–41, 143, 145, 151–2, 166, 184
Gaul/s, 20, 61, 77–8, 83–4, 87, 92, 95–6, 103, 106, 112, 125–7, 152–3, 162, 179–80, 182, 185, 187, 210, 212, 217–18, 224–5, 236, 238
Gelani, 168, 174, 176–7
Genzon, 234
Germanicus, 113, 126
Gibraltar, Straits of, 225
Gilan, 155, 177
Gladius, 25, 40, 102–3, 134, 170
Gnaitha, 29
Gordian, 129, 133, 150–1
Gothicus Maximus, 146
Goths, 20, 76, 128–33, 135–8, 140–4, 146, 151–3, 212, 214, 216–19, 221, 224–5

Granicus, River, 168
Gratian, 212, 217
Greece, 38, 58, 165
Grumbates, 169, 174, 177
Gumathena, 175
Gunderic, 225
Gundishapur, 160

Hadrian, 148, 185
Hamilcar Barca, 60
Hannibal, 49, 59–66, 68–74, 76, 79, 87, 92
Hanno, 61
Hasdrubal, 60–1
Hasta, 25, 32, 40, 80
Hastae velitares, 26, 40
Hastati, 24–6, 32, 38, 40, 43, 65, 80
Hecatompylos, 99
Hegemon, 37
Helena, 184
Helepolis, 197
Helvetia/n, 78
Heraclea, 42, 44, 49
Heraclea Sintica, 235
Heraclea, Battle of, 26, 34–51
Heraclius, 227–30, 235–6
Herennius, 129, 139, 145
   see also Etruscus
Hierapolis, 190
Hierius, 190
Hiero, 63, 66
Hieronymus, 48, 56
Hispania, 60–1, 63, 66, 77, 79–80, 83, 92, 95, 153–4, 162, 224–5, 236
Hispanic, 60, 66–8, 92
Histria, 129
Hoplite warfare, 5–7, 16, 20, 24–5, 42–3, 66
Hoplon, 25, 42, 66
Hormizd, 186
Hucumbra, *see* Symbra
Huneric, 225, 236
Huns, 214

Iatrus, River, 131, 137
Iberians, 25, 63–4, 67
Iceni, 115
Ichnae, 96, 101
Ignatius, 108
Illyricum, 217
Ingenuus, 162
Insubrian/s, 72
Ipsus, Battle of, 37
Isidore of Seville, 128
Italic Helmet, 135
Italic pectoral, 25, 27
Italo-Corinthian Helmet, 39

John, general under Basiliscus, 233–4
John (Joannes) Lydas (the Lydian), 226
John Malalas, 147, 183
John (Joannes) Zonaras, 148
Jordanes, 128–9, 131–2, 137–8, 141, 144–5, 212, 224
Jovian, 183, 209–10
Joviani, 209
Jugurtha, 79
Julian, 166, 182, 183–210

Ka 'ba-i Zardušt, 150
Kalkriese, 119, 123–4
Khosrow, 155
Khuzestan, 182
Kidarite, 168

Lactantius, 147–8, 158, 160
Laevinus, Publius Valerius, 42, 44–5, 49–50
Lancea Subarmales, 135
Lanciarii, 135
Larissa, 152
Latin War, 23
Latins, 23, 51
Lautha, *see* Zaitha
Lautulae, Battle of, 32
Legions: *IV Flavia Felix, VII Claudia, XIV Gemina*, 133
Leo, Emperor, 224, 226–8, 230–1, 235
Leves, 25
Libya, 229
Libyans, 61–4
Licinius, 95
Lilybaeum, 57
Limitanei, 171
Livy, 2, 4, 9–10, 12–13, 15, 18, 21–2, 24–6, 29–31, 33, 59, 67, 70, 72–3, 75, 112
Locri, 37
Loemedes, 179
Lollius, Marcus, 112
Longinus, Caius Cassius, 100
Longus, Lucius Cassius, 78
Longus, Quintus Sulpicius, 5
Longus, Sempronius, 62
Lorica Hamata, 38, 135, 170
Lorica Segmentata, 135, 170
Luca Bos, 48
Lucanians, 31, 36, 49, 53–4
Luceria, 29
Lucilianus, 193–4, 196
Lutatius, Treaty of, 60
Lysimachus, 37

Macedonia, 37, 53, 58, 96
Macepracta, 196

Macrianus, 161–2
Magister equitum per Orient, 167
Magister Militum, 171, 214, 235
Magister militum per Dalmatiae, 228
Magister militum praesentalis, 230
Magister scrinorum, 214
Magna Graecia, 36
Magnentiaci, 171
Magnentius, Magnus (usurper), 166, 171, 184
Magnus Maximus, 212–14, 221
Magnus of Carrhae, 183–4
Mago, 62–3
Maiozamalcha, 198
Majorian, 225–6, 230, 232, 235
Malalas, 147, 183–4, 235
Mallius, Gnaeus Maximus, 78, 84–91
Malta, 225
Maluginensis, Servius Cornelius, 5
Mamersides, 197
Maniple/s, 24, 26–7, 38, 53, 79–80
Maranga, Battle of, 206
Marcellinus, Ammianus, *see* Ammianus
Marcellinus *Comes*, 224
Marcellinus, Roman commander, 227–30, 234, 236
Marcianopolis, 132
Marcomanni, 113–14
Marian Reforms, 79, 102
Marius, Gaius, 75, 79–80, 82, 91–2, 94, 116
Maronsa, *see* Maranga
Marrucini, 51
Marsi, 51, 118, 126
Marsus, 229, 235
Massilia, 61
Maximinus Thrax, 129
Maximus, Gnaeus Mallius, *see* Mallius, Gnaeus Maximus
Maximus, Quintus Fabius, *see* Fabius
Meddix, 26, 29
Media, 96, 191
Megacles, 48
Megia, 194
Mercenary War, 60
Mercurium, *see* Cape Bon
Merena, 206
Mesopotamia, 98, 100, 108, 149, 154–5
Mesopotamiae, Dux, 165
Metus Gallicus, 20, 83, 92, 238
Minucius, Quintus, 32
Misiche, Battle of, 150
Mithradatkirt, 99
Mithridates, 96–7
Mithridatic War, 96–7
Moesia, 129, 131, 137–8, 141, 153–4

Moesia Prima, 131, 152
Moesia Secunda, 152
Mons Seleucus, Battle of, 166
Montefortino helmet, 38–9, 67
Mopsuestia, 185
Moxoëne, 191, 209
Mursa Major, Battle of, 166
Mus, Publius Decius, 50
Muthul, Battle of, 79

Naarmalcha, 200
Naples, 23, 49
Naqš-i Rustam, 147, 150, 153, 158, 161
Narses, 212, 224
    see also Narseus
Narseus, 202
    see also Narses
Nauta, 227
Nerva, 148
Nevitta, 193, 198
Nicias, 101
Nicopolis, 131, 137–8
Nisa, 99
Noorda, 205
Noreia, Battle of, 78
Noricum, 77, 154
North Sea, 113
Novae, 131–2, 137–8, 142
Numantia, 79
Numerian, 148
Numidia/ns, 62, 66–7, 225

Octavius, 108
Odenathus, 161–2
Oescus, 131–2, 137–8
Oplacus, 48
Optio, 39
Orodes II, 96–7, 99–101, 104, 107, 109
Orosius, 35, 76, 87, 91, 147–8, 211, 218, 221
Osrhoene, 98, 105, 107, 149, 154
Ostrogotha, 131–3, 138, 141–4
Ostrogouthos, see Ostrogotha
Oufentina, 31
Ozogardana, 194
    see also Zaragardia

Paeligni, 51
Palatina, 171
Palmyra, 161–2
Palmyrene Empire, 162
Pannonia, 114, 152–3
Parma (shield), 40
Parthia, 95–110, 147, 149, 155, 157, 160, 171, 207–8
Paterculus, Velleius, 75, 111, 115–16, 124

Pectoral, 25, 27, 38, 67
Pelta/stai, 43
Peroz, 150, 168
Persecution, 129–30, 145, 151, 160
Petronius Maximus, 225
Phalanx/Phalangites, 5–7, 24–5, 43, 53, 56–7, 66
Phathusae, see Anatha
Philip the Arab, 129–30, 133, 136, 150–1
Philippopolis, 132–3, 137–9, 142
Philippus, Marcus Julius, 150
Philostorgius, 211
Phissenia, 198
Phraates III, 96
Pigranes, 202
Pilum/Pila, 25, 27, 32, 39–40, 80–1, 102–3, 122, 170
Pirisabora, 196
Pirosen, 168, 178
Placidia, 225
Plague, 130, 153, 159, 179
Plague of Cyprian, 134
Plutarch, 2, 4, 9, 12–13, 15, 34–5, 43–5, 48, 54–7, 75–6, 83, 94, 97, 100–101, 104–5, 107–9
Po, River, 3, 63
Poetovio, Battle of, 214, 220–1
Poleto, 133
Pollio, Trebellius, 148
Polybius, 9, 35, 38–9, 53, 59–60, 62–4, 68–9, 72–3
Pompey, 91–2, 95, 110
Pontius, Gaius (Gavius), 26, 29–31
Pontus, 96
Pontes Longi, Battle of, 126
Porphyry, 147
Postumus, 162
Praetorian guard, 133
Praetorian prefect, 150
Praeventores, 171
Principate, 170, 181, 186
Principes, 24–6, 32, 38–40, 43, 65, 80
Priscus, 223, 226, 230
Priscus, Titus Julius, 132, 137
Procopius, 223, 226–7, 229–35
Procopius, general, 187–8, 191–2, 205
Propertius, 68
Provence-Alpes-Cote d'Azur, 84
Ptolemy II, 37
Ptolemy XII, 96
Pugio, 25, 40
Punic Wars, 1, 25, 34, 60–1, 74, 76
Pyrenees, 61, 224
Pyrrhus, 34–58, 63

Quadi, 161, 166
Quietus, 162
Quinctilius, 114, 116, 125
Quincunx, 24, 38, 40, 65, 79

Rehimene, 209
Res Gestae Divi Saporis, 147, 150, 154
Rhages, 99
Rhegium, 37, 49
Rhesaina, Battle of, 150
Rhine, River, 68, 112–15, 119, 124–7, 161–2,
    184, 217–18, 224, 239
Rhodes, 114, 154
Rhone, River, 61, 84–5, 87, 90
Rhyndacus, River, 168
Rome, *passim*
Rome, sacks of, 2, 10–11, 18–20, 35, 61, 67,
    76, 83, 92, 210–11, 221, 224–5
Rorarii, 24–5
Rufus, Publius Rutilius, see Rutilius, Publius
Rusenski Lom, River, 133
Rustaham, 97
Rutilius, Publius, 91

Saansaan, 168, 178
    see also Shahanshah
Sabines, 51
Sabinianus, 167, 178
Sacae, 174
Saguntum, 61
Sallentines, 54
Sallust, 75
Saltus Teutoburgiensis, 119, 124
Samarra, Battle of, 207–8
Samnite War, First, 22–3, 25
Samnite War, Second, 24–32, 35
Samnite War, Third, 35, 39, 51
Samnites, 12, 21–33, 36, 40, 44, 49, 53–4
Samnium, 26
Sampsigeramos, 152
Sardinia, 63, 225, 227–31, 236
Sarissa, 43
Sarmatia/ns, 137, 166
Sasanids, 109–10, 129–30, 149–50, 153–6,
    158–60, 162, 164–8, 171, 173–83, 185, 87,
    189, 194–5, 198–9, 206–7, 209, 217
Satala, 152
Satala, Battle of, 165
Saverrio, Publius Sulpicius, 50
Scaurus, Marcus Aurelius, 78, 85
Scipio Aemilianus, 59, 62
Scipio Africanus, 59, 62
Scipio, Publius, 61–2
Scriptores Historiae Augustae, 148
Scutum, 25, 37, 39, 67–8, 102, 170

Sebastianus, 187–8, 191–2, 205
Secundinus, 193
Segestani, 168, 174, 176–7
Segestes, 116
Segimerus, 115
Seleucia, 99, 199
Senones, 3–6, 10–11, 13, 15–20
Sentinum, 12
Sentinum, Battle of, 12, 55
Servian reforms, 5, 9
Servilius, Caepio, 84–6
Servilius, Quintus Servilius, 5, 63, 73, 78
Servius Tullius, 5
Severan Dynasty, 129
Shah, Gilan, 155
Shah, Meshan, 155
Shah, Sakastan, 155
Shahanshah, Sasanid, 154–5
Shapur I, 147, 149–61, 164
Shapur II, 165–9, 172–7, 180–2, 185–200,
    204–5, 209–10
Sibylline Oracle, 151
Sicily, 1, 11, 36–7, 57, 60, 62–3, 101, 230–1,
    234, 236
Sidicini, 23
Siege Engines, 192, 196, 199
Silaces, 96
Singara, 167, 171, 178, 182, 209
Singara, Battle of, 165
Sinnaca, 108
Siris, River, 44
Siscia, Battle of, 214, 220–1
Sitha, 194
Social War, 95, 103
Spahbad, 97, 99, 104
Sparta, 36
Spartacus, 95
Spatha/e, 134, 170
Sponsio, 30–1
Suebi, 113–14
Sueves, 224–5
Sugambri, 112–14, 118
Sulla, 92, 95
Superventores, 171
Surena, 97–9, 102, 104–6, 108–9, 195,
    197–8, 202
Susa, 99, 160
Symbra, 205
Synca, 206
Syncellus, 138–9, 141, 145, 158–9
Syracuse, 11, 19, 63, 66
Syria, 95–7, 108–9, 147, 150–1, 154, 167–8,
    175, 182, 188, 191

Taburnus, Mt, 29
Tacitus, Publius Cornelius, 111, 118–19, 125

Taifali, 131
Tairano, Mt, 27
Taq-e Bostan, 155
Tarentum, 23, 36–7, 43, 49, 63
Tarentum, Gulf of, 37
Taurini, 61
Taurus Mountains, 174–5
Teia, 212, 224
Telamon, Battle of, 67, 84
Tervingi, 210
Tetricus, 162
Teutobod, 84
Teutoburg, 111–27, 135–6, 145, 239
Teutones, 77–8, 82–4, 87–8, 90–2, 94
Thebaid, 229
Theodorus Lector, 227, 232
Theodosius I, 211–21
Theodosius II, 211–12
Theophanes, 235
Thesprotians, 53
Thessalia/n, 48, 53
Thessalonica, 213–14
Thilutha, 194
Third Century Crisis, 128, 148–9
Thrace, 136, 165, 216, 235
Thracian, 129, 132, 138
Thureophoroi, 43
Thureos, 43
Thurii, 37
Tiber, River, 12–13, 16, 18
Tiberius, 114, 125–6
Tiberius Coruncanius, 49
Ticinus, Battle of, 61–2, 66, 74
Tigranes, 96
Tigurini, 78
Timesitheus, Gaius Furius Sabinus Aquila, 150
Trajan, 137, 200
Trajan, Decius, *see* Decius
Trasimene, Lake, Battle of, 59–74
Trebia, Battle of, 62, 66, 69, 74
Trebonianus Gallus, *see* Gallus
Triarii, 24–6, 38, 40, 43, 65, 80–1
Tripolis, 229–31
Tripolitania, 228, 236
Truceless War, *see* Mercenary war
Tubantes, 126
Tummara, 207
Turmae, 117
Tyre, 147

Umbrians, 12, 51
Uranius Antoninus, 152
Ursicinus, 167, 171, 178–9
Usipetes, 113, 126

Valentinian I, 210
Valentinian II, 212–14
Valentinian III, 225, 236
Valens, 210, 217, 232
Valerian, Emperor, 152–4, 157–62, 164
Valerian, Life of, 148
Vandal/s, 131, 223–36
Vargonteius, 108
Varus, Publius Quinctilius, 114–17, 119–25, 127
    see also Quinctilius
Veii, 18
Velites, 25–6, 40, 42, 45–6, 53, 62, 65–7, 135
Venusia/ns, 44
Vercellae, Battle of, 92, 95
Verina, 224, 230, 235
Verona, 129
Vestals, 18
Vesuvius, 55
Vetranio, 207
Vexillatio Palatinae, 171
Vexillationes, 133–4, 154
Vibelius, Decius, 49
Victo, general, 193, 196, 198, 200, 202–3
Victor, Sextus Aurelius, 129, 139, 144, 147, 160
Victor, son of Magnus Maximus, 214
Vidimarius/Virdomarus, 68
Viminacium, 133
Vinicius, Marcus, 114
Visurgis, River, *see* Weser, River
Volscians, 51
Vorrano, Mt, 27

Weser, River, 112–13, 115, 119, 126

Yoke, passing under, 31, 78

Zabdicene, 209
Zaitha, 151, 193
Zama, Battle of, 74
Zaragardia, 194
    see also Ozagardan
Zeno, 235
Zenobia, 162
Zenodotia/ium, 96
Zephyrus, 175
Zeugma, 97, 100, 108
Zhayedan, 155
Zianni, 207
Zonaras, 35, 139–41, 145, 148, 151, 158–9
Zosimus, 128, 136–7, 141–6, 148, 157–8, 183, 186–8, 190–201, 204–8, 210, 212, 223